SELECTED READINGS SERIES

SEVEN

D0941080

# Citizen Participation in Urban Development

## Volume I—Concepts and Issues

*Edited by*

HANS B. C. SPIEGEL

CENTER FOR COMMUNITY AFFAIRS

NTL INSTITUTE FOR APPLIED BEHAVIORAL SCIENCE

# Preface

This volume is the seventh in the NTL Institute's[1] *Selected Readings Series* and the second of the series to be focused on issues in community development. Thus it represents the Institute's continuing and continually intensifying effort to bring behavioral-science knowledge and skill to bear on the crucial social problems of our day. From the first venture in applying the laboratory method of education to training for community leadership, NTL Institute's community program has expanded into the Center for Community Affairs, with a network of behavioral scientists engaged in a wide range of research, training, and organization-development activities in a variety of community contexts.

In two ways this volume represents issues central to the philosophy and goals of the Institute. It is, first of all, devoted to the question of "participation." To discover (and to help others discover) the nature and consequences of various modes of participation—in interpersonal relations, in groups, organizations, and larger social systems—is one way of expressing a major Institute goal. Early questions asked of community leaders at Institute training laboratories were, "Do we really want participation?" and "How do we get genuine participation?" Research on the consequences of different patterns of participation (like the classic Lewin, Lippitt, and White studies and the work of Douglas McGregor) are essential landmarks guiding the NTL Institute's explorations in learning and change. In the issue of citizen participation in urban development, the behavioral scientist's theories of par-

1 The NTL Institute for Applied Behavioral Science, formerly National Training Laboratories, a division of the National Education Association, is now an autonomous organization associated with the National Education Association.

ticipation, and the practitioner's ability to make use of theory, are put to a crucial test.

This reader also represents the traditional multidisciplinary and outreaching quality of NTL Institute; for the contributors are sociologists and city planners, action leaders and government officials, such contrasting figures on the national scene as Saul Alinsky and Senator William Proxmire. The editor, Hans Spiegel, an active member of the NTL Institute, is associate professor of urban planning in the Institute of Urban Environment at Columbia University. He has served as Deputy Assistant Commissioner for Relocation and Community Organization in the U.S. Urban Renewal Administration, as a member of the President's Task Force in the War Against Poverty, and as staff member of the President's Task Force on Urban Problems. He therefore represents the broad orientation to public human problems of the NTL Institute Center for Community Affairs, and his selections for this volume reflect that orientation.

The second volume of "Citizen Participation in Urban Development," subtitled "Cases and Programs," will highlight the work of a number of behavioral scientists and practitioners in varied community-development ventures, including some of the endeavors of the NTL Institute.

## A Note on the Selected Readings Series

The series which this volume joins was initiated in 1961 to bring together papers bearing on major concerns in human relations training. Previous numbers in the series are:

GROUP DEVELOPMENT, edited by Leland P. Bradford
LEADERSHIP IN ACTION, edited by Gordon L. Lippitt
HUMAN FORCES IN TEACHING AND LEARNING, edited by Leland P. Bradford
FORCES IN COMMUNITY DEVELOPMENT, edited by Dorothy and H. Curtis Mial

ISSUES IN TRAINING, edited by Irving R. Weschler and Edgar H. Schein

CONFERENCE PLANNING, edited by Richard Beckhard

The NTL Institute is pleased to add *Citizen Participation in Urban Development* to that list.

Washington, May 1968          H. Curtis Mial, Director
*Center for Community Affairs*
*NTL Institute for Applied Behavioral Science*

# Table of Contents

# Introduction

Probably no other issue is as vital to the success of solving America's urban crisis than the viable participation of urban residents in planning the neighborhoods and cities in which they live and the social programs which directly affect them. City dwellers are demanding to be heard. They want in—they want to help control—not only indirectly through their elected representatives in the councils of central government but also on the block and neighborhood level.

The selections in this book will stress the participation of low- and moderate-income individuals in our cities. This is not to suggest that better-to-do individuals and groups are either unimportant or aquiescent vis-a-vis urban development. The undeniable fact is, however, that the poor and the have-nots have been largely excluded from the charting of the urban environment and only recently has their quest for codetermination gained a measure of legitimization.

It is recognized, of course, that citizens actively involved in committees and action programs will not, themselves, succeed in reshaping the run-down central cities of America into attractive and creative areas, free from poverty and contempt. More than a participative process is needed. Substantive programs to create new jobs and to upgrade existing employment, housing, health services, and related endeavors must be strengthened or newly initiated. But these programs can only succeed if programs, on the one hand, and participating citizens, on the other, are effectively linked.

It is difficult to rank the various ingredients making for competent urban communities. A strong case could be made, however, that citizen participation, even more so than housing subsidies, new jobs, or rat control, is basic to helping people tackle a variety of community and individual problems. Citizen participation is the process that can meaningfully tie programs to people.

## The Focus of the Reader

As the first essay in this volume suggests, citizen participation has many faces. Numerous actions of citizens can be subsumed under the broad umbrella of this term: party politics on a national scale, a self-help suburban beautification campaign, volunteer work for the Red Cross, and participation in riots.

This Reader focuses primarily on the efforts of urban residents, especially in low-income neighborhoods, to improve their own community and individual conditions through group actions. Most of the contributions describe resident actions that are "political" in the boadest sense of this difficult term, that is, of residents organizing to meet their own ends, which may include the confrontation of governmental bodies.

The Reader stresses the more theoretical and valuative aspects of the topic. In a sense, it is concerned with the "know why" of citizen participation. "How is the problem defined by various authors?" is the lead question. The "know how," on the other hand, is the focus of a second volume, subtitled "Cases and Programs." Here concrete situations will be discussed and solution-oriented endeavors examined. The question that runs through the second volume might simply be stated as, "What can be done about the problem?" Together, it is our hope that the two readers will form a comprehensive guide to a crucial national issue.

## Acknowledgments

I am grateful, first of all, to the authors and publishers whose works are reprinted here. Without exception they have been most generous in permitting this volume to be printed— and printed on schedule.

The Institute of Urban Environment at Columbia University, ably directed by Professor Chester Rapkin, has given me considerable freedom and encouragement to explore the social aspects of urban planning. The invaluable assistance of Stephen Mittenthal of the Institute deserves particular acknowledgment and gratitude. Carolyn Tillotson, of the NTL Institute editorial staff, handled with exceptional skill the technical details of publication within formidable deadlines.

The moment this Reader is published, new titles will have appeared in the literature, new conceptualizations formulated, and new programs advocated. The selections in this volume need no apology, but only this qualification: As events dealing with citizen participation move with lightning speed across our societal landscape, new works will be written on this subject. The editor, mindful of the value of feedback from persons in the field, would greatly appreciate hearing from persons wishing to suggest new material for a possible revised edition.

Hans B. C. Spiegel
*Associate Professor*
*Institute of Urban Environment*
*School of Architecture*
*Columbia University*
*May 1968*

# Who's Who
## Among the Authors

**SAUL ALINSKY**
Executive Director
Industrial Areas Foundation
Chicago, Illinois

**EDGAR S. CAHN**
Director
Citizens Advocate Center
Washington, D. C.

**JEAN CAMPER CAHN**
Professor of Law
National Law Center
The George Washington
  University

**ROBERT L. CRAIN**
Associate Professor
Social Relations
Johns Hopkins University

**HAROLD C. EDELSTON**
Executive Director
Health and Welfare Council
  of the Baltimore Area

**HAROLD GOLDBLATT**
Lecturer
Social Research
School of Social
  Work
Howard University

**FERNE K. KOLODNER**
Community Planning Staff
Office of the Commissioner
Social Security
  Administration
Dept. of Health, Education
  and Welfare
Baltimore, Maryland

**PETER MARRIS**
Research
Institute of Community
  Studies
London

**STEPHEN D.
  MITTENTHAL**
Staff Associate
Institute of Urban
  Environment
School of Architecture
Columbia University

**RICHARD C. MURRAY**
Assistant Professor of
  Sociology
University of Illinois
Chicago, Illinois

**FRANCES F. PIVEN**
Faculty
School of Social Work
Columbia University

**MARTIN REIN**
Graduate Department
Social Welfare and Social
  Research
Bryn Mawr College

**STEPHEN C. ROSE**
Editor
*Renewal* Magazine
Chicago, Illinois

**DONALD B. ROSENTHAL**
Associate Professor
Political Science
State University of New York
  at Buffalo

**ROBERT C. SEAVER**
Associate Editor
Office of Reports
The Ford Foundation

**THOMAS D. SHERRARD**
Professor of Urban Affairs
Director, Urban Development
  Institute
Purdue University—Calumet
Hammond, Indiana

**HANS B. C. SPIEGEL**
Associate Professor
Institute of Urban
  Environment
School of Architecture
Columbia University

**JAMES Q. WILSON**
Professor of Government
Harvard University

**LOUIS A. ZURCHER**
Department of Sociology
The University of Texas

# SECTION I

# An Overview

# The Many Faces of
# Citizen Participation:
# A Bibliographic Overview

HANS B. C. SPIEGEL and
STEPHEN D. MITTENTHAL

Despite the increased attention given to citizen participation by the Federal Government through a number of dramatic new social programs, the existing work in the field—theoretical and empirical—reflects a good many uncertainties about the phenomenon, the difficulty in coming to terms with its implications, and the absence of criteria by which to measure its effectiveness and overall worth.

Citizen participation in planning, a seemingly facile subject at first glance, becomes upon further analysis a phenomenon of infinite complexity and subtle dimension. Truly the more one explores the endless ramifications of citizen participation, the more one appreciates the old adage of "having a tiger by the tail." Every effort to reduce its protean-like substance to a definable, systematic, and comprehensible body of thought is resisted by inherent dilemmas—contradictions between myth and reality and even between different sets of observable social phenomena. Citizen participation virtually defies generalization and delights in reducing abstractions to dust.

A major reason for citizen participation having successfully resisted generalization is the absence of a sizable-enough body of empirical evidence from which to draw meaningful inferences and conclusions. The evidence we do have is contradictory, inconclusive, particularistic, and overly qualified by the dictates of time, place, and circumstance.

Another mitigating factor is bias. A scientific approach to citizen participation is extraordinarily difficult, suffused as it is with normative judgments, value-laden preconceptions, lack of objective criteria and standards of measurement, and a host of differentiated perspectives from which anyone can draw just about whatever meanings his predilections desire. If one concludes, for example, that citizen participation is, by nature, good and desirable, then nearly every instance of it demonstrates a modicum of value, regardless of how much rationalization is accommodated in the process; conversely, if one has reservations about the efficacy of the process, it is not at all difficult to uncover situations which substantiate such doubts. Few absolutes adhere to citizen participation. Much of it is relative and contingent upon a wide range of variables, not the least of which is the nonobjective perception of the beholder.

Citizen participation has become the scholastic province of a number of professional disciplines, each seeking to place the phenomenon under its rubric. Political scientists, sociologists, psychologists, lawyers, social workers, redevelopers, and planners alike have made forays into this fecund area of research, only to come up with sectional views of the whole picture, some proffering heuristic arguments, others asserting generalizations about human behavior that look better in print than they do in the context of ghetto reality. No one has written extensively about citizen participation, though many have written *something*. Bits and snatches can be elicited from the works of such established social scientists as James Wilson, Edward Banfield, Robert Dahl, Floyd Hunter, William Kornhauser, Roland Warren, Harvey Perloff, Martin Rein, Peter Rossi, and Robert Dentler.

The last two are associated with one of the classic works in the field, *The Politics of Urban Renewal*,* which exam-

---

* For full citation on this and following references, see bibliographical list at the end of the essay.

ines the history of the famous Hyde Park-Kenwood urban renewal project in Chicago. Rossi also has written a further analysis of citizen participation in "Theory, Research and Practice in Community Organization."

Dahl and Hunter frame their appraisals of citizen participation within their counterposed approaches to the power structure. Dahl sees greater potential for participation in the pluralistic system of New Haven in *Who Governs,* while Hunter warns in *Community Power Structure* that citizen participation cannot become a reality in Atlanta until the closed power system is opened to shared citizen authority and responsibility. Harvey Perloff and Royce Hansen do not dispute this contention when they state in "The Inner City and a New Politics," that "participation without power is a cynical ritual." Perloff and Hansen strongly urge the reform of inner-city politics by reinvigorating the processes of participatory democracy to transform slums into habitable environments.

Among the advocates of citizen participation, Jean and Edgar Cahn, Peter Marris and Martin Rein, and Milton Kotler underscore the value of citizen participation in satisfying a variety of social and political objectives in three separate works, all of an exceptionally high order.

The Cahns, in a penetrating analysis entitled *Citizen Participation,* reassert the importance of participatory action as an essential component of the faith we profess in the dignity and worth of the individual, as a mobilizer of the energies and resources of the poor, as a source of insight, knowledge, and experience in social programming (the consumer perspective), and finally as the only guarantee that, frail as it may appear, people are willing to abide by the terms of America's social contract.

The Cahns rebut James Wilson's thesis (described below) that the poor invariably succumb to the pressures of immediate needs–satisfaction, contending, rather, that they are capable and entitled to deliberate on the question of resource allocation to effect social change. When the Cahns assail the "fallacy of monolithic man," they direct their criticism at those professionals (and academicians?) who manipulate the poor into a position of responding as passive consumers and dependents.

In the *Dilemma of Social Reform*, Marris and Rein posit citizen participation as a countervailing force necessary to protect social and welfare programs against the encroachment of institutional self-interest. Their recitation of the experience of social-action agencies in Boston, New Haven, and New York dramatizes the inherent conflict between these agencies' ideological commitment to the poor and their own vested interests, which make them institutional pawns in the great organizational chess game of urban politics.

Marris and Rein view citizen participation as a twin force, capable of involving and accommodating target-area residents to the demands of urban society, while at the same time holding out the possibility of pressuring institutions to better adapt to the needs of their constituencies.

Milton Kotler regards citizen participation as a countervailing power on an even grander scale. In "Two Essays on the Neighborhood Corporation," the combatants are pictured not simply as poverty programs and their institutional environment, as Marris and Rein perceive them, but the entire body of poor versus the community at large. Kotler carries the implications of citizen participation to their logical extreme on the affirmative pole of the continuum—that of neighborhood control and self-rule. In what is essentially a fundamental reordering of the body politic, Kotler advocates the transference of a portion of authority from the municipal government to the new focal points of power in the poverty neighborhoods. With particular reference to the Black community, he advocates neighborhood corporations set up as legal public entities, enjoying a substantial measure of self-rule in what could be described as a reconstituted territorial community of the poor.

The Cahns, Marris and Rein, and Kotler all penetrate into the deeper realms of citizen participation, extending beyond involvement in decisions made by the power structure to an opening up of the structure itself—to a redistribution of political power and authority. For the Cahns, it is citizens participating in the original decisions to allocate community resources and frame institutions, on the choices necessary in any kind of "capital formation and investment." For Marris and Rein, it is citizens participating to organize their interests, defend their rights, and restore their self-confidence through a redistribution of power, presumably accomplished outside the confines of a governmentally sponsored social-action organization. For Kotler, it is citizens participating in the shared exercise of authority and the performance of certain municipal functions within a territorial structure based on neighborhood power and local self-rule.

Those authors who emphasize the more negative and problematic features of citizen participation, or who underscore its inherent disabilities, come armed with theoretical brickbats and empirical thorns.

The deep rooting of citizen participation in politics is examined by James Wilson and Edward Banfield in *City Politics*, where sharp distinctions are drawn between a "public regarding" and a "private regarding" political ethos, the former the province of high status, community-oriented middle-class elements, while the latter represents the immediate, need-satisfying predilections of the lower class. Wilson emphasizes the low efficacy of the poor in organizational situations in his provocative article, "Planning and Politics: Citizen Participation in Urban Renewal." Frances Piven, whose article on "Resident Participation in Community Action Programs: An Overview," is reprinted in this volume, extends the characterization of the low-income community to one in which lower-class interpretations of the world reinforce an inability to cope with societal conditions. Political inefficacy results, which serves only to dampen participation and compounds a sense of community powerlessness. No inducements exist to stimulate citizen participation, either on the part of indigenous leadership whose rewards from their disadvantaged constituency are marginal, or on the part of the mass community whose paucity of organizational and influence resources deprive them of access to central sources of power and decision making.

Some of the weaknesses of citizen participation are further elucidated by William Kornhauser who, in "Power and Participation in the Local Community," suggests that democracy does not necessarily imply continuous participation in community affairs, that low-income people have fewer attachments to the community, hence fewer organizational ties and ultimately less incentive to support the rules according to which community affairs are generally conducted. Kornhauser is not opposed to citizen participation *per se*—which, like James Coleman in *Community Conflict,* he argues can be conducive to stable government—but cautions that unorganized mass participation can lead to extremism (Kornhauser, *Politics of Mass Society*).

Roger Starr finds that citizen participation can plainly be a hindrance to attaining the goals of public programs. In "An Attack on Poverty: Historical Perspective," he further states that "it is a misunderstanding of the way in which the American form of government has worked to suggest that leadership depends on constant consultation with the governed."

Roberta Sigel thinks it naive to suggest that "inarticulate masses" can devise urban renewal schemes or other planning endeavors. In "Citizen Committees—Advice vs. Consent," she states that the bulk of members on citizen committees must have discernible skills, and that while the poor can be mobilized for action and implementation, their role in the process of translating general goals into programmatic detail is perforce limited.

The theme of citizen participation and its relationship to

community stability is picked up by Robert Crain and Donald Rosenthal in an extremely provocative article, "Community Status and a Dimension of Local Decision-Making." The authors hypothesize that there is a direct correlation between socio-economic status and the level of day-to-day citizen participation in community decision making (nothing new in itself: see Wendell Bell and Maryanne T. Force, "Urban Neighborhood Types and Participation in Formal Associations," for an earlier correlation of this type). But then they go on to suggest that the main effect of increasing citizen power vis-a-vis municipal authority is to promote high levels of controversy, partially immobilize political processes, and contribute to instability in government. Thus a paradox emerges, namely that middle-class, high-status cities are less stable than lower-class, low-status cities where conditions would seem more likely to engender community instability. The implications of a theory that demonstrates the immobilizing effects of citizen participation on exercise of government authority and decision making are interesting to speculate about, though conceivably quite destructive in their practical effect.

Part of the skepticism about citizen participation among the poor is validated by certain empirical findings. Harold Goldblatt in *Citizen Participation in Urban Renewal—Washington, D.C.,* demonstrates a lack of widespread participation among low-income groups in an urban renewal project, citing in the process the low estimate of citizen participation among certain professionals in clearance projects. Joan Ash, a British social critic, shows how equally ineffective citizen participation can be in rehabilitation planning in *Planning with People, U.S.A.* Harold Edelston and Ferne Kolodner ask more than a rhetorical question in *Are the Poor Capable of Planning for Themselves?* Based on a research and experimental design set up to test the thesis that the poor have a capacity to develop viable roles in planning, the authors conclude that there was no evidence to indicate that the poor actually wanted to participate in planning; they were in fact bored by the intellectual process of problem solving and lacked a basic understanding of what the program was all about.

Still further empirical evidence, this in the form of a case study conducted by Louis Zurcher entitled *Walking the Tightrope—Some Role and Value Conflicts Experienced by a Poverty Program's Indigenous Leaders,* shows the poor to be passive, not active, in their mode of interaction with formal organizations. Their orientation to present needs rather than future goals and their intolerance of program delays all combine to weaken their potential for effective participation.

*A Description and Evaluation of Neighborhood Centers,* a study done by Kirshner Associates, highlights another disturbing aspect of citizen participation, namely, the phenomenon of greater involvement among the upper stratum of poor than among those who are termed the "problematic" and "disreputable" poor.

Contraposed to these empirical evidences of some of the shortcomings or negative aspects of citizen participation is a group of studies demonstrating just the opposite—that lower-class citizens *do* care enough to become involved and have shown themselves to be effective in citizen-participation efforts: Frank Bonilla and Anne Sarka, *Metro-North-INRA-CRRA: A Report on a Unique Collaboration;* the ECCO project in Columbus, Ohio, Institute for Policy Studies Series; *Neighborhood Foundations Memoranda;* Gray Park in Philadelphia, described in one of the best studies on citizen participation, "Citizen Participation in Urban Renewal," *Columbia Law Review;* Washington Park and other neighborhoods as described in William Loring, et al., *Community Organization for Citizen Participation in Urban Renewal;* and Kansas City's grass-roots "Residents for Renewal" program described by Edmund Burke in "Citizen Participation in Renewal." Effective participation in Hyde Park-Kenwood, albeit among more middle-class elements, is outlined by Julia Abrahamson in *A Neighborhood Finds Itself*. Also of timely interest is the *Bundy Report* advocating a decentralization of New York's school system, to include citizen participation as an essential ingredient of the proposed reorganization.

The good and bad features of citizen participation emerge from J. Clarence Davies' study of *Neighborhoods and Urban Renewal*. Through a series of case studies of urban renewal in New York City, Davies describes how neighborhood groups were able to use citizen participation as a means to attack urban-renewal programs considered inimical to local interests. At the same time, he shows how the participatory weapon is more effective in opposition to existing or proposed programs than in formulation of new ones. The author seems to feel, nonetheless, that citizen participation holds out the promise of engendering a new community spirit by overcoming alienation and apathy and reasserting control over the indigenous environment.

The diversity of citizen-participation policies and practices from one community to another is underscored by Robert Seaver in an article entitled "The Dilemma of Citizen Participation." Disclaiming judgments on the matter, Seaver observes that the character of citizen participation is far more likely to be influenced by the functional compromise of divergent community interests in a given locality than by any set of abstract principles espoused by policy-makers. Seaver believes the dilemma of citizen participation arises not out of any inherent quality in the process itself (a conclusion to which some scholars would take exception) but out of real differences that exist over the proper nature and scope of social-welfare efforts, the relation of these efforts to renewal and planning, and the substance of the relationship between professional and lay opinion in public affairs.

Citizen participation as both concept and reality has moved a long way in a short time. It is interesting to observe the evolution from the rather tenuous and rudimentary state of the art of several years ago to the more sophisticated analysis of today. As long ago as 1959, Gerda Lewis was groping for higher forms of citizen participation in her overview of urban renewal involvement entitled "Citizen Participation in Renewal Surveyed." Expressing the view that citizen participation consists of stimulating dissatisfaction with what is, demonstrating what can be, and providing opportunities to do something about both, she goes on to describe the relatively disappointing progress that had been made up to that time in making participation an integral part of the educative process. At this embryonic stage in its development, information-giving was the most advanced form of participatory action. Lewis concluded that citizen participation, as of 1959 at least, had not reached a point where it could be said to "represent a revitalization of the democratic process."

Four years later, in an issue devoted exclusively to citizen participation, the *Journal of Housing*, September 1963, reproduced a series of reports from across the country on the contributions of citizens groups to urban renewal. Unfortunately, the level of profundity of these short, descriptive pieces is epitomized by the pictures of happy public housing tenants, dancing, cultivating their flower beds, and playing tug-of-war. Evidences of the real tug-of-war, the political imbroglio between citizens and institutional authority, is occasionally manifested in articles on the New York Housing Authority, which reveal tensions between tenants and their governmental landlord, and on Freedom House in Boston, where it is not difficult to discern the between-the-lines story of institutional maneuvering and rivalry. But even by 1963, the poverty program and its notion of "maximum feasible participation" was a year away. Citizen participation had yet to come into its own.

As we have seen, citizen participation can occur in partnership *with* a governmental unit as well as *against* it. Its nature can be cooperative and integrative or conflicting and oppositional, or in the words of an international report, citizens can exercise *convergent* or *divergent* influences on governmental operations (Mumtaz Soyal, *Public Relations in Administrations: The Influence of the Public on the Operation of Public Administration*). Among the latter category should be mentioned the work of the Industrial Areas Foundation, headed by Saul Alinsky, and its profound influence on community organization as creating a power base capable of challenging City Hall. Nor can any description of citizen participation in the 1960's be complete without reference to black nationalism, on the one hand, and nonviolent, but militant civil rights advocacy on the other. It is likely that this area will be the subject of a growing body of literature over the next decade.

The discussion of "citizen participation" so far has centered on the relationship established between area residents—usually in groups—and governmental bodies. Of course, generically speaking, citizens participate in many other ways—within the family, in friendship groups, at work, in the voting booth. We will not discuss these forms of participatory behavior, except to say that their study is not irrelevant to our topic. Indeed, the serious student of "citizen participation" must not ignore the impressive literature that deals with the participatory process from other perspectives. For example, there are sociological and psychological writings that deal with small-group studies, organizational behavior in many settings, intergroup contacts, and related topics. The individual as a participating actor in a social setting is central to an understanding of these researches. Whether the individual participates in a community-improvement group or a work team in a factory, the sociopsychological processes involved are, we suggest, of the same cloth.

We also notice with interest the emergence of new interdisciplines which, similarly, conceptualize the individual as part of a participatory process whose central focus is the community. We are referring to community psychology, community psychiatry, and community mental health. Each field is gaining increased legitimization in the councils of their parent disciplines, and each is represented by a growing literary output.

A polarization exists in the literature on citizen participation between what are essentially theoretical, normatively oriented arguments, and empirical studies which proffer their own arguments on the basis of actual field experiences. Both have their advantages and disadvantages.

It is important to ask, for example, whether the low-income community can make a rational allocation of resources within the decision-making process as the Cahns suggest they can, or whether they lack the inherent capacity by dint of their own conditions of deprivation. It is interesting to speculate as well on the correlation between high socioeconomic status and consequent citizen participation on the one hand and evidences of community instability on the other.

But do we then, as Crain and Rosenthal suggest, accept the tautology that "if public officials are going to do the right thing, the people should leave them alone while they do it?" In other words, should we deemphasize citizen participation because it induces community instability? The logical implications of this and other theoretical questions on citizen participation can become counterproductive if accepted as the premises of public policy and action.

# Bibliography

Abrahamson, Julia. *A neighborhood finds itself.* N.Y.: Harper, 1959.

Adrian, Charles (Ed.) *Social science and community action.* East Lansing, Mich.: Institute for Community Development and Services, 1960.

Ash, Joan. *Planning with people, USA.* London: Ministry of Housing and Local Government, 1965.

Banfield, Edward C., & Wilson, James Q. *City politics.* Cambridge: Harvard Univer. Press, 1963.

Bell, Wendell, & Force, Maryanne T. Urban neighborhood types and participation in formal associations. *Amer. sociol. Rev.*, Vol. 21, February 1956.

Bonilla, Frank, & Sarka, Anne. *Metro-North-INRA-CRRA: A report on a unique collaboration.* N.Y.: International Research Associates, Inc., April 1966.

Burke, Edmund M. Citizen participation in renewal. *J. Housing*, Vol. 23, January 1966, pp. 18-25.

Cahn, Edgar S., & Cahn, Jean C. *Citizen participation.* Mimeographed draft, 1968.

Citizen participation in urban renewal. *Columbia Law Rev.*, Vol. 66, March 1966.

Coleman, James. *Community conflict.* N.Y.: Free Press of Glencoe, 1957.

Crain, Robert, & Rosenthal, Donald. Community status and a dimension of local decision-making. *Amer. sociol. Rev.*, 32 (6), December 1967.

Dahl, Robert A. *Who governs: Democracy and power in an American city.* New Haven: Yale Univer. Press, 1961.

Davies, J. Clarence. *Neighborhoods and urban renewal.* N.Y.: Columbia Univer. Press, 1966.

ECCO Project, *Institute for Policy Studies Series: Neighborhood Foundations Memoranda,* Washington, D.C. Undated.

Edelston, Harold, & Kolodner, Ferne K. *Are the poor capable of planning for themselves?* Address before the National Association of Social Welfare Conference, Dallas, 1967.

Goldblatt, Harold. *Citizen participation in urban renewal—Washington, D.C.* Health and Welfare Council of the National Capital Area, January 1966.

Hunter, Floyd. *Community power structure.* N.Y.: Doubleday, 1953.

Kirshner Associates. *A description and evaluation of neighborhood centers.* For the Office of Economic Opportunity, Washington, D.C., 1966.

Kornhauser, William. *Politics of mass society.* Glencoe, Ill.: Free Press, 1959.

———. Power and participation in the local community. *Health Education Monographs No. 6,* Oakland, Cal.: Society of Public Health Educators, 1959.

Kotler, Milton. Two essays on the neighborhood corporation. *Urban*

*America: Goals and problems.* Materials Prepared for Subcommittee on Urban Affairs of the Joint Economic Committee, Congress of the United States, Washington, D.C.: G.P.O., August 1967.

Lewis, Gerda. Citizen participation in renewal surveyed. *J. Housing,* Vol. 16, March 1959.

Loring, William C., Jr., Sweetser, Frank L., & Ernst, Charles F. *Community organization for citizen participation in urban renewal.* Housing Assoc. of Metropolitan Boston, for the Dept. of Commerce, Boston, Mass. Cambridge Press, Inc., 1957.

Marris, Peter, & Rein, Martin. *Dilemma of social reform.* London: Atherton, 1967.

Perloff, Harvey, & Hansen, Royce. The inner city and a new politics. *Urban America: Goals and problems.* Materials Prepared for Subcommittee on Urban Affairs of the Joint Economic Committee, Congress of the United States, Washington, D.C.: G.P.O., August 1967.

Piven, Frances. Resident participation in community action programs: An overview. In George A. Brager & Francis P. Purcell (Eds.), *Community action against poverty.* New Haven: College and Univer. Press, 1967.

*Reconnection for learning: Community school system for New York City.* McGeorge Bundy, Chairman, Mayor's Advisory Panel on Decentralization of the New York City Schools, N.Y., November 1967.

Rossi, Peter H., & Dentler, Robert A. *The politics of urban renewal: The Chicago findings.* N.Y.: Free Press of Glencoe, 1961.

Rubin, Lillian. Maximum feasible participation: The origins, implications and present status. *Poverty and Human Resources Abstracts, 2* (6), November-December 1967, pp. 5-18.

Seaver, Robert. The dilemma of citizen participation. *Pratt Planning Papers, 4* (3), September 1966.

Sigel, Roberta S. Citizens committees—Advice vs. consent. *Transaction,* Vol. 4, May 1967, pp. 47-52.

Soyal, Mumtaz. *Public relations in administration: The influence of the public on the operation of public administration.* Int. Inst. of admin. Sci., Brussels, 1966.

Starr, Roger. An attack on poverty: Historical perspective. *Urban*

*America: Goals and problems.* Materials Prepared for Subcommittee on Urban Affairs of the Joint Economic Committee, Congress of the United States, Washington, D.C. G.P.O., August 1967.

Wilson, James Q. Planning and politics: Citizen participation in urban renewal. *J. Amer. Inst. Planners,* Vol. 29, November 1963, pp. 242-249.

Zurcher, Louis. *Walking the tightrope—Some role and value conflicts experienced by a poverty program's indigenous leaders.* Paper presented at American Sociological Association Meetings, Miami Beach, August 28, 1966.

# SECTION II

# Housing and
# Urban Renewal

# Introduction

The urban renewal program illustrates the evolution of citizen participation as a program component. In the early years of the program—for perhaps ten to 15 years after the passage of the Housing Act of 1949—the most frequently utilized vehicles for citizen participation were community-wide citizens advisory committees. These committees were often so broadly constituted that urban renewal area residents were only a weak voice compared with the more powerful articulations of business, labor, organized religion, social welfare, industry, and education. To be sure, there were requirements for public disclosure and information concerning plans for site residents, a public hearing, and, of course, approval by the local governing body.

The planning and execution of the renewal process, however, was principally determined and run by the local renewal agency, with approval of the local governing body and expert consultants. In 1966 Congress passed the Demonstration Cities Act mandating "widespread citizen participation" in a comprehensive program of community development, coming on the heels of the anti-poverty program's requirement for "maximum feasible participation" of the poor. Model Cities promised to usher in a higher level of citizen involvement in contrast to urban renewal's reliance on information-giving and consultation. This is all the more significant in light of the fact that both Urban Renewal and Model Cities are administered by the same federal agency—the Department of Housing and Urban Development. It is instructive to compare these two programs. The first two selections in this section, therefore, present recent HUD publications concerning 1) citizen participation in the "old line" HUD programs

through the Workable Program for Community Improvement and 2) citizens participation guidelines of the new Model
Cities program. It should be noted that the Model Cities program mandates the active participation of residents in planning while Urban Renewal's Workable Program only im-
plicitly encourages resident participation as a component
of broader, community-wide representative involvement.
The difference between these two federal postures is not lost
on local officials.

In the second selection, Harold Goldblatt gives a balance
sheet of reasons for and against the active involvement of
area residents in urban renewal. Goldblatt writes in the context of an appraisal of the Adams-Morgan urban renewal
project in Washington, D.C. which was planned, but never
executed.

James Q. Wilson, a political scientist, renders a rather so-
bering assessment of the political aspects of citizen participation in renewal activities. He elaborates on a point of view
which was summarized in another article as follows: "Citizen
participation is not an end in itself, but a means to other
ends and it should be judged in terms of the ends it is likely
to serve. There is nothing but confusion to be gained from
insisting that urban renewal and grass roots democracy are,
and always should be, compatible." ("The Citizen in the
Renewal Process," *Journal of Housing*, Vol. 29, 1963, p. 627.)

In the final selection in this section, Robert C. Seaver
points out the dilemmas of citizen participation posed to the
public administrator. He does not question whether resident
involvement is good or bad, but how best to incorporate it in
the governmental process.

# Federal Regulations and Advice

## Citizen Participation under the Workable Program for Community Improvement*

Through a Workable Program a community demonstrates its determination to use all of its resources to eliminate and prevent slums and blight and to provide a sound base for securing maximum results from the Federal aids. A successful long-term Workable Program depends in large measure upon active participaton by local citizens. Every citizen benefits in some degree from the Program. Every citizen has something to contribute to it. The citizen participation requirement of the Workable Program provides a means whereby citizens can come to understand the Program benefits. They can make a positive contribution so that a Program can be planned and carried out to meet their needs and command their support.

Citizen participation, therefore, is the keystone of a community's Workable Program. It is the means by which citizens

(1) inform themselves of their community's activities—in progress and contemplated—and the needs for improvement with respect to planning, code adoption and enforcement, housing, public facilities, urban renewal and other Workable Program activities;

(2) assist in developing objectives and goals for improvement;

* Reprinted from the Department of Housing and Urban Development's *Workable Program for Community Improvement—Answers on Citizen Participation,* Program Guide No. 7. Washington, D.C., February 1966.

(3) inventory the community resources—public and private, present or needed—for accomplishing these objectives;
(4) learn and pursue the methods and means for achieving the determined goals for improvements; and
(5) serve as the medium for bringing private resources into the Program.

## How is Citizen Participation Organized?

Experience has demonstrated that effective citizen participation over the extended period necessary to carry out a successful Workable Program is based on an active citizens advisory committee. This is community wide and representative in scope, officially designated by the mayor and/or council, in accordance with local custom. The designation of such a committee is a Workable Program requirement. Also, because of the almost universal difficulty in communities over the country in making adequate housing available to minority groups, it is generally expected that there will be established a subcommittee or special committee on minority group housing. Both the overall advisory committee and the minority group subcommittee or special committee should have minority group representation.

## What is Meant by Community-Wide?

The citizens advisory committee should include a cross-section of all elements in the community. It should not be confined to any one segment of the population. It should include persons from all the principal neighborhoods. Where neighborhood organizations exist, they should be included. However, in large cities where it may not be feasible to include representation from each neighborhood organization, representatives might be designated by councils or associations of neighborhood groups which are usually overall bodies of neighborhood organizations.

## What is Meant by Representative?

Within every community there are organizations and committees whose interests, activities, and memberships relate in some way to the Workable Program elements. Other groups having a relationship to the Program may not be formally organized. The first step should be to study and identify these and determine which can make a positive contribution in attaining the goals of the Workable Program.

The members of the citizens advisory committee should be able to speak on behalf of established groups in the community. Such persons may be officers or recognized leaders in existing organizations although formal leadership is not essential. These persons should be able to communicate the interests of their group or organization to the committee and to public officials concerned with the improvement programs of the community. They should also be capable of explaining to their group or organization the policies and programs put forward by the official bodies concerned with planning, housing, urban renewal, and so on.

The following outline will be useful in achieving a citizens advisory committee which is community-wide and representative in scope. To utilize it the mayor and governing body might list the groups and organizations in their own community which belong in each category. The selection of suitable persons to represent these groups and organizations will follow. It will be advisable to consult with the leaders of these groups and organizations in order to identify suitable representatives.

Economic groups: Business; retail and manufacturing, finance, building, real estate, professional groups, labor groups.

Civic groups: Civic clubs, community improvement groups, taxpayers' groups, League of Women Voters, and the like.

Church groups:   Ministerial organizations, church councils, individual churches.
Educational:     Schools, colleges, libraries, and so forth.
Families:        Consumer groups, PTA's, neighborhood organizations.
Government:      Agencies concerned with planning, housing, urban renewal, include State and regional representatives where available. City employees should not be designated as members but may well serve unofficially from time to time to assist with particular problems.
Minority groups: Ethnic or racial groups.
Welfare:         Social service, health and welfare organizations.
Information:     Press, radio, television.

While it will hardly prove feasible to have every organization represented, every representative element of the community should be included. Some elements will be more strongly represented than others. For example, in most communities business and civic organizations will be prominent in matters affecting the community as a whole. Where this is so, it would be well to enlist their support through adequate representation. This representation, however, should not be exclusive of other elements in the community. Since the Workable Program affects every segment of the community, it will prove useful to have every element represented. Individuals should be selected who are deeply interested in, and who are able and willing to work for, improvement of the total community.

## What is the Job of the Citizens Advisory Committee?

The primary functions of the committee and its members are:
(1) to learn about the nature and extent of deficiencies and the means and methods for remedying them;

(2) to make recommendations for improvement; and
(3) to help inform other citizens and groups as to the need for the improvements and thus develop united community understanding of this need.

A work program should be established for the overall committee and the minority group committee or subcommittee, and for any other subcommittees designated. Regular meetings should be scheduled not less than quarterly for the full committee and, perhaps, monthly for subcommittees. Notice of meetings should be given, minutes kept, and—at least annually —a report prepared to the chief executive and governing body showing the progress which has been made by the community and outlining new goals to be accomplished in the future.

## How Large Should the Citizens Advisory Committee Be?

The size of the overall committee will depend somewhat upon the size of the community and the breadth of representation. Generally it will call for specialized subcommittees, in addition to the minority-group committee, to most effectively tackle the various subjects of concern to the committee. Subcommittees should be made up of the committee members who have a special knowledge of or interest in the particular subcommittee subject.

It is important that the person or persons responsible for making the appointments understand why they are appointing the committee and have an appreciation of the job which they will be asking the committee to do. It is equally important that the committee members fully understand their job and the responsibilities of membership. Special care should be given to the selection of a capable leader as chairman who is willing to devote considerable time to the work necessary to make the advisory committee an efficient instrument for community improvement.

## How Does the Citizens Advisory
## Committee Organize To Do the Job?

Organization of the committee and development of its work program may well begin with an *Executive* (or steering or planning) *Committee* composed of the chairman and other officers of the full committee and the chairmen of any subcommittees. The Executive Committee should meet regularly to:

1.  Set policy, develop rules and by-laws;
2.  Plan the overall advisory committee program; and
3.  Coordinate the activities of the subcommittees.

Subcommittees may be designated and their chairmen appointed at the time the full committee is appointed, or this function may be given to the Executive Committee.

The preferred form of citizen organization combines continuity of organization with considerable flexibility in day-to-day operations. For example, some subcommittees can be formed on an *ad hoc* basis and disbanded when their specific function has been served. Others can be added as new needs develop. Some of the subcommittees, because of the subject and problems they deal with, will be permanent and continuing.

# Citizen Participation in Model
# Cities Program*

## Introduction

Section 103 (a) (2) of the Demonstration Cities and Metropolitan Development Act of 1966 requires that a Model Cities program provide for "widespread citizen participation in the program."

---

* Reprinted from the Department of Housing and Urban Development, Model Cities Administration's *CDA Letter No. 3*. Washington, D.C., October 30, 1967.

## Policy Statement on Citizen Participation

The implementation of this statutory provision requires: (1) the constructive involvement of citizens in the model neighborhood area and the city as a whole in planning and carrying out the program, and (2) the means of introducing the views of area residents in policy making should be developed and opportunities should be afforded area residents to participate actively in planning and carrying out the demonstration.

This requirement grows out of the conviction that improving the quality of life of the residents of the model neighborhood can be accomplished only by the affirmative action of the people themselves. This requires a means of building self-esteem, competence and a desire to participate effectively in solving the social and physical problems of their community.

HUD will not determine the ideal organizational pattern designed to accomplish this objective. It will, however, outline performance standards for citizen participation which must be achieved by each City Demonstration Agency. It is expected that patterns will vary from city to city, reflecting local circumstances. The city government, as the principal instrument for carrying out the Model Cities program, will be responsible for insuring that whatever organization is adopted provides the means for the model neighborhood's citizens to participate and be fully involved in policy making, planning and the execution of all program elements. For a plan to be approved, it must provide for such an organization and spell out precisely how the participation and involvement of the residents is to be carried out throughout the life of the Model Cities program.

## Performance Standards for Citizen Participation in Model Neighborhood Programs

In order to provide the citizen participation called for in the Act, there must be some form of organizational structure, existing or newly established, which embodies neighborhood residents in the process of policy and program planning and program implementation and operation. The leadership of that structure must consist of persons whom neighborhood residents accept as representing their interests.

The neighborhood citizen participation structure must have clear and direct *access* to the decision-making process of the City Demonstration Agency so that neighborhood views can influence policy, planning and program decisions. That structure must have sufficient information about any matter to be decided for a sufficient period of time so that it can initiate proposals and react knowledgeably to proposals from others. In order to initiate and react intelligently in program matters, the structure must have the technical capacity for making knowledgeable decisions. This will mean that some form of professional technical assistance, in a manner agreed to by neighborhood residents, shall be provided.

Where financial problems are a barrier to effective participation, financial assistance (e.g., baby sitting fees, reimbursement for transportation, compensation for serving on Boards or Committees) should be extended to neighborhood residents to assure their opportunity to participate.

Neighborhood residents will be employed in planning activities and in the execution of the program, with a view toward development of new career lines, including appropriate training and modification of local civil service regulations for entry and promotion.

# Arguments For and Against Citizen Participation in Urban Renewal*

HAROLD GOLDBLATT

Urban renewal means the intervention of government in the processes of urban change. The practical questions from the perspective of the planner and official are, how can change be introduced into the locality in an orderly way with 1) a minimum of disruption to the area as a social system? 2) a minimum of damage to the interests of residents influential enough to secure a veto of the plan? and 3) a minimum of distrust on the part not only of the residents affected but of bystanders as well? For we are not so far removed from the view of government as "best when it governs least" as not to be wary of the exercise of political power particularly when it sets itself in opposition to private economic power. In short, the problems from this perspective is how to make change by governmental authority least threatening and resistance to it least effective.

"Citizen participation" is advocated by many as a practical answer to the problem of facilitating change in the renewal area or of it. Co-opt the residents of the area, so the argument goes, into the processes of planning the renewal and of implementing the plans as a practical matter of ensuring the success of the renewal program. One might call this the "argument from social necessity."

* Reproduced by special permission from the author and the Health and Welfare Council of the National Capital Area, from *Citizen Participation in Urban Renewal—Washington, D.C.,* January 1966.

Thus, Slayton and Dewey writing in 1953 (Slayton was not then Commissioner of Urban Renewal) had this to say: ". . . redevelopment projects . . . have been killed because of opposition within the redevelopment area . . . If residents of an area know nothing about its proposed development until they read about it in the papers, they are likely to take a dim view of its value . . . Thus from a purely practical point of view, as a means of easing redevelopment through the perils of resident opposition, the community organization . . . can become a valuable tool."[1]

. . . A sociologist, John M. Foskett, writing on "the influence of social participation on community programs and activities," states the argument of participation for the sake of co-operation in these terms: ". . . Support for a program exists only when the proposal grows out of the thinking of the wider group. The best way to insure support at the solution level is to secure full participation at the problem-defining and decision-making level."[2] Translated, this means,

If broad social support is needed for a renewal program,

and if maximum involvement of citizens in the definition of the problem, and in the making of decisions to solve it is obtained,

then citizen support for the proposed solution of the problem will be maximized.

Another example of this rationale for the involvement of residents in urban renewal comes from William C. Loring, Jr., Frank L. Sweetser and Charles F. Ernst. These sociologists writing about "community organization for citizen participation in urban renewal" in Boston report that ". . . the Housing Association [of Metropolitan Boston, Inc.] had in 1953 come to the conclusion that all types of official action by

[1] William L. Slayton and Richard Dewey. "Community Organizations and Redevelopment," in Coleman Woodbury, Ed. *The Future of Cities and Urban Redevelopment,* University of Ohio Press, 1953. P. 427.

[2] John M. Foskett, "The Influence of Social Participation on Community Programs and Activities," in Marvin B. Sussman, Ed. *Community Structure and Analysis.* New York: Thomas Y. Crowell Co., 1959. P. 326.

themselves would not check blight and improve living standards in residential neighborhoods, unless there was active citizen participation in the effort."[3] Here citizen participation seems to connote activity more immediately related to the later implementation phase of renewal than to the earlier problem-definition and planning-decision phases.

Having offered the same warning as the others of what must befall the planners' hopes if they ignore the local residents these writers go on to promise positive assistance to the planners if they do include them in the program. "When there is citizen participation in the planning stages of a renewal program, plans can be formulated which reflect the desires and needs of residents as they perceive them. Moreover, having had a hand in the planning, residents are already predisposed to accept the plans which they feel they have helped create, even though the plans finally involve changes in the neighborhood they would not have agreed to without prior discussion and change of their attitudes."[4] Or, in other words, if citizens do *not* participate in the renewal program

then residential neighborhoods will continue to decline despite official action,

and living standards will not improve.

If citizens *do* participate in the renewal program,

then official plans will change to reflect citizens' perceptions of their desires and needs,

and citizen attitudes toward official plans will become more favorable.

We are seeking to examine the expectations which prompt urban renewal officials and their professional advisers to favor the involvement of citizens in the renewal process. The

---

[3] William C. Loring, Jr., Frank L. Sweetser, & Charles F. Ernst. *Community organization for citizen participation in urban renewal.* Prepared by the Housing Assoc. of Metropolitan Boston, for the Massachusetts Dept. of Commerce, Boston, Mass. Cambridge Press, Inc., 1957.

[4] *Ibid.*, p. 220.

first reason, then, is the expectation that the help of the residents will be needed in the implementaion of the plan and to secure this they had better be allowed into the planning of it. A second practical reason advanced for citizen participation is that the citizens may be needed as allies in the political contest for official acceptance of any renewal program. Thus, Loring, Sweetser, and Ernst: "... the planners, being the most optimistic group of city employees [Boston, Massachusetts] were found to be discounted by, if not in disrepute with, all the rest of the official family. They needed evidence of citizen support if their plans were to gain any chance of being taken up by politicians and administrators."[5] In other words:

If urban renewal officials are distrusted by their colleagues, then the support of influential citizens may reduce their distrust.

A similar reason for citizen involvement was voiced locally [in the District of Columbia] by Hylan Lewis in these words: "The District is a city where a very large number of gate keepers have veto power over community action proposals. Citizen participation might provide leverage for prying open the doors they keep. The change in the racial composition of the District and anticipated developments have been influential in making people receptive to suggestions who, six years ago, would have dismissed them as too academic, impracticable, or too Negro."[6]

Renewal officials may need the local citizens as allies "against" their colleagues in a different way: James Lash, speaking from extensive personal experience with citizen participation in urban renewal for Action, Inc. had this to say in its favor: "Citizen participation means pushing officials for services. It has the advantage that this can be done without embarrassment to the urban renewal officials who are their colleagues. Also, people low in social status are suspi-

[5] *Ibid.,* p. 93.
[6] Hylan Lewis, Director of Center for Community Studies, Interview on March 29, 1965.

cious of government officials and of the established welfare
agencies but less so of community organizations with a technique of involving the indigenous leadership."[7]

We have described above instances of the expectations of
urban renewal officials and their professional advisers that
without citizen participation the urban renewal program
must fail of acceptance or of implementation or both, whereas, with citizen participation, saving modifications in the official plans resulting from the give and take among citizens,
officials, and planners will ensure success. We might term
these expectations "practical" reasons for advocating citizen
participation. A different order of reasons, however, is also
offered by many based on quite another kind of expectation.
These are the reasons of propriety.

The significance of the distinction between citizen participation advocated as a necessary condition to the success of
the urban renewal program and citizen participation advocated as the right and proper mode of procedure is, of
course, the distinction between means and ends. In the one
case procedure may be evaluated in terms of efficiency and
effectiveness, that is to say, pragmatically. In the second case
only consistency with other values may be invoked for evaluation.

What may be called "the argument for democracy,"
for example, does not evaluate citizen participation as a
*means* to the objective of a successful urban renewal. Rather
citizen participation is viewed as the procedure to follow *regardless* of the consequences for the particular renewal program. Citizen participation is considered to be nothing less
than *democratic* procedure and, hence, a self-justifying end
in itself.

... The case for citizen participation includes among its advocates some who believe it valuable as a militant watch-dog
in civic affairs. Paraphrasing Clemenceau, who remarked that

[7] James Lash (New York Office of Action, Inc.). Interview in Washington,
D.C. May 4, 1965.

"war is too important to leave to the generals," are those who believe that urban renewal is too important to leave to the officials and planners. The late Hugh Pomeroy,[8] a city planner with a distinguished career, himself believed as much: "Shall [planning] then be left entirely in the hands of bureaucrats—like me, for instance?" he asks. And answers his own philosophical question: "Not at all. I do not trust myself to make decisions *for* the community. Planning is making decisions profoundly affecting the whole form and character of the community and the manner of life of its people. That calls for deeply rooted citizen participation."

... J. Allen Young,[9] Director of the University Neighborhood Council at Howard University, comments:

"We want citizen participation for the purpose of changing the system: to pressure the United Planning Organization, the Federal Housing Authority; to organize rent strikes; to align the community on the need for change. Groups are beginning to form around this problem, to pressure to bring about change. Everybody's in a protest mood. The need for change has become a moral issue, not only an economic one. The technique is to embarrass people who have functional responsibility."

So much for *types* of expectations and justifications offered as arguments for the involvement of "citizens" in urban renewal. We cannot claim to have exhausted all the varieties of argument but certainly these are the common ones which are phrased in general terms. We turn next to consider the arguments offered against the involvement of laymen in urban renewal.

... Perhaps the most telling of the arguments against citizen participation is that, far from being an indispensable means

[8] Hugh R. Pomeroy. "The Planning Process and Public Participation," in *An Approach to Urban Planning,* Gerald Breese and Dorothy E. Whiteman, Eds. Princeton University Press, 1953.

[9] J. Allen Young, Director of University Neighborhood Council. Interview on April 1, 1965.

to the achievement of the goal of urban renewal, it should rather be seen as a self-defeating mobilization of antagonistic sentiment. Many have commented to this effect both locally and as observers of events in other cities.

... From Loring, Sweetser, and Ernst[10] who, as we have seen, themselves advocate the involvement of "citizens" in urban renewal, comes the report that "some renewal administrators express a misgiving ... that neighborhood citizens would not act responsibly, would be needlessly aroused too early, and would continue to act in all the months of participation with griping, fantasy, and negative and suspicious rather than constructive attitudes. . . . To some of the redevelopment administrators, private redevelopers, and real estate promoters whom the senior author has met in various cities of the country, it is evident that citizen participation in renewal is considered worse than a nuisance. It is imagined by them to be a hazard, a potential which could thwart their professional judgments and render risky their business endeavors."

. . . Phil Doyle,[11] previous Executive Director of the Redevelopment Land Agency, expressed this point of view in an interview to the writer about as follows:

"Organization for participation means mobilizing the community to veto renewal plans. It is self-defeating for government to do this. You can't take a plebiscite about every official action or proposal and a plebiscite is what citizen participation is. The leisure time spent in participation in neighborhood discussion of local issues would be more effectively spent in a political club. Since it lacks home rule, the District of Columbia is in a special category. But elsewhere citizen participation is through the political process that elects officials who when they become unresponsive 'rascals' are then 'turned out.' "

An evaluation of citizen participation by the present director of the Redevelopment Land Agency, Thomas Appleby,

[10] op. cit., p. x.
[11] Phil Doyle. Interview, April 15, 1965.

was given in an interview to *The New York Times Magazine* shortly before he came to Washington from New Haven, Connecticut. "...in the late fifties 'planning with the people' became a major theme in urban renewal... But there are limits. 'Planning with the people' cannot always be as dandy and democratic as it sounds. What happens when a neighborhood says it wants no Negroes, no low-income public housing, no site for a public high school? Sometimes that's exactly what the people in the area themselves want, but it is a little hard to work with on a community-wide basis."

A second argument against citizen participation is that it is a lobbying for locality-based vested interest or special privilege. Participating citizens grind their axes on behalf of their own geographical locality and at the expense of the total community and of other localities. The outcome if they are successful is a disproportionate allotment of total community resources to the specific locality whose participating citizens have been influential with the professional planners and the government officials.

Thus, Phil Doyle[12]: "Citizen participation is, in effect, a splinter group instead of a city-wide effort. Because it is local it perceives renewal in local terms; it is a pressure group, a lobby for local vested interests as opposed to the interests of the total community. It assumes that the responsible department has budget which it isn't spending. Actually neighborhood improvement lowers the level of service in other neighborhoods by diverting personnel and material from them to the lobbying neighborhood. The philosophy of city officials, on the other hand, is equal treatment of every section of the community."

...The third argument against citizen participation in urban renewal has already been anticipated... Many have noted that inevitably the participants are a proportion, sometimes only a small proportion, of all those from the

---

[12] *Ibid.*

neighborhood eligible to take part. Nathan Volkman,[13] deputy director of the D.C. Office of Urban Renewal, who took a major role in the organization of Adams-Morgan [urban renewal project] noted: ". . . it must be remembered that even in well-organized neighborhoods it is far from total or totally representative. It does not include the uneducated, inarticulate. They are not consulted nor informed about impending changes." And Anita Bellamy,[14] who organized Girard Street for self-improvement, commented: "Citizen participation in urban renewal has not been tried. What we thought was citizen participation was not. What would be citizen participation was prevented from happening. In true citizen participation there would be a dialogue between planners and representatives of the residents. The latter would be indigenous: if from a Negro neighborhood they would themselves be Negro; if from a low-income neighborhood they would themselves be low-income. They would learn what they needed to know in conference with technical planners and the latter would modify their proposals in the light of the on-going dialogue. Instead, non-representative Negro ministers whose concern was that their churches not be relocated or that they receive compensation adequate for a replacement, or social work professionals, or businessmen, were chosen for membership on city-wide citizen advisory committees."

. . . Still another argument against reliance on citizen participation for urban renewal is that even at its very best local citizens cannot directly improve the neighborhood substantially in its physical aspects. This is most obvious in the case of redevelopment. The role of citizen participation is admittedly limited here since the total present population will be displaced nor will many be readmitted to the area once it has been redeveloped.

[13] Nathan Volkman, Office of Urban Renewal, Interview on April 6, 1965.
[14] Anita Bellamy, Community Organizer, Redevelopment Land Agency. Interview on March 5, 1965. See also Dagmar H. Perman, *The Girard Street Project*, Washington, D.C.: All Souls Church Unitarian, 1964.

Andrea Maddox,[15] who has seen citizen participation both in connection with rehabilitation and with redevelopment, said, "Stay or go makes all the difference. Citizen participation can be much more extensive and varied if the residents are to remain in the area while it has much less of a role if they are to leave it."

But even when rehabilitation or conservation is the renewal mode, citizen participation can, it is argued, accomplish little of what is needed. If, for example, compliance with the housing code would suffice "to save" or to upgrade the area why has not compliance already been forthcoming? In the case of home-ownership the answer may be that the home-owners could not afford the repairs necessary to maintain their property despite the economic incentive to do so. In the case of absentee ownership, similar considerations apply except to the unscrupulous slumlords who buy property to "milk" its rental value. In the latter case such "citizens" can scarcely be persuaded to "participate" voluntarily in a do-good program when they have deliberately set themselves to ignore the needs of the area.[16]

... A fifth argument advanced against citizen participation is that it is essentially without authority even within its own domain, in conservation as well as rehabilitation situations. Citizen participation organized in a council of neighborhood associations expressly set up for the purpose of planning and implementing urban renewal constitutes, in effect, a local "government," though one without the legitimate authority of real government—namely, the authority to coerce dissenters to abide by the will of the majority.

Moreover, Phil Doyle added[17] that citizen participation or organization, in the long pull, has little influence on official decisions, certainly not on the large ones which are made

---

[15] Andrea Maddox. Inaerview on April 9, 1965.

[16] Mrs. Anne Tolliner, President of Reliance Realty Company. Interview on April 13, 1965.

[17] Doyle, *op. cit.*

from the perspective of the total community. On the other hand, it offers little dependable support to officials in need of support for city-wide programs.

Doyle would not go so far as to say, as other officials have, that citizen participation is a usurpation of the responsibilities and authority of government officials. The latter are not so jealous of their rights and duties; rather, citizen participation is ignored when the major decisions are to be made.

He saw only a social role, as distinct from a political or economic role, for citizen participation: It can support supplementary services such as private trash disposal additional to city service, or added services to schools through the P.T.A. or private police protection. It has a role in areas receiving relocatees: to make them welcome and to assist in their rehabilitation.

A sixth argument against citizen participation is that it prolongs the planning process excessively, endangering the hoped-for success of the renewal effort. Urban renewal, it is argued, is at best a process which spans years of activity; to add to the time span delays consequent to citizen participation is to increase the risk of ultimate defeat or obsolescence of the renewal plans.

Other reasons for and against the involvement of citizens in urban renewal could doubtless be added to the inventory of those cited here. But enough has been set down to show what a hopeless task it would be to attempt to assess the worth of citizen participation in urban renewal if discussion must continue on the present level.

The arguments for and against the participation of citizens in urban renewal, when formulated in general terms, do not seem to differ materially from arguments for or against their participation in other spheres of activity. They are *generic* arguments. In other words, they relate to the *general problem* of the role of the citizen in a democracy and of the technically expert civil servant in relation to the government official, elected or appointed. This is the triumvirate which jockeys for influence over governmental decisions. But citizen participation is not one single activity; it is a wide variety of specific activities by a variety of persons occupying different status positions in the city. And the same must be said for urban renewal, which is not one but a variety of modes of procedure for the improvement of urban areas, both in their physical and social aspects. . . .

# Planning and Politics: Citizen Participation in Urban Renewal*

JAMES Q. WILSON

Few national programs affecting our cities have begun under such favorable auspices as urban renewal. Although public housing was from the very first a bitterly controversial policy, redevelopment and renewal by contrast were widely accepted by both Democratic and Republican administrations and had the backing of both liberals and conservatives, labor and business planners and mayors. Yet today, almost fourteen years after urban redevelopment was inaugurated as Title I of the Housing Act of 1949, the program is beset with controversy and, what is even more dismaying to its supporters, lagging far behind its construction goals.

Although there are nearly 944 federally-approved slum clearance and urban renewal projects scheduled for over 520 different communities, only a little more than half have proceeded to the point where the cities are authorized to begin assembling and clearing land. And most important, of all the projects authorized only 65 have been completed.[1] In New York, the city which has been the most active in renewal programs of all kinds, all the publicly supported projects undertaken over the last quarter century cover less than one per

* Reprinted with permission of the author and publisher, *Journal of the American Institute of Planners,* XXIX, No. 4, November 1963, 242-249.

[1] Housing and Home Finance Agency, *Housing Statistics: Annual Data,* April 1962, p. 76.

cent of the city's surface.[2] Further, most of the projects completed can be found in or near the central business districts of cities rather than in residential areas, and they have often involved clearing, not slums, but deteriorating commercial and industrial structures.

Some of the reasons for the relatively slight accomplishments of urban renewal are not hard to find. Federally sponsored projects such as renewal require dealing successfully with almost endless amounts of red tape; it has taken a long time for city governments and private developers to acquire the knowledge and experience required for this. Furthermore, even though the federal government pays most of the cost of assembling and clearing the land on which a project is planned, it is not always easy to find a private developer to whom the land can be sold.

An additional reason for slow progress in urban renewal is racial. Blighted areas are often Negro areas. The political and social problems involved in relocating Negroes in other areas of the city are often sufficiently formidable to make opposition to the renewal program as a whole very powerful.

But the most important reason for controversy and slow progress is the mounting disagreement over the methods and even the objectives of urban renewal. The coalition among liberals, planners, mayors, businessmen, and real estate interests which originally made renewal politically so irresistible has begun to fall apart. Liberals, who still see the rehabilitation of the central city as a prime goal for government, have begun to have doubts, particularly about redevelopment that involves wholesale clearance by bulldozers. They are disturbed by charges from many Negro leaders—whom liberals are accustomed to regarding as their natural allies—that liberals have aided and abetted a program which under the guise of slum clearance is really a program of Negro clear-

[2] See Raymond Vernon. *The myth and reality of our urban problems.* Cambridge, Mass.: Joint Center for Urban Studies of MIT and Harvard, 1962. P. 40.

ance. They have been disturbed and even angered by the elimination of whole neighborhoods, like the Italian West End of Boston; by the reduction in the supply of low-cost housing to make way for high-cost housing built with federal subsidies; and by what they take to be the inhuman, insensitive, and unrealistic designs of some city planners. Jane Jacob's book, *The Death and Life of the Great American Cities*, is expressive of one powerful segment of opinion in this regard.[3] The liberals are everywhere demanding that redevelopment (that is, wholesale clearance) be abandoned in favor of rehabilitation—conserving as many existing structures as possible.

Mayors and other city officials in some cities (although not yet in all) have seen in these debates a sign that a program which began as "good politics" has turned into something which at best is difficult politics. When it seemed possible that a vigorous and ambitious mayor could place himself at the head of an alliance of liberals, planners, businessmen, and newspapers on behalf of restoring the central city, urban renewal became a top priority civic objective. An initial burst of enthusiasm greeted renewal in almost every city where the idea was broached. But after the first few projects were undertaken, the hidden political costs began to become evident. Voters who did not like being called slum-dwellers and who liked even less being forced out of their old neighborhoods began to complain. As the enthusiasm of the civic boosters began to wane, many mayors began to wonder whether they were going to be left alone on the firing line to answer for projects which the boosters had pushed them into in the first place.

[3] See also, as an example of liberal objections to renewal, Staughton Lynd, "Urban Renewal—for Whom?" *Commentary*, January 1961, pp. 34-45. The consequences of urban renewal for the underprivileged in American cities are discussed in Peter Marris, "The Social Implications of Urban Redevelopment," *Journal of the American Institute of Planners*, XXVIII (August 1962), 180-186.

What in many ways is the most interesting aspect of the controversy surrounding urban renewal is not the breakup of this coalition, however, but the growing resistance of neighborhoods to clearance and renewal programs. The growth of neighborhood resistance to urban renewal has been gradual and cumulative. Many of the earliest redevelopment projects were completed with little organized opposition. Somehow, however, people have learned from the experience of others, and today, in cities which have been engaged in renewal for several years, the planners often find prospective renewal areas ready and waiting for them, organized to the teeth. In Chicago, for example, the Lake Meadows redevelopment project met with relatively little organized indigenous opposition (although considerable opposition from forces outside the area). The Hyde Park-Kenwood project, undertaken a few years later, was greeted with considerably more opposition. Today, plans for the Woodlawn and Near West Side areas have been met with impassioned opposition from many of the residents of the neighborhoods involved. Similarly, the West End project in Boston had relatively little difficulty in dealing with people in the area; the project planned for Charlestown, begun some time later, has been—at least for the time being—stopped dead in its tracks by organized neighborhood opposition. Today, according to Robert C. Weaver, Administrator of the Housing and Home Finance Agency, "in nearly every major city in the country and many small cities there are heated debates over urban renewal projects that are underway or under consideration."[4]

Mr. Weaver might well be concerned over these debates, for federal policy requires local citizen participation in the formulation of local renewal plans before federal money can be spent on them. As he himself stressed on another occasion, "We mean [by citizen participation] not just a passive acceptance of what is being done, but the active utilization of

[4] Quoted in *St. Louis Post-Dispatch*, February 27, 1963.

local leadership and organization which can profitably assist in the community's efforts."[5]

Local citizen participation on a city-wide basis is usually not difficult to obtain. "Civic leaders" representing various groups and interests in the community can always be assembled for such purposes. But getting the participation, much less the acquiescence, of citizens in the renewal neighborhood is something else again. Although federal law does not require participation at this level, the increased vigor of neighborhood opposition has made such participation expedient if not essential—particularly with the new emphasis on rehabilitation and self-help.

### The Hyde Park-Kenwood Experience

The fullest account we have of such participation is that found in the book, *The Politics of Urban Renewal*, by Peter H. Rossi and Robert A. Dentler. This study dealt with one neighborhood—Hyde Park-Kenwood in Chicago—which in many ways is remarkable if not unique. The site of the University of Chicago, it is heavily populated with University professors and business and professional people, all possessing an inordinate amount of education, experience, and skills, and all having a strong commitment to the community. From 1949 on, these people were organized into the Hyde Park-Kenwood Community Conference, a neighborhood group with a professional staff, dedicated to conserving the area against blight. Actual planning for the area was not, of course, done by this organization—that was beyond its resources—but by the planning staff of the University of Chicago and by various city agencies.

The Community Conference took a deep and continuing interest in the $30,000,000 urban renewal plan for the area and meticulously examined and discussed every part of it. Local and federal authorities judged the Conference to be an

---

[5] From an address to the 50th Anniversary of the Family Service Association of America, New York City, November 13, 1961.

excellent example of genuine grass-roots participation in a major renewal effort. After the plan was finally approved by the Chicago City Council, it commanded widespread (although not unanimous) citizen acceptance, even though about 20 per cent of the buildings in the community were to be torn down.

In evaluating the work of this local citizens group, Rossi and Dentler conclude that the Hyde Park-Kenwood Community Conference played two important roles. First, it stimulated public awareness of the necessity and practicability of change and gave people confidence that something could be done to save their neighborhood. Second, the Conference managed to create a climate of opinion in which the actual planning was done, and although it is impossible to tell exactly what impact this climate had on the planners, it is likely that the general mood of the community as articulated by the neighborhood organization influenced at least the most general goals that were embodied in the final plan.

But it is also important to note what the Conference did not do. According to this study, the organization did not play a crucial part in influencing the specific details of the plan. Instead, it created broad popular acceptance for a plan which was not entirely in keeping with its own objectives. Rossi and Dentler conclude that the "maximum role to be played by a citizen-participation movement in urban renewal is primarily a passive one."[6]

Considering what I have said about the rising opposition of local neighborhoods to urban renewal, the acquiescence of this grass-roots organization seems to require explanation. In the narrowest terms, this support was due to the fact that the Hyde Park-Kenwood Community Conference represented that part of a very heterogeneous community which would ultimately benefit from renewal. The upper-middle-class professors, housewives, and business and professional men (both

[6] Peter H. Rossi and Robert A. Dentler. *The Politics of Urban Renewal— The Chicago Findings* (New York: Free Press of Glencoe, 1961), p. 287.

white and Negro) who made up the bulk of the Conference
were mostly people who were going to remain in the community and whose peace, security, cultural life, and property
values would probably be enhanced by a successful renewal
plan. The persons who were to be moved out of the community and whose apartments and homes were to be torn down
were usually lower-income Negroes who, with very few exceptions, were not part of the Community Conference.

But this narrow explanation in terms of self-interest is only
partly true, for if low-income Negroes were not directly represented on the Conference they were often represented
vicariously—at least in the eyes of the Conference members.
Time and again the Conference, or leading members of it,
pressed the city to provide middle- and low-income public
housing in the renewal area in part to accommodate persons
who would be displaced by demolition. The Conference was
firmly committed to the idea of a multi-racial community;
some of its members were committed in addition to the idea
of a multiclass community.

I would argue that this broader consideration was equally
as important as the narrower one in explaining the positive
and constructive role of the Conference. The organization
was made up to a large degree of persons who attached a high
value to community-wide and neighborhood-wide goals, even
(in some cases) when attaining those goals entailed a sacrifice in
personal, material satisfactions. They are people who partake to an extraordinary extent of what Edward C. Banfield
and I have called in a forthcoming book the "community-
regarding" or "public-regarding" political ethos.[7] This ethos,
which is most likely to be found among citizens who rank
high in income, education, or both, is based on an enlarged
view of the community and a sense of obligation toward it.
People who display it are likely to have a propensity for looking at and making policy for the community "as a whole"

[7] Edward C. Banfield and James Q. Wilson. *City politics.* Cambridge,
Mass.: Harvard University Press, 1963. Chap. xvi.

and to have a high sense of personal efficacy, a long time-perspective, a general familiarity with and confidence in city-wide institutions, and a cosmopolitan orientation toward life. In addition, they are likely to possess a disproportionate share of organizational skills and resources.

It is just these attributes, of course, which make such people most likely to participate effectively in organizations whose function—whatever their ostensible purpose—is to create a sense of community and of community confidence and to win consent for community-wide plans. They are, in short, precisely those attributes which are likely to produce "citizen participation in urban renewal" that planners and community organizers will consider "positive and constructive"—that is, participation which will influence some of the general goals of renewal and modify a few of its details, but allow renewal to proceed.

## Social Differences in Citizen Participation

Most neighborhoods which planners consider in need of renewal are not, however, like Hyde Park-Kenwood in Chicago and are not heavily populated with citizens like the ones who organized the Hyde Park-Kenwood Community Conference. Most renewal areas are likely to be low-income, often Negro sections, many of whose inhabitants are the opposite in almost every respect from the cosmopolitan elite of Hyde Park-Kenwood. Such people are more likely to have a limited time-perspective, a greater difficulty in abstracting from concrete experience, an unfamiliarity with and lack of confidence in city-wide institutions, a preoccupation with the personal and the immediate, and few (if any) attachments to organizations of any kind, with the possible exception of churches.[8] Lacking ex-

[8] Cf. Seymour Martin Lipset, *Political man* (Garden City, N.Y.: Doubleday & Co., 1960), chap. iv, and Robert Agger, *et al.*, "Political Cynicism: Measurement and Meaning," *Journal of Politics*, XXIII (August 1961), 477-506. See also the vivid account of the culture of a lower-income Italian section of Boston in Herbert J. Gans, *The urban villagers* (New York: Free Press of Glencoe, 1963).

perience in and the skills for participation in organized endeavors, they are likely to have a low sense of personal efficacy
in organizational situations. By necessity as well as by inclina-
tion, such people are likely to have what one might call a "private-regarding" rather than a "public-regarding" political
ethos. They are intimately bound up in the day-to-day struggle
to sustain themselves and their families.

Such people are usually the objects rather than the subjects
of civic action: they are acted upon by others, but rarely do
they themselves initiate action. As a result, they often develop
a keen sense of the difference between "we" and "they"—
"they" being outside, city-wide civic and political forces which
seek to police them, vote them, and redevelop them. It is quite
natural that the "they" are often regarded with suspicion.

Although such people are not likely spontaneously to form
organizations to define and carry out long-range very general
civic tasks, it is wrong to assume that they are not likely to organize—or to allow themselves to be organized—for any purpose. The important thing is not that they are unorganizable,
but that they can be organized only under special circumstances and for special purposes. Except for organizations
which are in some sense extensions of the family and the
church, lower-income neighborhoods are more likely to produce collective action in response to threats (real or imagined)
than to create opportunities. Because of the private-regarding
nature of their attachment to the community, they are likely
to collaborate when each person can see a danger to him or to
his family in some proposed change; collective action is a way,
not of defining and implementing some broad program for the
benefit of all, but of giving force to individual objections by
adding them together in a collective protest.

The view which a neighborhood is likely to take of urban
renewal, then, is in great part a product of its class composition. Upper- and upper-middle-class people are more likely to
think in terms of general plans, the neighborhood or community as a whole, and long-term benefits (even when they

might involve immediate costs to themselves); lower- and lower-middle-class people are more likely to see such matters in terms of specific threats and short-term costs. These differences account in great measure for some of the frustrations of the planners, redevelopers, and community organizers who are involved in urban renewal. Whereas it is relatively easy to obtain consent to renewal plans when people are thinking in terms of general goals and community-wide benefits, it is much harder—often impossible—when people see the same set of facts in terms of possible threats and costs.

This interpretation of lower-class behavior applies in its full force only in the extreme case, of course. There are many stable working class neighborhoods where indigenous leadership can be developed and involved in urban renewal programs on a "constructive" basis. The Back of the Yards area of Chicago is an example of one neighborhood of blue-collar families with strong local leadership (although even here, it should be noted, one powerful impetus to community organization was the fear of Negro invasion). But many potential renewal areas, particularly in Negro sections, do not even qualify as "stable working class." Half of all urban Negro families had an income of less than $3,000 a year in 1960. Thus, although the contrast I draw between middle-class and lower-class with respect to their attachment to neighborhood and community is deliberately extreme, it must be remembered that urban renewal is a policy intended in great part to apply to "extreme" areas.

## Community Organization Strategies

Among community organizers, two radically different strategies have been evolved to produce citizen participation under such circumstances. One recognizes the special character of depressed lower-income neighborhoods and seeks to capitalize on it. The most prominent and controversial exponent of this approach is Saul D. Alinsky, executive director of the Industrial Areas Foundation of Chicago. He has created in a lower-income, heavily Negro area near the University of Chicago an organization ("The Woodlawn Organization") built in large part upon the residents' fears of urban renewal. According to a recent account, "Alinsky eschews the usual appeals to home-owners' interests in conserving property values or to a general neighborhood spirit or civic pride—appeals, in his view, that apply only to middle-class neighborhoods." Instead, he "appeals to the self-interest of the local residents and to their resentment and distrust of the outside world."[9] If residents do not have what I have called a "public-regarding" ethos, Alinsky is perfectly willing to appeal to their "private-regarding" ethos and to capitalize on the fact that collective action among such people is possible only when each person fears some threat to his own interests.

By stimulating and focussing such fears, an organization is created which can then compel other organizations—such as the sponsors of an urban renewal project—to bargain with it. Often the only terms on which such negotiations are acceptable to the neighborhood organization are terms unacceptable to the sponsors of renewal, for they require the drastic modification or even abandonment of the renewal plan. When an organization is built out of accumulated fears and grievances rather than out of community attachments, the cost is usually the tearing up of any plans that call for really fundamental changes in the landscape. On the other hand, such an organization may be very effective in winning special concessions from city hall to remedy specific neighborhood problems.

Many, probably most, planners and community organization specialists reject Alinsky's tactics. To them, his methods produce and even exacerbate conflict rather than prevent it, alienate the neighborhood from the city as a whole rather than

[9] Charles E. Silberman. "The City and the Negro," *Fortune*, LXV (March 1962), 88-91. See also Saul D. Alinsky, "Citizen Participation and Community Organization in Planning and Urban Renewal," address before the Chicago chapter of the National Association of Housing and Redevelopment Officials, January 29, 1962.

bring it into the normal pattern of civic action, and place a premium on power rather than on a cooperative search for the common good.

The alternative strategy of most community organizers is to stimulate the creation of neighborhood organizations which will define "positive" goals for their areas in collaboration with the relevant city agencies and in accord with the time schedule which binds most federal renewal efforts. In Boston, for example, a new quasi-public agency—Action for Boston Community Development, or "ABCD"—has been created with both public and Ford Foundation funds in part for the purpose of stimulating the formation of neighborhood associations which will provide citizen participation in (and citizen consent to) the renewal plans of the Boston Redevelopment Authority. So far, it has been put to the test in two neighborhoods selected for renewal. In one, Washington Park-Roxbury, where it assisted in creating an organization "from the top down" by gathering together ministers and others prominent in this Negro community, it was able to win from the middle-class Negroes who would benefit from the plan consent "in principle" to a rehabilitation program the details of which are not yet entirely clear. In the other case, Charlestown, an old, lower-middle-income Irish neighborhood, ABCD brought many existing grass-roots organizations together for the purpose of ratifying a renewal plan. The citizens of Charlestown, however, knew their own interests well enough to cripple, at a public hearing, the proposed renewal plan with a flood of objections and conditions which, at least for the time being, the renewal authorities could not meet.

## Implications for Renewal Programs

If one's goal is urban renewal on any really large scale in our cities, the implications of these observations are disturbing. The higher the level of indigenous organization in a lower-class neighborhood, the poorer the prospects for renewal in that area.

To say that the prospects are poorer does not, of course, mean that renewal will never occur with the consent of strong indigenous organizations in lower-class areas. But the difficulty is substantially increased, and a protracted, subtle, and assiduous wooing of neighborhood sentiment must first take place.[10] Perhaps this explains why, at least until very recently most local urban renewal directors made no effort to encourage citizen participation except on a city-wide basis—with little or no representation from the affected neighborhood.[11]

In short, while the devotion of some planners today to the concept of "planning with people"—that is, citizen participation in neighborhood rehabilitation—may be an improvement over old-style urban development which ignored or took little account of neighborhood interests, the enthusiasm with which the new doctrine is being advocated blurs many important problems. The most important of these is that "planning with people" assumes on the part of the people involved a willingness and a capacity to engage in a collaborative search for the common good. The willingness is obviously almost never present when the persons involved will be severely penalized by having their homes and neighborhoods destroyed by wholesale clearance. Nor will that willingness be present when "rehabilitation" means, as it usually does, that the residents must at their own expense bring their homes up to standards deemed satisfactory to the renewal agency or have their homes taken from them. But what is less obvious is that it may not be pres-

[10] See the account in Alfred G. Rosenberg, "Baltimore's Harlem Park Finds 'Self-Help' Citizen Participation is Successful," *Journal of Housing*, XVIII (May 1961) 204-209. The initial reaction in the neighborhood to a renewal plan was bitter and got worse for three years. Patient community organization managed to overcome some of this resistance after much effort.

[11] See the survey reported in Gerda Lewis, "Citizen Participation in Urban Renewal Surveyed," *Journal of Housing*, XVI (March 1959), 80-87. Questionnaires returned by about half the local renewal directors in the 91 cities which had approved "workable programs" as of July 31, 1956, showed that "the residents of project areas . . . seem to be relatively uninvolved in urban renewal"; representation from these areas on citizens' committees dealing with renewal was "almost totally absent."

ent, even when such clearance is not envisaged, because of important class differences in the capacity to organize for community-wide goals. This means that middle-class persons who are beneficiaries of rehabilitation will be planned with; lower-class persons who are disadvantagd by rehabilitation are likely to be planned *without*.

The fact that some people will be hurt by renewal does not, of course, mean that there should be no renewal. There are scarcely any public policies which do not impose costs on someone. What it does mean is that planners might more frankly take such costs into account, weighing them against the benefits renewal may confer on individuals and the community. There is little except obfuscation to be gained from attempting to maintain, as the slogan "planning with people" implies, that urban renewal and perfect democracy are and always should be compatible; that not only can the city be revitalized, it can be revitalized with the consent of all concerned.

If we decide to try to obtain the consent of those neighborhoods selected for renewal, we had better prepare ourselves for a drastic reevaluation of the potential impact of that program. Adjusting the goals of renewal to the demands of the lower classes means, among other things, substantially reducing the prospects for assembling sufficiently large tracts of cleared land to make feasible the construction of dwelling units attractive to the middle-class suburbanite whom the city is anxious to woo back into its taxing jurisdiction. This, in turn, means that the central city may have to abandon the goal of recolonizing itself with a tax-paying, culture-loving, free-spending middle class and be content instead with serving as a slightly dilapidated way-station in which lower-income and minority groups find shelter and a minimal level of public services while working toward the day when they, too, can move out to a better life. That, of course, is in great part the function that at least the older central cities of this country have always performed, and until we run out of lower classes (a day unfortunately far in the future), that may be the function they must continue to perform.

## Political Effects

Not only does the question of citizen participation in urban renewal have important implications for the goals of planning and even for one's conception of the function of the central city; it also goes to the heart of a fundamental problem in the urban political process. Resolving this issue is not simply a problem in planning priorities, but in addition a problem in electoral politics.

American mayors today are faced with the problem of governing cities in which to a great extent the traditional sources of political power have been dispersed or eliminated. The old-style political machine is gone except in a very few big cities. Party organization generally is weak. Mayors must still assemble the power to govern but they can rarely do so today by relying on loyal party lieutenants who occupy the lesser city offices and who sit on the council. Instead, the mayor must try to piece together that power out of the support he can receive from city-wide interests, such as newspapers, civic associations, business organizations, and labor unions. Support from such sources, valuable as it is, does not always carry with it the assurance that the support of the rank-and-file voter will also be forthcoming. Average citizens have a way of not sharing (or sometimes not even knowing about) the enthusiasms of the top civic leadership.

To insure against this possibility, many "new-style" mayors are trying to build up new neighborhood associations and enter into relationships with old ones in order to provide themselves with a way of reaching the average voter and of commanding his support. In Boston, for example, it is an open secret that Mayor John Collins is hoping that the support and attention he has given various neighborhood associations will be reciprocated, on election day, by the support of their members for him.

To the extent that these neighborhood associations are courted by mayors, they attempt to extract in return concessions on matters of city policy (such as street sweeping, garbage collection, or playground maintenance) which affect their areas. They see themselves as instruments for adapting the programs of an impersonal city bureaucracy to the various and often conflicting needs of neighborhoods. In a sense, they perform (for entirely different reasons, of course) the same function which the political machine once performed.

The neighborhood civic association is widely regarded as not only a new mechanism for representing citizen wants to the city bureaucracy, but a means of ending the political "alienation" of those citizens. Much has been written of late to suggest that a large and perhaps growing number of people are "alienated" from the American political process, but particularly from the political process in their communities. In Boston,[12] Cambridge,[13] Detroit,[14] Nashville,[15] upstate New York,[16] and various other places where studies have been made, the voters—usually (though not always) those with little income or education—feel, we are told, estranged from and even threatened by the political life of their cities. To the extent

[12] Murray B. Levin, *The Alienated Voter* (New York: Holt, Rinehart & Winston, 1960), pp. 58-75. See also Murray B. Levin and Murray Eden, "Political Strategy for the Alienated Voter," *Public Opinion Quarterly*, XXVI (Spring 1962), pp. 47-63.

[13] See William A. Gamson, "The Fluoridation Dialogue: Is It An Ideological Conflict?" *Public Opinion Quarterly*, XXV (Winter 1961), pp. 526-37, and Arnold Simmel, "A Signpost for Research on Fluoridation Conflicts: The Concept of Relative Deprivation," *Journal of Social Issues*, XVII (1961), pp. 26-36.

[14] Arthur Kornhauser, *Attitudes of People Toward Detroit* (Detroit: Wayne University Press, 1952), p. 28.

[15] E. L. McDill and J. C. Ridley, "Status, Anomia, Political Alienation and Political Participation," *American Journal of Sociology*, LXVIII (September 1962), pp. 205-213.

[16] Wayne E. Thompson and John E. Horton, "Political Alienation as a Force in Political Action," *Social Forces*, XXXVIII (March 1960), pp. 190-5 and Horton and Thompson, "Powerlessness and Political Negativism: A Study of Defeated Local Referendums," *American Journal of Sociology*, LXVII (March 1962), pp. 485-93.

that this alienation exists (and the studies are not very precise on this), the neighborhood civic association is seen as an important way of giving the citizen a meaningful and satisfactory relationship with his community—a way, in short, of ending his "alienation."[17]

It is not yet clear, however, whether such neighborhood groups will provide a means whereby citizens overcome their "alienation" or whether they will simply provide a forum in which citizens can give expression to it. These groups, after all, are usually concerned about neighborhood, not city-wide, problems, and the member's attachment is often at most only to his immediate family and neighbors, not to the community as a whole. Neighborhood associations seek many goals in their dealings with city hall. Generally speaking, however, they want higher levels of community services but they oppose extensive physical changes in their areas, as would be caused by highway construction or urban renewal programs.

For city-wide officials, such as mayors and planners, the crucial problem is how to make attention to these neighborhood demands compatible with city-wide programs, almost all of which will, to some extent, impose hardships on some neighborhoods. The old-style political leaders who were bosses of city machines were not faced to the same degree with this problem. Whenever they could, they avoided the conflict between neighborhood and city by not proposing any extensive programs designed to appeal to city-wide interests. When such programs were politically unavoidable, they resolved the inevitable conflict by "buying off" their neighborhood opponents. The bosses used the jobs, favors, and patronage which they controlled to enforce their wills on neighborhood political leaders and to compensate the neighborhood voters for their distress.

[17] William C. Loring, Jr., Frank L. Sweetser, & Charles F. Ernst. *Community organization for citizen participation in urban renewal.* Prepared by the Housing Assoc. of Metropolitan Boston, for the Massachusetts Dept. of Commerce, Boston, Mass. Cambridge Press, Inc., 1957. Pp. 232-238.

Today's mayor can neither avoid proposing large programs to satisfy city-wide interests nor can he buy off the neighborhood opponents of such projects. Under these circumstances, the mayor must move cautiously between the twin evils of doing so little as to disappoint community-regarding voters and doing so much as to antagonize private-regarding voters.

Citizen participation in urban renewal, then, is not simply (or even most importantly) a way of winning popular consent for controversial programs. It is part and parcel of a more fundamental reorganization of American local politics. It is another illustration—if one more is needed—of how deeply embedded in politics the planning process is.

# The Dilemma of
# Citizen Participation*

ROBERT C. SEAVER

In the broadest sense, citizen participation in public affairs, particularly at the local level, is a fact of political life that applies no more and no less to urban renewal and city planning than it does to any other function of government. At the ballot box, in public hearings, and through all the other less formal avenues that our system provides, the people will make their views known and their interest felt. This phenomenon is intensified today by the growing expectations and militancy of groups not formerly recognized in the traditional urban power structure. So in a way it is misleading to speak of a dilemma of citizen participation for it implies some choice, however equivocal.

Yet in a more limited sense there is a dilemma. It is not whether to have citizen participation in the broad sense—that is taken for granted—but whether to incorporate as a part of official process a more positive form of citizen engagement. In this limited sense, the dilemma goes this way: Experience shows that failure to get across to the people the rationale of a given proposal may evoke opposition based more on emotion than on the merits of the case, and therefore far more virulent. Yet in some cases, efforts to bring the community into the process early enough to create understanding has seemed to do

* Reproduced by special permission of the author and the publisher from Pratt Planning Papers, 4, The Pratt Institute, New York City. Written when the author was Chief of the Bureau of Community Affairs, City of New York Housing and Redevelopment Board, 1960-65.

more to forearm the opposition than to win support. So arises the argument that the best citizen participation is the least citizen participation.

This argument is superficial and probably frivolous. There are too many instances—regrettably eclipsed by the horror stories—to indicate that it is possible to work with the community with benefit to both sides. The critical question seems to be whether or not the conditions necessary to successful citizen engagement are tolerable to the administrative, political, and professional establishment in whose hands the initiative lies. Some of these will be suggested later. They do not necessarily imply the surrender of integrity or the abdication of responsibility. But they do imply some sharing of the decisions in the process. So to many responsible people in the field the question—whether to accept the conditions will accomplish more than to reject them—is very real.

It will become more real. A new body of thought in the social welfare field—the client as partner rather than recipient, the poor as abused rather than delinquent—has been given a firm shove forward by the statutory requirement of "maximum feasible participation" by the poor in community programs under the federal war on poverty.

Congress has, in effect, set a new national standard of citizen interest and involvement that, however hazy, goes far beyond anything ever contemplated in more than a few localities prior to the antipoverty program. The two chief features of this standard are that it recognizes the vested interest and certain corollary if unspecified rights of the people who are directly affected by public programs, and that it places at least a part of the power to shape or respond to such programs in their hands. This standard is being established in the very communities where renewal is most likely to be needed, and long-range planning finds its maneuvering room. Even if it were not, the tide of events is such as to sweep the underlying philosophy into such areas. Advent of these ideas has already led to instances where community residents were mobilized by personnel paid with antipoverty funds by one local agency, to oppose the renewal or planning proposals of another agency. Some renewal and planning veterans, looking ahead, wonder if it will be possible to live with this standard. They are far from sure that the answer is yes, but fearful of the implications if it is no.

One reason the question is so opaque is that within the urban renewal field, and to an even lesser degree in city planning, there never has been an adequate resolution in policy or practice of what citizen participation is, can, or should be or do. Indeed, the central difficulty in discussing it is that almost everyone has a different view based on unspoken assumptions and perspectives that in turn spring from differing personal imperatives, political philosophy, social understanding, and other variables. The basic idea that somehow the parties in interest should have some voice in the process commands almost everybody's assent. But who the parties are, what kind of a voice they should have, about what aspect of the process, and with what degree of influence, are questions that evoke the most diverse array of strongly—even combatively—held opinions.

Policies and practices in citizen participation reflect this diversity from one locality to another. More importantly, they reflect it in the quality of the engagement effort in any given locality. That is, the substance of the exchange between citizen and agency in any community is much more likely to be the result of a functional compromise among the respective views of the various people responsible for action than it is to reflect the abstract principles of participation espoused by policy-makers. Beyond a certain point, this discrepancy is one practical measure of how productive or destructive the exchange will be.

These gaps are not merely semantic. They reflect real differences over the proper scope and nature of social welfare efforts, whether renewal and planning are properly concerned with these, and the proper relationship between profession and lay opinions in public affairs. Detailing these is beyond the scope of this short paper. The point is that the dilemma of citizen participation arises from these differences and not from some inherent quality of the process itself. The more they can be resolved or at least made explicit the clearer the substantive issues become, and the brighter the prospects for honest and even productive collaboration between city and citizen.

Nobody can claim a magic formula to insure such a happy outcome. Probably none exists. But it is possible to suggest some common-sense steps in a more rational approach to communication between citizen and agency.

One is to recognize that there are formidable obstacles to productive citizen-agency exchange, acknowledge them and ventilate them as freely as possible in discussion. If in the course of this some of them disappear, so much the better. At least they are in the open and can be taken into account.

First of all, virtually everyone who is a party to the renewal or planning process operates from a different set of imperatives. With the certainty of oversimplification, the situation may be typified this way: The elected executive hopes if possible to offend no one—the voters directly affected, their legislators, the "responsible" elements of the community, various other segments of the local power structure; he may also hope to satisfy some secondary aims or commitments in the process of getting something constructive done. So he proclaims his administration's willingness to listen to all views in its pursuit of progress and betterment, and hope for the best. The appointed administrator may be more or less sensitized to the web of interests surrounding the matter, and have greater or less skill in coping with it. But he is most likely to respond to the need for tangible achievement. So he listens, but subordinates what he hears to what he has been told—or himself believes—is the most important objective. Under him, the bureaucrats will fit what remains of the message into the iron maiden of procedures and programs at their disposal, and the technicians will further select what they are capable of responding to in light of their own professional disciplines and personal capacities. The result of this process may be a response that comes as a shock to the citizens who are unaware of the hazards of transmission loss and filtration that beset their original statements. This model presupposes good faith on all sides. It does not take into account attempts to exploit the issues for ulterior purposes—though the situation offers fertile ground for such tactics.

Secondly, there is gross disparity between the actual capabilities of renewal and planning programs as such, and the results citizens expect of them, or have been led to expect. This is a manifestation of the more general disparity between the global manner in which citizens perceive community wants and needs, and the compartmentalized structure of public programs designed to meet them. The bureaucrat or technician is frustrated at the citizen's apparent inability to understand that he cannot solve all problems because they are not all his responsibility. The citizen is frustrated at the bureaucrat's apparent indifference to the richness and diversity of his wants and needs. This is particularly true of renewal, which may be the first public program to touch intensively a deprived area with a dreary history of neglect. It will unleash a flood of complaints, resentments, and demands which far outreach the limited tools of the program itself. Yet the far-reaching power of those tools to change the makeup of a neighborhood somehow lures planners and politicians alike into a grandiosity of expression that only serves to reinforce the popular misconception that renewal is a panacea. Essentially an instrument of physical change, it is spoken of as if it could solve all social and economic problems as well. The people, dazzled at the prospect of so much so soon, are naturally disappointed and hostile when the bulldozer (or some lesser form of displacement) issues forth instead of milk and honey. The long-range prospects offered by planning are sometimes even more disillusioning in their short-term product. To gloss over the realistic limits of what renewal and planning can accomplish directly, and what they must leave to coordinated efforts through other forms of public action, can only lead to misunderstanding and bitterness. So, too, however, will refusal to discuss concerns outside their immediate scope.

Thirdly, but related, is that within their direct scope, renewal and planning are beset by goal conflicts which must be balanced out in the development of specific proposals. To cite a few: tax base preservation vs. housing the poor; minimum cost vs. maximum amenities; minimum disruption and relocation vs. maximum housing improvement and production. Some of these are products of renewal's split personality: its conception as an instrument of physical and economic betterment, with social benefits important but indirect aims, vs. growing efforts to satisfy immediate social needs directly. Others spring from conflicts within the social goals: integration vs. neighborhood preservation (especially in ghetto areas) for example.

Turning from these general observations, a second step is to recognize certain realities about the process of citizen engagement that may seem self-evident to many, but are often ignored or forgotten in practice. Officials at all levels often seem to fail to understand what they are setting in motion when they undertake to engage the community. This failure, more than any real threat in the process, seems to produce most of the disfunctions and bad experiences, which are exacerbated when the foregoing obstacles are encountered. One of these realities has already been noted. It is that the engagement process cannot be neatly confined to an agenda of pure planning or renewal questions. Once engaged, the community will not be patient with the procedural niceties and delays of renewal, nor will it be satisfied with simply discussing a roster of future benefits and satisfactions. A city that undertakes to engage the community in the renewal and planning processes must anticipate the likelihood that supplemental services and interim activities will be required. It should be prepared to see the community, once engaged, steadily press its concern with immediate problems—with special emphasis on social and community services—even while discussing more remote solutions. Another reality is that, once begun, engagement is not something that can readily be turned off or manipulated to some predetermined end. Its initiation represents a commitment on the part of local government and its professional establishment to let the people have their say and to respond reasonably to their expressions. Failure to fulfill the commitment will not end the process, only escalate it via other channels. Sometimes when the community begins to ask hard or embarrassing questions, professionals retire beneath a mantle of experience and qualifications to demand that their judgments be accepted as revealed truth; administrators retreat behind a smoke screen of procedural objectives. Neither satisfies the community, who see the process as directed toward their welfare (and why not—that was what they were told, wasn't it?) not toward the observance of rules or standards that seem to them arbitrary or artificial. The inevitable result of such a failure to fulfill the commitment is a continuing miasma of hostility and mistrust that communicates to other neighborhoods as well, and other areas of government activity.

So in addition to flexibility and responsiveness to concerns outside the scope of renewal and planning, the engagement process must entail a continuing two-way communication rich with education as well as information. This is the only way that emergent proposals can be shown as reasonable to the lay people on the other side of the table, and the procedural requirements made understandable.

It will not take long, either, for at least some in the community to sense it if the process of participation is not genuine. To attempt a pro forma engagement process with the idea of obtaining sanction without giving some options is to risk a schism that may well wreck sound and basically acceptable plans. The community must have a chance to make some contribution, exercise some real choice. Fortunately, situations are rare where there is one and only one technically, economically, and politically acceptable solution to a given set of prob-

lems. But among the choices may be one that is more acceptable to the community for reasons that may appear completely
irrelevant to the official or professional. To learn which it is
should be a primary goal of the engagement process. The bare
minimum of reality should be an opportunity for the community to choose among sound options.

In no reasonably diverse community is there likely to be
found a single "voice" that may be engaged with assurance
that its sanction will mean sanction of the whole community
or even a majority within it. There are in most communities
many interests, usually advancing demands which are at cross
purposes or mutually exclusive. To elicit as many as possible
of these is essential if the community is to be presented with
choices among possible options that are meaningful as proposals are developed. More important, if these diverse positions are not made explicit in full view of all factions, it will
be impossible to arrive at compromise or choice among them
through community consensus, and agency decisions about
them are likely to appear—and be branded—capricious or arbitrary. To try and keep diverse interests separate or under
wraps is to invite all factions to turn their fire on the agency.

Furthermore, it is a virtual certainty that the "organized"
community as it is first encountered does not represent the full
range of interests which will be affected by the ultimate proposals. Even the most assiduous engagement efforts will probably leave some of these untouched, only to later awake to the
implications of formulated proposals, and come forward to
state their interest—at a time when it is least possible to accommodate them.

Even if late-blooming demands are kept to a minimum, the
engagement process is unlikely to be orderly, predictable or
even rational. The subject is inherently volatile and explosive—
charged with profound implications for the lives and fortunes
of many, and hence with emotion. Social and economic factors
influence the citizen's ability to understand and respond to
information provided to him, and the level at which he may

engage in dialogue about it and his own wants and needs. They will also influence the individual and community view of the trustworthiness and good faith of the source, whether it be official, community leader, community worker, or other. Communities themselves vary widely in structure and composition, problems and available solutions. So just as there is no single renewal plan or technique which will meet the needs of all communities everywhere, there is no single format or procedure for citizen engagement that applies to all. The sole key element seems to be genuine collaboration. Without it, nothing is mobilized but opposition.

The importance of skilled, specialized staff in dealing with these realities has already been discovered by most cities with experience in citizen participation. Their experience indicates that a wide range of skills and backgrounds can work effectively in the process, and that procedures can vary widely with good results. But only in relatively small communities with relatively simple problems and structures—in effect, where the administrator is at the project manager level—is it possible for him as principal official to handle all community relations single-handed. Even then, the degree of continuing personal contact required, the sustained nature of the education, information, and service activities necessary to a productive dialogue, is likely to be burdensome. When the burden is underestimated at the outset, or let fall somewhere along the line, problems are certain to arise.

However, no number of specialized community liaison staff, or degree of skill among them, will guarantee a successful engagement process. The community worker can only facilitate communication. Planners and officials who are responsible for the formulation of substantive proposals are the ones who must actually engage, for they are the ones with the power to respond in practical fashion to community views and demands. If they take no part in it, the engagement process will lack the essential element which is required for any prospect of success.

Some will ask, why bother? For planners at least, one answer

suggests itself. Among the pervasive inconsistencies and conflicts that characterize renewal and planning as public programs is one between the technical operations themselves and
the medium of their implementation—politics. The former are
abstract, usually long-range, anti-crisis, and contingent. The
latter is concrete, immediate, crisis-oriented, and definitive.
Thus many planners see cherished concepts and objectives
lost in the ordeal of compromise and accommodation through
which their work must pass on the way to realization. Sometimes they may feel that the end product bears little important
resemblance to their original concept.

Is it possible that the reason lies somewhere in a failure of
planners to build a constituency for their competence? That
instead of identifying their efforts with some consensus in the
battle, they have remained aloof and let their efforts fall among
the factions, to be torn apart? If so, perhaps planners should
insist on working in the closest possible collaboration with
the community, not apart from it—in effect making themselves
consultants to the community rather than prescribers for it.
There have been instances where planners, working within
the entire context of stresses, limitations, and conflicts of a
given situation, have helped a community arrive at a viable
solution which was implemented by the political and administrative authorities. But such advocate planning, whether
done from within or outside the official establishment, imposes
some grave responsibilities. Where these attempts have led
to professional and political conflicts, little has been accomplished without the most painful kind of controversy and furor.
Where they have led to community demands for solutions
which are beyond the capacity of available economic, administrative, or political resources, nothing has been accomplished.

There is nevertheless a good deal to suggest that planners—
and others in the renewal and planning fields—have more to
gain than to lose in embracing the action horn of the citizen
participation dilemma. Like all sharp objects, it needs to be
treated with respect. But it need not gore. And there may be

no choice. The waves of community action and citizen interest that are building on the entire local government front may force the choice unless it is made with good grace and skill first. It is worth thinking about.

# SECTION III

# The Anti-Poverty
# Program

# Introduction

Inconspicuously lodged in Section 201 of thte Economic Opportunity Act of 1964 is a definition which has caused considerable controversy, action, and reaction in all parts of the country. The definition holds that "The term 'community action program' means a program . . . which is developed, conducted, and administered with the maximum feasible participation of residents of the areas and members of the groups served." Thus, the phrase "maximum feasible participation" entered the lexicon of community action to be interpreted and reinterpreted with almost as much anxious scrutiny as the phrase "with all deliberate speed" that emanated from the 1955 Desegregation decree of the U.S. Supreme Court. In both cases a principle or policy was mandated which had to be implemented ultimately through new administrative machinery.

In retrospect, it is interesting to observe that the abbreviated section-by-section analysis that usually accompanies bills in Congress did not even mention citizen participation at the time of the poverty hearings and that Sargent Shriver's articulate presentation of the merits of the program included merely the innocuous sentence, "Above all, it [the community action program] includes the poor people of the community whose first opportunity must be the opportunity to help themselves."

The fledgling Office of Economic Opportunity had the difficult task of issuing regulations affecting citizen participation in the community-action program. On the one hand, the new poverty agency was obliged to advocate consequential, meaningful resident involvement while on the other, it was equally responsible to avoid overstepping a tenuous Congressional mandate. Initially, OEO pursued a course of calculated ambiguity. It advised local anti-poverty programs on a number of ways to help the poor to participate through the establishment of new, indigenous-based organizations, actual employment in component projects, and assurances of representation in the governing bodies of the community action agencies. At this point OEO policy took two simultaneous courses. It virtually mandated the inclusion of representatives of the poor to the amount of one-third of the CAP Board membership. At the same time, the agency insisted on an open-ended flexible stance. An early entry in the CAP Workbook stated, ". . . tested knowledge on maximum resident participation and political influence is minimal. We are only beginning objectively to explore this issue. In all probability, there are no uniform methods that fit all situations. Ways and means will vary from community to community." Eventually, the duality of policy positions was resolved when OEO issued firm administrative regulations establishing the one-third quota.

How did neighborhoods and communities respond to Washington's administrative dictum? Did the poor become genuinely involved in decisions affecting their lives? What participatory patterns emerged? Did power struggles ensue? At this writing, definitive answers have not as yet found their way into the poverty literature. A number of studies are presently underway, exploring some of these questions. Partial data have become available through the U.S. Senate's Subcommittee on Employment, Manpower, and Poverty's "Examination of the War on Poverty." Several hearings and staff papers have resulted in the summarization of important empirical data. But the last chapter on citizen participation in the OEO's Community Action Program will not be written for a while. For the present, at least, it seems no exaggeration to claim that the war on poverty has ushered in a new federal posture toward the poor. The underlying ideology of this posture—one that is still in a state of flux—might be characterized as a departure from the view of the disadvantaged as welfare recipients to one of citizens actively engaged as decision makers.

The writings in this section represent some of the more thoughtful reflections on citizen participation in anti-poverty programs. Whatever theory may ultimately evolve out of this area of social planning, the following selections capture, we hope, certain crucial themes that reflect hardcore realities about the phenomenon. All three contributions have the unique advantage of being written by persons thoroughly knowledgable in the war on poverty, and are based on extensive first-hand participation and observation.

# Selection of Indigenous Leadership*

## LOUIS A. ZURCHER

The case history to be presented and analyzed in this monograph is that of the Indian Community Action Committee, one of the Special Audience Committees represented in the Topeka OEO. As mentioned above, the Indian Committee does not represent a specific target neighborhood as designated by the Topeka OEO. However, their subcultural, blood, and social ties, plus the pressures resulting from being an ethnic minority, summate to give them a feeling of groupness that transcends neighborhood boundaries. It was this feeling, plus an awareness of the physical and social ills among them, that prompted some of the Indians eventually to establish a Community Action Committee of their own.

That all of the members of the subject committee were Indian-Americans could be viewed as disadvantageously limiting the generality of interpretations presented in this study. On the other hand, the life situation of the Indian—who traditionally has been treated as a Government welfare problem and who manifests marked ambivalence toward authority figures and organization representatives and expects his leader, as a "Chief," to solve insolvable problems—may establish a set of conditions that makes the interaction between the beneficiaries and the Topeka OEO, the development of indigenous leadership, and the phenomena of socialization and "followership" more clearly discernible within this group than any

* Reproduced by special permission from the author and the publisher, *Genetic Psychology Monographs*, Vol. 76, 1967, pp. 31-56.

other Community Action Committees with less significant
subcultural influences. In other words, some of the processes
that are manifested in minor key by other Committees seem
to be manifested in major key by the Indian Committee. Historical and contemporary subjugation, and styles of life to
cope with it seem to be common factors among the poor. Since
the Indians have had many generations of experiencing and
reacting to subjugation, their striking responses to the sudden
opportunity for "maximum feasible participation" may be
valuable for understanding the reactions of others who are
thrust into the same situation.

An important anthropological field study of the Prairie
Potawatomi has been and is being conducted by the Department of Anthropology at the University of Kansas. The study
yields insights pertinent to cultural influences upon the members of the Indian Committee. Data from the study—particularly those concerning value orientation, bases for role expectations, and traditional forms of interactions with white organizations—will be introduced throughout this monograph
when relevant.

## A. The Indians of Topeka

Approximately 300 Indians, most of them Prairie Potawatomi,
live in clusters of families in five different sections of the City.
Thirty miles to the North of Topeka, at Mayetta, Kansas, is
the 11 square mile Prairie Potawatomi Reservation. According
to a 1963 census, another 503 Indians reside on or immediately around the Reservation[1]. There is considerable interaction
between the Topekans and the Mayettans: frequent relative
and friend visitations, clubs and religious memberships in
common, and traditional gatherings and ceremonies. Evidence
has been presented for a growing sense of community among
the Prairie Potawatomi, partially as a result of increasing ac-

[1] Clifton, J. A. & Isaac, B. The Kansas Prairie Potawatomi: On the nature
of a contemporary Indian community. *Transactions Kansas Acad. Sci.*, 1964,
*67* (1), 1-24.

culturative stress from interaction with the white community.[2, 3]

Virtually all of the male Indians who are employed are blue collar workers or laborers. The employed female Indians work primarily in jobs that do not require special skills or training, with the exception of a few who are registered or practical nurses.

The majority of the Topeka Indians would qualify as "poor" (less than $3000 annual income for a family of four). This generally low-income level is due to a number of factors: lack of education, which keeps them from getting jobs requiring advanced skills or training; job discrimination against Indians; and the seasonal or temporary nature of the jobs that are open to Indians. In a number of cases, the human needs of the Indians are critical: inadequate nutrition, housing, and health facilities. In short, the Indians living in Topeka are numbered among those for whom the programs of the War against Poverty were intended.

## B.  First encounter with the OEO

In June 1965 the Assistant Director of the Topeka OEO, a Mexican-American former factory machinist and union official, contacted, as a normal part of his task to organize Community Action Committees, several ministers who had Indians within their congregations. Of the ministers who were asked to make announcements from their pulpits concerning the Topeka OEO, one in particular, Rev. H. of the Methodist Indian Mission, seemed especially interested. Rev. H. volunteered his church as a meeting place, and on an evening in July 1965, eight Indians joined Rev. H. to hear the Assistant Director explain "what the Topeka OEO was all about." According to the Assistant Director, the Indians who attended were "suspicious, very skeptical that such a program could

---

[2] Clifton, J. A. Culture change, structural stability and factionalism in the Prairie Potawatomi Reservation community. *Midcontinent Amer. Stud. J.,* 1965, *6* (2), 101-122.

[3] Clifton & Isaac, *op. cit.*

work, and really only asked a few questions that indicated they were interested at all." The Assistant Director "left it up to them whether they wanted to know any more about the Topeka OEO, and about forming a Committee of their own." The Indians agreed to meet again, in the same place, two weeks later to see whether or not the Assistant Director would "tell the same story a second time."

The second meeting was held on schedule, but was not chaired by the Assistant Director, since he had to attend an emergency meeting in another part of town. Instead, the meeting was conducted by the Director of the Topeka OEO, a white Methodist minister with three terms' experience as a Representative in the Kansas State Legislature. Fifteen Indians attended this meeting, and the Director reported a response from the group quite similar to that of the first meeting. He indicated that the Indians were "pretty quiet, seemed rather skeptical that the Program could do them any good, and seemed only mildly interested." Nevertheless, the Indians agreed to schedule a third meeting, to be held again in the same place and again two weeks later. (At this time, the other established Community Action Committees were meeting on a twice-monthly basis.)

In the interim between the second and third meetings, primarily because of the influence of the Director of the Topeka OEO, the local press became interested in "what the Indians were starting to do for themselves," and decided to send a reporter and a photographer to the forthcoming Indian Committee meeting.

Thirty-five Indians attended this third meeting, which was officiated by the Assistant Director of the Topeka OEO. As indicated by the response of the press, and the report of the Assistant Director, the Indians were far more outspoken at this meeting than they had been at the previous two. Several of the statements recorded pointed to a feeling among the attending Indians that they should "do something for themselves, because nobody else really cared about Indians." One of the participants commented, "We're getting to be like the white man—we don't take care of our own anymore." A number of questions were raised by those attending concerning the organizational structure of the Topeka OEO, its goals, and what it might mean to the Indian. According to the Assistant Director, most of the questions still were "suspicious and skeptical. They wanted to know how much the Director and I were getting paid for running the Topeka OEO. They wanted to know about the Director's politics, and whether or not this was just a political organization. They asked a lot of questions at this meeting, but almost all of them seemed to challenge us to prove that we weren't there just to take advantage of the Indians, but rather to offer them ways that they could help themselves through OEO Programs." At this meeting, as he had during the first meeting, the Assistant Director suggested to the group that they should think about electing a chairman, a vice-chairman, and a secretary, thus establishing themselves as a *bona fide* Community Action Committee within the Topeka OEO structure. The Assistant Director commented that "they seemed hesitant to elect leaders, almost as if nobody wanted to take that responsibility. Some of them even commented, 'You'll never get an Indian to be a leader!' " Though the Indians were still not "sold on the program" they agreed to get together for a fourth meeting, to be held two weeks later.

It was now September, and the Indians had not yet established direction from indigenous leadership. The fourth meeting of the Indian Committee found the Assistant Director again unable to attend, and the Director substituting for him. At this meeting, according to the Director:

... all hell broke loose. They aggressively questioned me about my politics, my motivations for running the Topeka Program, and about the worth of their becoming involved in such a program. Everytime I would answer a question, they would sharpshoot another one at me. I was just getting my feet on the ground in the OEO Program, so some of their questions I couldn't answer directly, but I told the group that I would try and find out for them as soon as I could. They seemed to take great delight in catching me with questions for which I didn't have ready answers. In general, I got the feeling that they were less interested in finding out about the Topeka OEO, than they were in giving me a bad time!

The Director further indicated that during the meeting, when the Indians were

... obviously harassing me, they very carefully continued to call me "Sir." Almost everyone of the questions that they asked me was anteceded by "Sir," as if they were using that exaggerated politeness as another way of being hostile. Many of them seemed to be having fun trying to get my goat, or trying to embarrass me. When one of them would succeed in coming up with some question, for example about the way the Bureau of Indian Affairs' policies overlapped with OEO policies, he would be rewarded by laughter and encouragement from his friends.

This fourth meeting ended with no indication whether or not any other meeting would ever be held by the Indians concerning the Topeka OEO. The Director indicated that he was "discouraged about that group," and wondered whether or not it would be best to forget about trying to help them organize into a Committee. The Assistant Director decided to make a final attempt to get the Indians together, and arranged with some of them to hold a fifth meeting within the next two weeks. During the time between the fourth and fifth meetings, the Assistant Director contacted a number of the Indians to "find out what happened at the fourth meeting." He discovered that during the previous meeting many of the participants saw the Director as an "agency official," and, therefore, determined that he was "no more than another Indian Agent," and his program was no more than "another one of those Government handouts like they have on the Reservation. It's another one of those deals where we're always told what to do, and told what we'll get."

An interesting discovery by the Assistant Director, and, through subsequent interviews with the Indian participants, by this author, was the fact that several of the Indians who attended that meeting seemed actually to enjoy themselves. One of the participants responded, "I haven't had such a good time giving an official a bad time for as long as I can remember." Another participant commented, "Boy! We really had him going! I'll bet he knows what old Custer felt like!" The zest with which the Indian participants baited the Director during the fourth meeting and the apparent enjoyment that many of them seemed to gain from being harassers point to an interesting phenomenon among the Indians that was best described by an Indian respondent in an unstructured interview. He commented, in referring to the fourth meeting and also to other experiences that he and several of his friends have had with agency officials, that "the Indian has a way of 'putting on' people who are big shot agency representatives." The respondent then, with great glee, told a story about

. . . the time when the Government gave us a bunch of old cows that they had left over from somewhere. They told us that all we had to do was to give back to the Government the first calf that any of these old cows might have. They told us that we were supposed to use the cows to improve our livestock. Well, about a week or so after the Government official had left the reservation, we started killing off those cows, and had some of the biggest feasts that you'll ever see in your whole lifetime. After awhile, the Government official came back again, looked around and said, "Say, where have those cows gone?" We all put on our most innocent faces and told the Government man that "You know, sir, those cows up and got sick, and just seemed to die off." The Government man then sat us down and began to tell us all about the diseases that could kill off cows, and the ways that we could prevent those diseases. We still kept our innocent faces on, and asked him all kinds of questions about the diseases and about how we could save our cows in the future. Inside we were all busting our guts to keep from laughing! When the Government man left again, we rolled around on the ground, laughing until tears came to our eyes! We tell that story over and over, and everytime we tell it, we laugh almost as hard as we did when it happened. Even now, just telling it to you, I can't keep from laughing out loud.

In a discussion about the Indians' participation in OEO

Programs, the supervisor of an eight-state Indian poverty intervention organization reported that he had observed, time and time again, the Indians' ability to "play games with people." He described the Indian as "having a way of engaging in verbal repartee, almost like role playing, with representatives of agencies." In response to a question about the dynamics underlying the "putting on" behavior, the supervisor, himself an Indian, said, "I'm certain that the interaction of the Indians with Government officials has led them to adopt such a facade behind which they can offer to agency officials what they expect, and yet can maintain some control over the situation. It's a chance for them to take the lead, aggressively, in a situation with a power authority figure, in a situation where they usually never have the opportunity to take the lead."

The Assistant Director, with the cooperation of Rev. H., managed to get together eight Indians for a fifth meeting, held in the same place as the previous meetings, the Methodist Indian Mission. This meeting focused primarily on what had happened during the meeting two weeks earlier. The participants told the Assistant Director not to let the Director "ever come out to talk to us again," and they said that the Director "was more confused than we were, and he reminded us of the Indian Agents that our forefathers had to put up with on the Reservation." The participants stated, "We want nothing to do with him in the future." Thus, the Indians soundly rejected what they perceived to be "just another agency official." Yet, they did not reject the Assistant Director, who, objectively, was as much an agency official as was the Director. The difference seemed to be that to the Indians the Assistant Director, because of his working-man background and his membership in a minority ethnic group, was "someone just like us." Furthermore, the Assistant Director, having served a long apprenticeship in union organizing, approached at the onset a number of Indians directly and established personal rapport with them. They had a chance to get to know him as a person, rather than as an agency official, before any formal meeting had been held. This provided a basis for understanding between the Indians and the Assistant Director, and established him as a "regular guy." One of the Indians summed up their view of the Assistant Director, saying, "Well, once in a while, he's got to wear a suit and tie and sit behind a desk in that OEO office, but he's not the kind of guy who is going to forget that he used to roll his sleeves up and get his hands dirty like the rest of us. He talks our language."

The Director, therefore, as perceived by the Indians, was from the beginning stereotyped as an "agency official," who should, if possible, be "put on." Any chance that he might have had successfully to negotiate with the Indians, for the purpose of their establishing a Community Action Committee was severely impeded by the expectations that they had for him as a "big wheel from the Government." On the other hand, the Assistant Director was able to take a more personal approach to the Indians; as one of the Indians put it, "A Mexican-American has a lot of the same kind of problems as an Indian." Because of his more direct manner and language in dealing with them, the Indians seemed willing to go along with him and "take a closer look at this white man's war on poverty."

By the conclusion of this fifth meeting, the few Indians who were attending agreed that "maybe we ought to get some officers pretty soon," and scheduled elections for a meeting to be held two weeks from that night. The participants further agreed among themselves to "get the word back out to the people who said they wouldn't come to any more of these meetings, and tell them it might be worth another try."

Reports of the first five meetings between the Indians and staff members of the Topeka OEO revealed several consistent and interesting patterns of interaction. It seemed quite clear that the staff of the Topeka OEO took very seriously the goals of the War Against Poverty; and earnestly were attempting to afford the Indians an opportunity, with no strings attached, for full participation in the decision making, formulating, and implementing basic to the program. Yet, the staff, particularly the Director, were met with an immobilizing admixture of skepticism, suspicion, passiveness, verbal aggression, and ridicule. Apparently, only their evolving perception of the Assistant Director as a "regular guy who might be trusted" encouraged some of the Indians to remain passingly interested. The nature of these interactions provokes analysis.

It is not surprising that the Indians' initial reaction to the presentation by the Topeka OEO was skepticism and suspicion. With good historical reasons, such attitudes toward Government organizations and the people who officiate them are endemic to Indians—and the Potawatomi are no exception. The Indians who were curious enough to come to the first few meetings found it very difficult to perceive the Topeka OEO as being anything different from the Bureau of Indian Affairs or county welfare agencies. Thus, at the onset, the Indians enacted the passive-aggressive role noted by other social scientists observing their behavior *vis-a-vis.* Leon, for example, describes Indians' interactions with the Bureau of Indian Affairs as "passive compliance with what is expected and a tendency to sulk and be stubborn. Aggression is rarely expressed openly"[4] Spindler and Spindler[5] and MacGregor[6] also discuss the passiveness manifested by Indians toward agency authority, born of a series of defeats and the failure of physical aggression, and agree with Leon that covert resistance and subtle and controlled expressions of hostility remain significant components of the passivity pattern. Writing specifically about the Potawatomi, Searcy[7] reports that historical

[4] Leon, R. L. Maladaptive interaction between Bureau of Indian Affairs staff and Indian clients. *Amer. J. Orthopsychiat.,* 1965, 35, 723-728.

[5] Spindler, G., & Spindler, L. American Indian personality types and their socio-cultural roots. *Ann. Amer. Acad. Political & Soc. Sci.,* 1957, 311, 147-157.

[6] MacGregor, H. Task force on Indian affairs. *Hum. Organization,* 1962, 21 (2), 125-137.

[7] Searcy, A. The value of ethnohistorical reconstructions of American Indian typical personality: The case of the Potawatomi. *Transactions Kansas Acad. Sci.,* 1965, 68 (2), 274-282. (a)

accounts of Potawatomi behavior, many of them recorded by acculturating agents, indicate a cultural theme of coexisting passivity and aggression. Referring to Vogt,[8] she adds that the conflict between passivity or dependence and aggression is found in many American Indian groups, especially the more acculturated groups.[9] The Prairie Potawatomi, by virute of the characteristics of their community, are a highly acculturated group.[10]

The first two meetings of the Indians with the Topeka OEO followed, therefore, what might have been the expected and typical pattern—the Indians relatively quiet, passive, and covertly resistant through mechanisms of suspiciousness and skepticism. The third meeting, however, and the intensified discussions, explanations, and publicity that preceded and followed it demonstrated to the Indians that the Topeka OEO, unlike the Bureau of Indian Affairs or county welfare agencies, possessed no sanctions for nor controls over the Indians. Here was a white man's agency, symbolic of all the historical, physical, social, and psychological torments imposed upon the Indians by the white man—and it could not hit back! By the fourth meeting, consequently, there was no longer a need for enactment of the traditional passive role, and covert resistance quickly and easily became active verbal aggression. The opportunity for the expression of hostility became doubled when the white Director rather than the Mexican-American Assistant Director appeared at the meeting and was systematically and vigorously "put on." The flames were fanned when the Director was perceived to express his authority defensively and to attempt to "put some order" into the meeting.

Gossen writes that the Reservation-dwelling Potawatomi, who as pointed out above have close ties and frequent meetings with their relatives and friends in Topeka,

[8] Vogt, E. Z. The acculturation of American Indians. *Ann. Amer. Acad. Political & Soc. Sci.*, 1957, 311, 137-146.

[9] Searcy (a), *op. cit.*

[10] Clifton & Isaac, *op. cit.*

. . . find themselves almost totally dependent on stable and satisfactory relations with white men and their institutions; i.e., county welfare agents, public health agents, local law enforcement agencies, the Bureau of Indian Affairs, tribal lawyers, loan agents, creditors, and white farmers to whom they rent their allotted lands. It is definitely not in the Potawatomi's best interests to antagonize these individuals and agencies, but, at the same time, these very persons and institutions may have consistently exploited, cheated, and deprived him of the social and economic means to better his minority situation. Injustice will seek expression and resolution—even if the only available vent is a traditional animal fantasy.[11]

Gossen reports on Potawatomi folklore and the function it serves as an escape valve for acculturative stress. In particular, he presents, in its modern context, an intensive study of one traditional tale—the "Coon-Wolf Cycle." The story is essentially a series of episodes in which the coon (clearly identified as the Indian) dupes and destroys the wolf (clearly identified as the white man). The pattern of the coon's success and the wolf's downfall is consistent from episode to episode. The wolf attempts to take the coon's food. The coon, however, cleverly distracts the wolf by lying to him about the source of the food and how much more the wolf can get if he goes directly to the source. The wolf, motivated by his greed, inevitably rushes to follow the suggestions of the coon, and just as inevitably meets with disaster, usually at the hands of the farmer. Thus the coon, verbally and with much amusement, beguiles (or "puts on") the wolf, who is safely and indirectly eliminated by a third party. In the same fashion, covert resistances and "putting on" are indirect ways of thwarting representatives of agencies perceived as powerful and oppressive. However, when, as in the case of the Topeka OEO, the wolf in effect has no teeth, the general level of overt aggression, including the vehemence of "putting on," can safely be

---

[11] Gossen, G. H. A version of the Potawatomi coon-wolf cycle: A traditional projection screen for acculturative stress. *Search: Selected Stud. by Undergrad. Honors Students Univ. Kansas*, 1964, *4*, 8-14.

heightened. Relevant to the nature of "putting on," Searcy reports, when discussing major psychological traits of the Potawatomi, that aggression typically tends to be channeled into hostile and at times humorous verbalizations.[12]

The passive-aggressive mode of interaction with power figures has been reported as representative of other ethnic minorities having a history of subjugation and impoverishment. Pettigrew[13] describes aggressive meekness and an impervious mask of passive acquiescence adopted by Negro-Americans individually interacting with white authority. Other writers have described a similar pattern within the subculture of Mexican-Americans.[14, 15] Unwilling compliance with and controlled hostility toward components of society perceived to be responsible for their powerlessness and alienation seem also to be a significant pattern among impoverished whites.

A few of the Indians, in spite of the disaster and apparent finality of their fourth meeting, had agreed again to meet with the Assistant Director. Cardinal among the reasons for their continuing interest was the fact that the Assistant Director did his utmost to present himself informally, as a person rather than an official. As he explained:

I make personal contact with them, and talk to them plain, and straight from the shoulder. If I walk into their houses, sit down and have a cup of coffee or a beer with them and just be one human being to another, then they'll listen, and maybe believe what I say. But if I walk in there waving a bunch of papers around and using a bunch

[12] ———. Contemporary and traditional Prairie Potawatomi child life. K. U. Potawatomi Study Research Report Number Seven (mimeographed), Department of Anthropology, University of Kansas, Lawrence, Kansas, September 1965. (b)

[13] Pettigrew, T. F. *A Profile of the Negro American*. Princeton, N.J.: Van Nostrand, 1964.

[14] Meadow, A., & Stoker, D. A comparison of symptomatic behavior of Mexican-American and Anglo-American hospitalized patients. *Arch. Gen. Psychiat.*, 1965, *12* (3), 267-277.

[15] Zurcher, L. A., Jr., & Meadow, A. On bullfights and baseball: An example of the interaction of social institutions. *Internat. J. Comp. Sociol.*, 8 (1), 66-84.

of big bureaucratic words, they'd throw me right out of the door. How do I know that? I know that because if some guy came into my house with a bunch of double talk, I'd throw *him* out of the door!

The same thing goes for someone standing up in front of a group at a meeting. If the fellow uses big, fancy words and I don't know what he's talking about, I'll holler out "Wait a minute! Let me go get my sledge hammer and break up those big words so I know what you are talking about!" I try to remember that myself whenever I'm standing up in front of a group of people who haven't had a chance to get used to those college degree words.

It's the same thing with titles. You know, if you work for a big organization with a lot of other people who have worked for big organizations, they'll listen to you if they're impressed by the title that you have. It doesn't make any difference whether they know you or not personally, the title is what counts. But with the people out here in the target neighborhoods, and it seems especially true with the Indians, just to announce yourself with a title doesn't do the trick. As a matter of fact, a lot of times a title makes them suspicious of you! It's the person that counts, and not the letters before or after his name.

Take the Indians for example. What have titles and big words meant to them? All they've meant are reminders of a big Government organization far away that has, over the generations, taken away their land and, in a lot of cases, their rights. I guess what I'm trying to say is that with low-income people in general, and with the Indians in particular, you've got to get them to accept you as a person, and to trust you, before you can even begin to talk to them about an organization like the Topeka OEO and what it can help them accomplish.

It is not remarkable that the Potawatomi accept individuals in terms of how they are as "people" rather than what official status they have. Not only have they had generations of negative experiences with "officials," but theirs was, and to a large extent still is, a social system of extended families.[16, 17] Cohen writes that "the world view" of individuals in the type

[16] Callender, C. Social organization of the Central Algonkian Indians. Milwaukee Public Museum Publications, No. 7, Milwaukee, Wisconsin, 1962.
[17] Searcy (b), *op. cit.*

of society that fosters extended kinship contains definitions of human relationships in terms of "propinquity, intimacy, and solidarity," and influences the perception of social situations in terms of "close personal bonds."[18] Redfield describes behavior in the ideal type familial society as "personal, not impersonal. A 'person' may be defined as that social object which I feel to respond to situations as I do; a person is myself in another form, his qualities and values are inherent within him, and his significance for me is not merely one of utility."[19]

The Assistant Director clearly was sensitive to the Indians' value orientation for personal relationships and the influence of the value orientation upon perception, evaluation, and acceptance of unfamiliar individuals, things, or ideas. His own people, Mexican-Americans, have a history of and in many cases still maintain extended family or *compadre* systems, and have been reported to manifest a similar value orientation for personal rather than impersonal interpretations.[20, 21, 22]

As much as possible divesting himself of his "officiality" and approaching the Indians as "just another guy looking at what OEO is all about," the Assistant Director campaigned to interest more of the Indians in the scheduled sixth meeting.

## C.  The Election of the "Chief"

It was at the sixth meeting of the Indians that the author began participant observation within the group and was introduced as "a good friend" by the Assistant Director (the previous five meetings had been reconstructed from interviews with

[18] Cohen, Y. A. Patterns of Friendship. In Y. A. Cohen (Ed.), *Social Structure and Personality*. New York: Holt, Rinehart, & Winston, 1961. Pp. 353-383.

[19] Redfield, R. The folk society. *Amer. J. Sociol.*, 1947, *52*, 293-308.

[20] Dozier, E. P. Folk culture to urbanity: The case of Mexicans and Mexican-Americans. Unpublished paper, University of Arizona, Tucson, 1964.

[21] Loomis, C. P., & Beegle, J. A. *Rural Social Systems*. New York: Prentice-Hall, 1950.

[22] Zurcher, L. A., Jr., Meadow, A., & Zurcher, S. Value orientation, role conflict, and alienation from work. *Amer. Sociol. Rev.*, 1965, *30* (4), 539-548.

the participants). It was now early October, and the Indian group was over ten weeks old. Yet the group still had in no way identified itself with the Topeka OEO, nor had they viewed themselves as a Community Action Committee. Those who had participated in the previous meetings did so for a number of reasons, none of which seems to align itself with the goals of the poverty program. Some came because they were "curious about what this was all about." Others attended because "it was a nice opportunity to spend some time chatting with friends who lived across town." A few sat in on the meetings because "it was fun to needle some Government man a little bit." The Assistant Director hoped that tonight's meeting would be different from those held earlier. He had a feeling that "the Indians are, I think, beginning to see the opportunities that the Program has to offer, and I think that they may be about ready to elect themselves some officers. Also, I think they're beginning to trust us, and to see that maybe we aren't like the bad picture they have of Government officials." During the week prior to this evening's meeting, the Assistant Director had made personal contact with about 20 Indian families, felt that he had begun to establish rapport with some of the Indians, and that they were beginning to have confidence in him. Thus, he had hopes that the meeting shortly to start would reveal, more than any of the meetings had before, the beginnings of an Indian Community Action Committee.

While we were waiting for the meeting to begin, several of us, including the Assistant Director, Rev. H., and the author, stood in front of the Indian Mission and quietly talked. All of the Indian men were wearing work clothes, but had at least one Indian accoutrement on their person—a beaded belt, a silver jade buckle, an ornamental watch fob, and the like. The men were talking about how tough times were now and how difficult it was to "get jobs that paid a living wage and didn't seem to end just when you were beginning to get your head above water." The general tone of the conversation was depressed until one of the men excitedly said, "Remember how it was right after the war?" The other Indians perked up, and one of them exclaimed, "Yeah, man. In '45 and '46 *anything* went!" These comments kicked off a lively and spirited conversation in which the men shared with each other "sea stories" of drinking, fighting, and seducing (the latter was largely implied, sometimes with careful looks at the minister who was standing nearby), and with several references to the "way we could go anywhere we wanted to because we were veterans just like anybody else." As the Indians continued to relive the time when society allowed them more status and more freedom than perhaps at any other time in their lives, other Indian couples approached the Mission. Invariably, the woman went inside the church and sat with the other wives, while the man joined the growing circle of "braves."

The meeting was scheduled to begin at 7:30 p.m. At 7:45 p.m., the Assistant Director suggested that we all go inside the church and "get the show on the road." The Indian Mission was an old, worn, two-story frame house, with one room set aside as the place for worship. The furnishings were mismatched and secondhand. On the peeling walls were a crucifix, a few faded religious pictures, a notice of the record highest Sunday donation ($35) and last Sunday's donation ($1.40), and a crayoned announcement of a forthcoming revival meeting. There were 15 people in attendance, six of them women. All of the members besides the Assistant Director and the author were at least part Indian. One of the women had a small baby in her arms.

When all of us were seated and settled, the Assistant Director opened the meeting. After a very brief review, he came right to the point, stating that "the purpose of the meeting tonight is to find out if you are interested in this program, and if you are, for you to elect officers." He re-emphasized to the group that the Topeka OEO was not a welfare program, and anything that was to be accomplished would have to be started and supported by the people here. He asked if there were any questions.

During all of the Assistant Director's five-minute talk, the people sat and listened attentively. When he asked for questions, they continued to sit silently and look forward attentively. All that could be heard was the occasional gurgling of the baby. Finally, the baby belched loudly, and the group laughed. One Indian man commented loudly, "That's the way I feel about it, too!"

One of the men asked the Assistant Director, "Well, what are we supposed to do now?" The Assistant Director responded with a suggestion that they think about electing officers. Another of the men said, "Maybe we should think about this some more." The same man asked if there was any literature on the Program, and the Assistant Director, responding in the affirmative, went out to his car to get some. While he was gone, an Indian man said loudly, "I don't know what the hell this is all about. That Assistant Director guy is okay, but what are *we* supposed to do—*it's their Program!*"

The Assistant Director returned and handed out some pamphlets which contained pictures of poverty families and dwellings and outlined some of the programs available through the Office of Economic Opportunity. The Indians looked through them with interest, and as they did they made a number of embarrassed, yet amused self-references. "Where did they get a picture of my house!" "Where, what page?" "Page 13." "Hell, that's *my* house, not *yours!*" (The picture was of a broken-down shanty.) "Look, here's a picture of me and my family!" (Laughter) "I ought to charge them for this!" (More laughter) "Well," voiced one disgruntled female, "at least they don't have any teepees in this book." One could immediately feel the sensitivity the people had to being labeled as "poverty" types. The comment about teepees especially seemed to highlight an aversion to being stereotyped or "pointed out" in a negative fashion: It is quite reasonable to assume that these people, or, in fact, any people in poverty situations, do not necessarily view themselves as "problem" people. They have struggled to maintain an adjustment in a world restricted to them by poverty and prejudices, and in most cases take some pride in "making out in this lousy world." In a later interview, one Indian pointed out, "That's part of the reason why it's so hard to get a group of Indians together into a Committee with the Topeka OEO. No Indian is ashamed of not having a lot of money, but he doesn't like the other things that go along with being labeled as 'poor.' He knows that when most people use the word 'poor' they also mean worthless, lazy, shiftless, and just plain no-good."

The self-references stimulated by the pamphlets served as a basis for a number of questions from the Indians. They wanted to know more specifically what the "programs were that had been *started by his office*." The Assistant Director reminded the group that programs were not "started" by his office, but that his office only implemented the ideas of the Community Action Committees. An Indian then asked, "Well, what are you going to do *for* us?" Again, the Assistant Director repeated that this was not a welfare program. "Whatever is going to be done has to be started and supported by you." One of the Indian men then straight-forwardly suggested, "The Indians would be interested in forming a committee if you guaranteed them that they would have food and clothing for the winter when they're out of work." A very clear difference could be seen between the expectations that the Indians had for the Topeka OEO, and the expectations that the Topeka OEO had for the Indians and other target neighborhood residents. The Indians, at this stage, still viewed the Topeka OEO as a Government agency, and saw the Assistant Director as a "good guy who will help us get what we've got coming from this War on Poverty Program." The Indians were judging the Topeka OEO in accord with their longstanding experience with the United States Government—an experience that is based firmly upon the principles of paternalism. On the

other hand, the Topeka OEO, reflecting the rationale and
goals of the "War on Poverty" expected the Indians, as it expected other target neighborhood residents, to become actively involved as participants in the war against poverty: to
assess and vocalize their needs, to select feasible programs to
meet these needs, and to use the Topeka OEO as a service. The
key component in this conflict of expectations is the process of
active beneficiary participation in a social amelioration organization, as opposed to traditional passivity to and dependence upon such organizations. As the Assistant Director continued to interpret the Economic Opportunity Act to the people, there were several objections raised that "this was not
President Johnson's program! That's not what President
Johnson wants to do for us!" The parallel could be seen, his-
torically, with promises made by the "Great White Father"
to the Indian, only to be exploited by some criminal Indian
agents. In spite of the Assistant Director's closeness to the participants this evening, in spite of the fact that they were not
attacking him personally, there were still some misgivings about
the Topeka OEO's being like unto an interfering Indian agent.

One of the Indian men asked the Assistant Director, "Why
don't we just write down on a piece of paper the programs that
we want, and then you send these back to Washington for us?"
The Assistant Director explained that it wasn't quite that
simple, and if they wanted a Day Care Center, a Neighborhood
Aide Program, and so on, they would have to become active in
demonstrating the need, planning, and carrying out a number
of the specifics for the program. The same Indian replied, "Well,
you know we've never had to do too much planning for things
like that. Usually, somebody else does all the planning for us.
Where do we begin?" The Assistant Director suggested to the
group that they talk with their friends and neighbors and try
to put together a list of specific needs that the Indians might
have, such as employment, housing, education, and so on. "Why
do we need this here Topeka OEO anyway? Why don't we just
send this list of needs directly to Washington," inquired an

Indian man. Another answered, "Washington's a long way from here. Maybe if we got together with this OEO thing here in Topeka, then anything we write down would carry a lot more weight." "Yeah," another commented, "maybe we had better string along with this deal." "Say," asked a third, "you said that there were some other committees already going great guns. What are they doing?" The Assistant Director explained to the group about the Day Care Centers, Neighborhood Aide Programs, Neighborhood Center Programs, etc., fostered by other Community Action Committees. "Those ideas came from them?" the man further inquired. The group was visibly impressed with this, and it seemed that the program, at this instant, became more believable to them. "Those other committees that have gotten these different programs, you say they already have officers?" asked an Indian woman. The Assistant Director replied in the affirmative. An Indian man then argued, "Well, let's get us some officers too!" All the group members vocally agreed to the suggestion, but then the action dramatically ceased.

Several dynamics worked to engender this silence. First, the participants were not familiar with nomination and election procedures. Clifton and Isaac[23] and Searcy (b)[24] have reported that the Potawatomi have had relatively little experience with tribal self-government and, thus, with the procedures associated with such self-government.

Second, as a later interview with a participant indicated, there was some feeling of clumsiness about *electing* a leader: "You know, we just don't *elect* chiefs." Third, and again revealed in later interviews with the participants, there is a devaluation of volunteering for leadership among the tribes from which the Topeka Indians come. One of the respondents explained that he had quite early learned the lesson of not "trying to be the big-shot leader." He related:

My father told me that if you made it obvious that you wanted to be a number one man, then you would give other people a feeling that

[23] Clifton & Isaac, *op. cit.*
[24] Searcy (b), *op. cit.*

you thought you were better than they were, and that would be the worst kind of bad manners that there are.

Another respondent explained how

... grandpa gave us good advice whenever we wanted to play sports in high school. He used to tell us "Don't be *too* good at football, or anything else. Don't make people think you are showing off. If you are playing in a game, stay far enough out in front so you can win the game, but don't make anybody else look bad! I suppose there's nothing wrong with winning, but don't forget that it might be one of your brothers who is going to lose." We listened carefully when he told us about things like that.

A third respondent replied:

I can remember when I used to run in track meets, and I was as fast as the wind. I remember usually being able to win easily, but lots of times just staying a couple of feet ahead of the second man so that I would cross the tape first. Then after the race was over, I would turn to him and say, "Boy, you sure gave me a tough time," and I could see that he would feel good about it. I would do this even though I knew I could have run away from him at any time.

Thus, there appears to be a rather complex and somewhat ambivalent attitude toward leadership when the leadership may involve competitive activity or active pursuit. However, it appears to be another matter if leadership is thrust upon an individual by his peers. "If your people turn to you and *make you a leader*," commented an Indian respondent, "then you have no choice but to be a leader. To refuse, even though you may not want to be a leader and have done nothing purposely to get it, would be the same thing as telling your brothers that you think your opinion, the opinion of one man, is better than all of theirs." Apparently, the important element is, according to these respondents and these observations, that the individual should not appear to *want to be a leader* and should not overtly compete with his brothers. (This attitude, as revealed by the respondents, is generally intramural in nature. There seem to be fewer such feelings when an Indian group is competing with an Anglo group in sports or other kinds of extracurricular activities.) This complex reaction to the leadership role was nicely illustrated during a recent Potawatomi Pow-Wow. A visiting Chief was called upon by the group to lead them in prayer, and he responded, "The greatest honor that can be given to a man is to be asked to stand before his people and lead them. There are many others here tonight who are more worthy than I to have this honor. But, so that I will not embarrass them by naming them, I will do what you wish."

A fourth issue fostering the hesitancy of the Indians to present themselves as candidates for election or even to nominate others was the general ambivalence toward authority—including both having a hand in establishing authority or becoming authority. One of the participants, later interviewed, explained:

You know, we Indians seem to be afraid of authority. We know from our past history that we can't break through the power of authority. We learned this from the Federal Government. We don't particularly like sitting back and giving in to authority all of the time, and sometimes we'll take little digs at officials if we can get away with it, but usually we do what we've kind of learned the hard way—we sit back and let the authorities take care of us.

You can see this among the Indians themselves, too. I saw a great example of this with our bowling league. The league was to be a part of a Pow-Wow Club that we had started. It took us a couple of months to get anyone to be officers of that Pow-Wow Club, because of the same kind of problem I was just talking about. Nobody wants to be a leader, and it seems like nobody even wants to set up officers over them. Anyway, we drew names out of a hat to see how to divide our league into four-man teams. Just by chance, three of the officers of the club were placed on one team. On another one of the teams in the league, the four best bowlers were members. This was not by drawing out of a hat, but, by agreement, because this team was going to represent us in a bigger bowling league, and we thought that they should have experiences together.

Well, a funny thing happened. The team with the Indian officers on it bowled against the team with our top four bowlers several times. Now, on the record, the pin average of the officer team was many pins lower than that of the team of best bowlers. But the team with the best bowlers *never* defeated the team with the three officers on it during our league or even during practice games. They bowled together at least 10 times that I can remember. We used to tease the team of best bowlers after they would lose, and I remember them telling us, "How can you beat a team that has all chiefs on it!"

This is a fascinating parallel to William Fotte Whyte's[25] observations of the distribution of bowling scores according to status within the Gang of Street Corner Society.

None of these responses should indicate that the Indians participating in the meeting, or any Indians for that matter, inevitably cower in the face of authority or authority figures or totally avoid becoming a leader. Rather, these data indicate rather clearly an ambivalence toward authority and leadership—an ambivalence that quite understandably could impede or delay the development of indigenous leadership within a proposed Indian Community Action Committee. This ambivalence was further complicated by the fact that anyone elected at the meeting would be a leader *within* the Topeka OEO—itself identified as a Governmental agency. This would mean becoming a member of the very organization that the Indians had quite recently lambasted and toward which they were still quite skeptical.

After a rather lengthy and awkward silence, with considerable foot-shuffling, shifting in seats, and coughing, the Assistant Director explained briefly the standard nomination and election procedure, and called for elections, saying, "Don't any of you think you've got some leaders here?" There was another shorter pause, and then finally Mr. M., one of the older Indian men present, was nominated for Chairman. He stood, and very seriously said, "I consider this a very great compliment to be nominated as a leader, but I have to decline because my health is not good." He in turn nominated Mr. C., who thanked the group, but declined because he "didn't really have enough time."

[25] Whyte, W. F. *Street Corner Society*. Chicago: Univ. Chicago Press, 1943.

A few minutes before, while the Assistant Director had been explaining to the group the procedures for nominating and electing officers, Mr. A., a 48-year-old heavy-equipment operator, had gotten up from his chair and stepped outside the door "to have a cigarette." He stood quite near the entrance-way to the Mission and was within earshot of what was going on inside. Mr. A. had attended the fourth and fifth meetings of the Indian group and on both occasions had been the most outspoken, aggressive, and skeptical of the participants. He is an intelligent and verbal individual, with a quick and keen sense of humor, and was a key figure in the process of "putting on" the Director of the Topeka OEO a little over a month before. Mr. A. was one of the individuals with whom the Assistant Director had developed a personal friendship and a mutual respect.

After Mr. M. and Mr. C. had declined nominations for Chairman of the Indian Committee and while Mr. A. was still standing outside smoking his cigarette, an Indian man suddenly said, "Wait a minute! I know who a good man for the job is! It's Mr. A. He's a fighter, he is, and he'll be a good representative for us. He knows what's going on too! I put up Mr. A. for the job!" The group called Mr. A. back into the church and told him that he had been nominated. They asked him if he would accept the nomination and he replied, with a soft voice and a shrug of the shoulders, "I guess so, if that's the way you want it." He was elected by acclamation, and seemed visibly pleased as his friends congratulated him. Mr. A. later informed me that he had "gone outside because he had a feeling that he might be nominated by the people, and he didn't want to be around if he was." He also indicated later that he thought, at the time of the nomination meeting that "the job of Chairman might be worth a try, but I'm not going to work very hard to get it." It was quite clear that he didn't actively pursue the nomination, and, in fact, left the room before the nominations began. In this way, perhaps, he was able successfully to resolve a conflict between wanting to "take a crack" at being the Chairman and whatever ambivalences he had toward actively pursuing or accepting a position of leadership and authority. There was little doubt, at this moment, that Mr. A. was pleased by the fact that the people had elected him, even though, as he said in his brief acceptance speech, "I'm still not quite sure what the hell we're going to do, but if we hang on, maybe we'll find out."

The election of the Vice-Chairman was a far simpler matter. It seemed that once the Chairman, the head man, was established, anything else was secondary. Only one Indian man was nominated; he was accepted and was elected by acclamation. For Secretary, the group nominated Mr. A's wife. After looking to her husband for approval and receiving it, she accepted and was elected by acclamation.

The Indian Committee was now formally established as part of the Topeka OEO organizational complex, with all the rights and privileges of representation and votes due any other Community Action Committee. The newly elected Chairman discussed with the Assistant Director and the group a time for the next meeting, and the reconvening date was established for two weeks later. Mr. A. then adjourned the meeting, and there was another round of handshaking, congratulations, and some strong indications of a "we feeling" within the group. As the participants filed out of the door of the Indian Mission, one of the Indian men turned to the newly elected Chairman and loudly said, "Good night, Chief." Mr. A. beamed.

## D. The Committee Begins to Formalize

The day after Mr. A. had been elected Chairman of the Indian Committee, he began, as he reported, "going around to the houses of Indians that I know personally and talking up this OEO Program with them." He said that he chose to go to the homes personally because he "knew from working with his people before that sending memos or announcements about something was a waste of time. The fact of life is this: if I can get people to come to these next couple of meetings, it's mostly because they're my friends, not because they believe that the Program is going to do them any good." When describing what he referred to as "the Indian mind" and the responses he was getting to his efforts, he said:

It's rough going! The first question they asked me is what good will this do me *now*? They want to know if the Program can get them a better job *today*, not next month or next year. They want to know if the Program can guarantee that they'll have enough to eat during the winter when they're out of a job. I try to explain to them that this is not that kind of program; it's not welfare or anything like that. I try to explain to them that it's maybe a chance to take a part in running some of this War on Poverty themselves, but it's hard for them to understand that and it's hard for me to explain it. I don't know enough about all this OEO stuff yet. I know some of the other target neighborhoods are getting Day Care Centers, Neighborhood Aides, Neighborhood Centers and things like that, but that doesn't answer the meat and potatoes questions that the Indians ask me. For example, one of my friends asked me, "What would this OEO do to help me get a job?" I told him that the OEO would probably refer him to the employment people. He shrugged his shoulders and said, "Well, that's just the same old thing. I've been sitting down at the employment office day after day anyway, and nothing happens. If I want to be referred, I'll just look in the Yellow Pages of the phone book!"

Right now, the Indians aren't concerned with long-range programs that may help them in the future to get better jobs or better standards of living. As one of my friends put it, "We aren't interested in some big feast next year—what we want is a loaf of bread on the table now!"

There's another problem too, and that's the negative attitude that we seem to have. A lot of the people I've been talking to tell me, "What's the use. You know that Program isn't going to change anything for us! You know that we've been talked to by agency people until we're blue in the face, and then we find out that most of it is just talk and nothing more." There's a feeling among us of wanting not even to try to change things, because we don't think we can. Look at all the opportunities that we have had in the past. Indians can go to school, have all their tuition paid, their board and room, their clothes, their books; and not many of us take advantage of it. I remember when I was in school thinking, "What the hell's the difference whether I get an education or not, that's not going to open doors to me closed by prejudice." So, you kind of sit back, relax, and ride along with life, letting the Government take care of you, but not really liking it.

Well, you can see what you've got against you when you try and talk to the Indians about taking an active part in this OEO Program. First of all, they don't think it's going to work or it's going to help them; and, second, they don't want to take an *active* part in anything. I know how they feel about it, and they know that I know how they feel and that I feel pretty much the same way myself at times. But I tell them that maybe we ought to give this a try and see what happens. I think some of them will show up at this meeting coming up, but none of us are really believers yet.

Mr. A. was questioned about his willingness to work as a leader of a Topeka OEO Community Action Committee, even though he still was skeptical of the Program and was encountering difficulties in getting others interested. He admitted frankly that:

. . . at first I thought that the whole idea was just so much stuff, and it was just another one of those agency games that we have to play. But then it occurred to me that the way the Indian has been in contact with the Government before was on the basis of a whole Reservation. Here in Topeka, we aren't on the Reservation and so maybe we don't have to be so quiet. I thought that maybe if a bunch of us here in Topeka could get together, come up with some suggestions about ways to improve things that we're unhappy about, then the force of our group, through the Topeka OEO would give us a louder voice than we've been able to have before.

There's a Mexican-American organization here in town that started because of problems like we have; and now they're organized in 30 states and when they speak, people listen! I thought also this might be a good chance to change the picture that people here in Topeka have of us Indians. If we got into the OEO like the neighborhoods have, then maybe people would get a chance to see that Indians really aren't like the stereotype says.

I don't know if any of this makes sense or if I can do anything about it. I guess the thing that really sold me on taking the job of Chairman is that the people asked me to. You just don't turn that down.

At 7:45 p.m., on the evening of October 5, 1965, Mr. A. called to order the seventh meeting, held again in the Indian Mission and attended by 30 people. He told the group, "I'm not much of a talker, and I'm not quite sure how to go about this. As a matter of fact, my wife told me that I'm like the bottom half of a double-boiler—I make a lot of steam, but I don't really know what's cooking up above." Mr. A. then called upon the Assistant Director to explain again "what OEO is all about, and what the Indians can do about it." Following the brief talk by the Assistant Director, Mr. A. introduced Mr. G., an Indian who was the Director of a program to stimulate Indian participation in OEO programs throughout eight Midwestern states (not including Kansas). Mr. G. outlined what the Indians were doing, particularly dwelling upon the victory of the United Council of Tribes in South Dakota in a recent land and civil jurisdiction dispute. He impressed the group, stating, "You see what Indians can do if they get together—they can even beat the State." Mr. G. described the difference between Indian participation in the OEO programs and their traditional interaction with the Government. He said,

In OEO, the Indians have a chance to actively develop their own program. For a change, the Indian can be a decision maker and not the Government; he just doesn't have to take what the Government hands out to him. There are some disadvantages to having things handed to you all of the time. After awhile you get used to having things handed to you and you're not much good for anything else. The important thing is that you've got to get involved and take an active part, and you've got to get together into a group—because that way you have more power. You know, this reminds me of a story. There was once an Indian all by himself who was wandering across the plains, and he saw a large group of blue-coated soldiers. Being a brave, he wanted to attack the group, but then he figured, "I can't beat them by myself," and he started to go away disappointed. But then he thought to himself, "Maybe I should go back and get some other braves to join me." So he went back to the village, gathered a large group of braves, and together they went out and attacked the Army. That my friends, was how Custer lost his hair! See what you can do together!

Mr. G. had a visible impact upon the group. Here was an Indian who was repoting to them the fact that Indians *could* do something in this OEO Program. After Mr. G. had finished, Mr. A. added, "You see! There's power in numbers. If we can get together, and work through this OEO organization, maybe we can really get some things changed around here! Now I don't know a heck of a lot about organizing. When I'm at the local bar I can always get a pool game or a ball game organized, but that's a little different than this! That's why I've asked a couple of guys from this Mexican-American organization to talk to us about organizing, and how they did it." Mr. A. then introduced an officer from the local chapter of a national Mexican-American organization, who explained that:

... the only way we Mexican-Americans could get first class citizenship was by banding together and using the power of a group. Even lawyers, who know the law very well, joined together in an organization because they know that if they stand alone as individuals, they wouldn't be heard. The problems of the Mexican-American are very much like the problems of the Indian. The Mexican-Americans and the Indians are at the bottom of the ladder when it comes to prejudice and discrimination. Like the Mexican-Americans, the Indians have a very strong heritage of which they can be proud. This makes it easier to work together and to organize.

When the officer was finished, Mr. A. commented, "There's another example of how working together will get you somewhere. We owe it to ourselves as *friends and tribesmen* to help one another out. It's the only way that we can get along and get ahead!" Mr. A. was again hammering at the friendship obligations of one Indian to another. As described above, intuitively he had assessed the personalistic value-orientation among his people, and saw this as the first means of getting them together. He was aware that he couldn't immediately start talking about specific problems without first building a base of acceptance for the Topeka OEO within his group. "You've got to offer the Indians something more than just a bunch of program talk, at least at first. You've got to offer them, when they attend the meeting, something that's more important to them: like friendship. Then gradually, maybe they'll start talking about the specific things in the Topeka OEO on their own—and it will come from them, not pushed down on them from up above."

Mr. A.'s strategy, plus the stimulation from the testimony of the invited speakers of the evening, had the hoped-for effect. One of the Indian particupants asked, "Well, if we're going to get together, we might as well see what this OEO operation has that we can use. Why don't we write down all our needs and then take up these needs as subjects in future meetings? Maybe that way we can develop our own programs." There was general agreement within the group about this, and here was the first indication of the development of an agenda for meetings to come. Mr. A. followed up on this suggestion and told the group he would accept these lists any time the people wanted to give them to him. He said, "This would be something quite a bit more than getting a 'tough luck' slip to go see the chaplain and then getting nothing but a bunch of words in return. Here's a chance that maybe we can do something for ourselves.

The question came up about ways of getting more Indians involved in the meetings. One participant commented that "the only way you can get Indians together on a regular basis is to have a social or a pow-wow." Mr. A. agreed, adding, "You know, sometimes you have to fight Indians to get them to accept ideas that are really good for them." This opened a discussion among the group members about the fact that

"Indians don't really like to accept help from people, especially from people who aren't Indians. We like to prove that we can make it ourselves, and that we can go it alone." This was a fascinating kind of statement, seeming to contradict other comments that the Indians had made that same night about wanting the Government or the Topeka OEO to "give them food, jobs, and clothing *now*, not tomorrow." This apparent contradiction again revealed the complexity of Indians' attitudes and ambivalences toward traditional Government paternalism. It also revealed one of the basic difficulties in getting this group of Indians together on a relatively permanent basis under the auspices of the Topeka OEO.

Another question came from the floor, the Indian man inquiring, "What about paying dues? Maybe we ought to pay 50¢ a year or something." Mr. A. responded that he didn't think this was necessary. He felt that "the purpose of this organization doesn't call for dues." The man began to argue with Mr. A. and said, somewhat derogatorily, "Well, Mr. Chairman, Sir, you can't expect people to be interested if they're not going to pay a little dues." Mr. A. continued to disagree, saying, "'we only want people here who are interested. We don't want their money. We don't want anything more from them than just their participation." The questioner smiled and said somewhat softly, "Okay, Mr. Chairman, okay." This was the first show of disagreement between a follower and the leader. For a moment the interaction had almost the undertone of Mr. A.'s own previous interaction with the Director of the Topeka OEO; the undertones of "putting him on." In a subsequent interview, Mr. A. remembered this incident quite well, and said, "Well, you know that was the first time I felt uncomfortable being the Chairman." This incident was to be a harbinger for later indigenous leadership problems.

Mr. A. suggested to the group that they get some of the coffee and cookies that had been provided. Then, looking a little bewildered, he blurted out, "I don't know how to end this thing!" He asked the Assistant Director, "What do I do

now?" The Assistant Director explained to him the procedures
for adjourning the meeting, and Mr. A. began to do just that,
until he was loudly interrupted by several members of the
group. "Wait a minute! What about setting a time for the
next meeting?" Mr. A. apologized and the group agreed to
hold another meeting two weeks hence. There appeared to be
a genuine desire expressed by the members of the Committee
to continue their meetings.

It was then after 10 p.m., and the meeting had run its course
for two and a half hours. Several of the people went home, but
about 10 of the participants, all male, moved off to a side
room in the Indian Mission. Here, Mr. A. again began holding forth on "the Indian mind." He reflected with the group
that:

The Indian has been kicked around so much and promised so much
and faced with so many phonies that he has learned how to play the
game with them and how to lead them on. He knows how to get what
he can out of them and then laugh it off after it is over with. That's
what makes it so tough to get Indians interested in a program like
this OEO. Any program like that, coming from the Government, is
guilty until proved innocent. Well, this OEO Program looks to me
like it's a little bit different than the usual kind of stuff we get. I think
we ought to give it a fair look, but trying to convince other people
about it is really a tough job.

The members of the group agreed with Mr. A. One participant commented:

Yeah, you know it may sometimes look to others that Indians always
let themselves get pushed around, and never do anything about it.
Well, there's not a hell of a lot we can do, because we never had had
too much power and the other guys have usually always held the
cards, but we have our own quiet kind of ways of letting the pushers
know who is boss: like the way we ate up all those cows!

The group laughed loudly at being reminded of the famous
cow story (related above). Again, the need was manifested
by the Indian participants to demonstrate that they did, in

fact, have definite ways of maintaining some control over the various elements that influence their daily lives.

The conversation shifted to "the way that you get disgusted with programs and agencies and stuff like that because of all the red tape." Mr. A. told the group about how impressed he was with a juvenile officer, who was now no longer in Topeka. He said that he admired the man because

... he was a guy who could be respected. When any case came to him, he looked over the whole situation, what it meant to the people involved, and then he made a decision. He checked into the families, and you could approach him as a friend, and he talked to you that way. He didn't just go by some book or some rules and regulations that are written down like they had nothing to do with people. I tell you, that's the only way that things can be done right: you've got to approach people as one human being to another. This is especially true of the Indians, and I would guess it's true of other minority groups who are just damned sick and tired of being dealt with by agencies as if they were things and not human beings.

Mr. A. then commented on the Assistant Director's approach to the Indians, saying, "Now look at the Assistant Director here, for example. Suppose he had come to see us the same way that the Director did—with all that fancy talk, those titles, like he knew all the answers and he knew what was best for us. Well, if he had done that, there wouldn't have been any meeting tonight, or any other meeting of the Indians as far as OEO is concerned. Instead, he met us eye-to-eye, and got to know us personally. That makes all the difference in the world, and if the OEO doesn't realize that, then they're in big trouble The personalistic value-orientation and its powerful influence, was again sharply manifested.

At this point, the Indian man who had earlier raised the question about dues repeated his argument. "I still think," he said to Mr. A., "that if we're going to have a group here, we ought to have dues." Mr. A. again began to argue with him, "No, we don't want dues. We just want interest! We don't want to take anybody's money except maybe the Government's!" (The group laughed.) The questioner argued some more, and finally said very heatedly, "Well, you know damned well that in any *white man's club* they charge dues!" Following that statement he remained silent. It was easy to sense the resistance that this individual had to being labeled as a member of a "poverty" organization. He much preferred the Committee to be one to which members paid at least some token dues, like the clubs whose doors are always closed to the Indian. By paying some small amount, the member might also feel a sense of ownership in the organization—a sense of ownership that could extend to more active participation. One had the feeling the questioner was arguing that he couldn't believe active participation could be made available to the Indian unless he paid for it in one way or another. Mr. A. told the man that he "might have a point, and I'm going to give it a good deal more thought. Maybe we can talk more about it at the next meeting."

It was 11 p.m., and Mr A. suggested that "we all go home now, and then let's see what will happen at the next meeting." With that, Mr. A. went over to a small counter in the back room, reached under a shelf, and pulled out an old, battered brief case. He fumbled with the lock, and sheepishly mumbled, "I'm not used to working this damned thing yet." Finally, he got it open, stuffed in a few papers and rearranged them, then snapped the brief case shut, and with no less *savoir faire* than a Madison Avenue executive, Mr. A. left the Indian Mission.

# Participation of Residents in Neighborhood Community Action Programs*

## FRANCES F. PIVEN

*Strategies to obtain participation of residents must overcome the general lack of resources in low-income communities: scarce knowledge, apathetic beliefs, and few inducements by which to hold leadership or build organizations.*

The widespread advocacy of participation by residents of local communities in public programs by no means reflects agreement regarding the goals of such participation, the forms it should take, or the means for its effectuation. Some of the different concepts comprehended by "resident participation" and the problems these entail are suggested by a review of recent experiences with urban renewal and the early community action projects, predecessors of the antipoverty program.[1]

Both urban renewal and the antipoverty program can be viewed as policies for under-developed areas. They repre-

* Reproduced by special permission from the author and the publisher, *Social Work, II* (1), January 1966.

[1] Community action projects were initiated by the Ford Foundation's "Grey Areas Program" and by the President's Committee on Juvenile Delinquency and Youth Crime several years before the current spate of projects funded under Title II of the antipoverty legislation, according to which a "community action program means a program which mobilizes and utilizes resources, public or private of any 'community' in an attack on poverty." Public Law 88-452, Title II, Part A, Section 202.

sent a new move forward in the developmental functions of government, as distinguished from its more traditional regulatory functions. It follows from the tasks of these programs that they have extraordinary—and differential—impact on selected local communities.

## An Issue in Urban Renewal

Resident participation became a major issue in local areas earmarked for rebuilding under urban renewal programs. The dilemmas regarding resident participation followed in part from the fact that although local areas were selected as targets for redevelopment they were to be redeveloped in terms of assumptions about the welfare of "the city as a whole." Whatever diffuse benefits such a program might indeed come to have for the larger community, an immediately disruptive impact was felt by groups residing in the target area.[2] It was these groups that were hit most sharply by the costs of renewal, but it was not necessarily these groups that were to benefit from the new development. Economic and cultural revitalization of inner city areas was spelled out for slum residents by clearance and dislocation. The new developments chiefly included high rental housing. Existing residents in areas scheduled for renewal were confronted with the distress of upheaval, the loss of neighborhood, and the prospect of greatly increased rentals.[3] In consequence, adamant local protests came to be an earmark of renewal programs, often spelling political turmoil for the projects.[4] These experiences resulted

[2] Considerable outrage has been occasioned among the advocates of government action in housing and urban renewal by publication recently of an extremely critical study of urban renewal by a conservative economist. See Martin Anderson, *The Federal Bulldozer* (Cambridge, Mass.: MIT Press, 1964). For a general but more judicious review of urban renewal policies and problems, see Herbert J. Gans, "The Failure of Urban Renewal," *Commentary, 39* (4), April 1965, 29-37.

[3] For a review of problems in relocation, see Chester Hartman, "The Housing of Relocated Families," *Journal of the American Institute of Planners, 30* (4), November 1964, 266-286.

[4] For a discussion of the political dilemmas created by renewal programs,

in a growing concern with resident participation in renewal and also influenced the kinds of participation that were advocated and solicited by those responsible for the programs. In order to avoid local protests, which often rocked the projects when they were already well under way, steps were taken to initiate resident groups at an early stage in order to educate and win them to the plans.

Efforts to bring about resident participation in urban renewal were thus marked by an irony reflecting the dilemma of renewal policy. Programs for resident participation were developed to offset the spontaneous—but disruptive—participation of local protest groups. Critics came to describe such programs cynically as a mere "cooling-off" tactic. However, so long as renewal plans were oriented to the welfare of the city as a whole they would almost surely generate acute protest and conflict in local areas. Only the most blithe and happy faith in the democratic consensus could permit a program geared to the community as a whole to promote participation by and *influence of* local residents in renewal areas. It was virtually inevitable that educational forms of participation would be emphasized in renewal programs.

## Difference in Poverty Projects

The community-based poverty projects that are already under way also emphasize the place of resident participation. These projects have, however, been given a different public mandate than renewal programs in that they are oriented to the problems of the poor in the project community rather than to the larger urban community. Moreover, they have developed at a time when the civil rights movement has lent new force and meaning to political and organizational activity among the minority groups that form the bulk of the urban poor.

The new concern with resident participation reflects a

see James Q. Wilson, "Planning and Politics: Citizen Participation in Urban Renewal," *Journal of the American Institute of Planners, 21* (4), November 1963.

characterization of the low-income urban community as dis-organized and politically ineffective. Low-income people tend not to belong to organizations and do not participate in community affairs. They are relatively uninfluential in the formation of policies and practices of the major institutions that affect the course of their lives. This kind of social and political inactivity is viewed as an aspect of social disorgani-zation and is closely linked, therefore, with many of the prob-lems of the low-income community—having to do particularly with socialization of the young and also with the social pre-conditions for individual and family effectiveness generally.

Consistent with this characterization, new objectives and strategies are being associated with resident participation in the antipoverty projects. Three interrelated objectives can be identified:

1. Fostering the participation of low-income people in a variety of local associations.
2. Enhancing the effective influence of low-income people on the policies and practices of institutions that serve the low-income community.
3. Establishing the conditions for effective individual and family life by altering the social context of individual behavior.

These objectives for resident participation reflect the con-cern of the poverty programs with political problems per-taining to democratic participation and influence as well as concern with the social welfare problems to which the programs are principally addressed. The conception attributed to urban renewal programs, in contrast, emphasizes another kind of political problem—that of integrating local groups to the support of a larger public policy. It should be noted, however, that the poverty programs are only less immediately charged with the problem of reconciling divergent group interests. To the extent that the programs do pursue objectives oriented specifically to the interests of the poor they will, as they de-

velop, require changes and accommodations from larger
institutions. Problems of political conflict and integration
will inevitably arise and rebound on the objectives of local
resident participation and influence.[5] Recent contests between
city officials and neighborhood leaders for control of the local
poverty program structures may be an anticipation of these
developments.

## Characteristics of the Urban Poor

While the poor are obviously composed of diverse groups,
certain attributes can be identified that are pertinent to any
efforts to encourage resident participation among the poor,
in terms of the objectives outlined above.[6] The discussion
which follows is addressed specifically to the urban poor. The
problems and potentialities in involving the rural poor would
appear to be quite different and to require examination in
their own right. Several aspects of low-income urban life
contribute to disorganization and political ineffectiveness.[7]
Low-income people are overwhelmed by concrete daily needs.
Their lives are often crisis ridden, deflecting from any concern with community issues. They have no belief in their
ability to affect the world in which they live, and so they are
not easily induced to try to affect it.[8] Frequently they lack
the necessary resources of knowledge and information to enable

[5] There is already evidence of such problems in the controversy over Mobilization for Youth, an action-research project on New York's Lower East
Side. Recent testimony from local leaders before a Congressional committee
suggests, moreover, that such problems may smolder without becoming so
publicly evident.

[6] For a discussion of the different class and status factors used to identify
the lower class see S. M. Miller, "The American Lower Classes: A Typologi-
cal Approach," in Frank Riessman, Jerome Cohen, and Arthur Pearl, eds.,
*Mental Health of the Poor: New Treatment Approaches for Low Income
People.* N.Y.: Free Press of Glencoe, 1964. Pp. 139-154.

[7] For a review of the sociological literature on the lower class see Herbert
Gans, "A Survey of Working Class and Lower Class Studies," in Riessman
et al. Pp. 119-127.

[8] See Walter B. Miller, "Lower Class Culture as a Generating Milieu of
Gang Delinquency," *Journal of Social Issues,* 14 (3), July 1958, 5-19; and

them to scrutinize social policies. Leadership capabilities are also scarcer among the poor. Moreover, when leaders do emerge, the poor have few incentives to offer them and means of controlling them are scarce. Potential leaders therefore tend to take advantage of opportunities for their own advancement that move them quickly away from low-income concerns. Finally, the institutions whose services might offer incentives for low-income interest and activity are often effectively insulated from the low-income community by their structure, practices, and cultural style.[9]

These several aspects of low-income life are interrelated and cumulative in their effects. Thus, lower-class interpretations of the world stress the inability of most men to affect the conditions under which they live.[10] These beliefs take form in a sense of political inefficacy, which discourages political participation and thus further reinforces conditions of actual powerlessness. Low-income people have little to offer in the way of material resources as political inducements, and they are separated by their social location from the exercise of personal influence on decision-makers. Therefore they are not easily able to obtain the benefits of political influence that

---

Albert Cohen and Harold Hodges, "Characteristics of the Lower Blue-Collar Class," *Social Problems, 10* (4), Spring 1963, 303-334.

[9] This has been a major theme in recent criticism of social welfare services, and a problem that the employment of "indigenous" or "nonprofessional" workers in neighborhood service centers is designed to alleviate, by helping to bridge the cultural and bureaucratic gaps between client and agency. For a description of public welfare practices and how they are countered by such a service center, see Richard A. Cloward and Richard M. Elman, "The Storefront on Stanton Street," to be published in *Commentary*. For a critique of the service patterns of the private social welfare agency, see Richard A. Cloward and Irwin Epstein, "Private Social Welfare's Disengagement from the Poor: The Case of Family Adjustment Agencies" (New York: Columbia University School of Social Work, 1964). (Mimeographed.) See also Herbert J. Gans, "Redefining the Settlement's Function for the War on Poverty," *Social Work, 9* (4), October 1964, 3-12.

[10] For a discussion of the interrelationships between real powerlessness and attitudes of powerlessness, see Warren C. Haggstrom, "The Power of the Poor," in Riessman et al., *op. cit.*, pp. 205-223.

might serve as inducements for political participation and to overcome the disadvantages in education and skill that inhibit participation.

The organizational life of the low-income community both reflects these individual attributes and serves also to maintain the conditions that produce them. Participation and influence do not consist only of the relations between disparate individuals and official decision-makers. The influence of individuals is mediated by organizations. It is through organizations that diverse individual resources are co-ordinated into coherent patterns of effective influence. But lower-class people have few of the requirements out of which stable organizations are generated: they have less organizational skill, less professional expertise, less money, and fewer personal relations with officials.[11] In any case, they do not have the resources lent by a stable livelihood that are required merely for regular participation in organizations. The instability of lower-class life and the character of lower-class beliefs further discourage the poor from organizational participation.[12] It is, in turn, partly because of the meagerness of organizational life that the poor community is so little able to retain or control its potential leaders.[13]

This characterization of low-income urban life may be modified or even overcome when, for example, a community

[11] For a political scientist's discussion of the requirements for organizational influence in city affairs, see Wallace L. Sayre and Herbert Kaufman, *Governing New York City*. N.Y.: Russell Sage Foundation, 1960. Pp. 481-515.

[12] In fact, instability in occupational or family life has frequently been the criterion used to distinguish the lower class, or the poor, from the working class. See, for example, S. M. Miller, *op. cit.*; and S. M. Miller and Frank Riessman, "The Working-Class Subculture: A New View," *Social Problems, 9* (1), Summer 1961, 86-97.

[13] The sparse social texture of the poor community is suggested by a survey conducted by Mobilization for Youth on the Lower East Side of New York City. Over half the residents reported no informal group participation and only 15 percent got together with a group more than once a week, "just to talk, play cards, go bowling, or something else like that." "Codebook: Mobilization for Youth, Vol. I. Adult Survey." New York: Research Center, Columbia University School of Social Work, 1962. Mimeographed.

is bound by a strong ethnic culture.[14] It is a characterization that tends to apply to vast numbers of the urban poor today, however, and one that marks those groups who share least in organizational and political life. The meager success of traditional approaches to involving the poor, which rely on exhorting them to participate or on civic education, can be understood in terms of the interlocking and reinforcing relationships between actual powerlessness, apathetic beliefs, and scarce skills and resources. These circumstances, in turn, both produce and are maintained by the paucity of organizational life in the low-income community.

## Program Strategies

The antipoverty projects can address these problems in resident participation in two different contexts. They can attempt to facilitate resident participation in a variety of areas of community life and with regard to a variety of institutions. This is typically the approach of community organization efforts. The antipoverty project is, however, also itself a public policy arena. The focus may, therefore, be specifically on resident participation in the policy and program of the local project.

Various strategies for facilitating resident participation in community life generally are being used by projects already under way. These can be identified and reviewed in terms of early experiences.

1. Concrete services are provided, such as help in processing housing complaints or in consumer problems. These services are located in places easily accessible to local people and are expected to attract low-income people as recipients. The effort, however, is to induce recipients to take on more active roles through associations formed around the provision of service.

[14] See, for example, Herbert J. Gans's study of an Italian community in Boston in *The Urban Villagers: Group and Class in the Life of Italian-Americans.* New York: Free Press of Glencoe, 1962. See also William F. Whyte, Jr., *Street Corner Society.* Chicago: University of Chicago Press, 1955.

Thus tenant associations may be organized in housing clinics, with the aim of interesting tenants in sponsoring and operating the clinic and the hope that eventually, as a group, they will become more articulate and aggressive concerning the issues in housing policy that their daily problems reflect. Mobilization for Youth, for example, opened storefronts where residents could get not only advice on housing problems, but the intervention of staff in dealings with landlords and housing agencies. The staff first gave individual help and then attempted to induce the tenants in a building to get together in order to register joint complaints and in some instances for joint withholding of rent. These different building organizations were, in turn, invited to join a neighborhood-wide tenants' council for further group action.

2. Existing low-income organizations in the project area are helped with staff and facilities. It is expected that adding to the resources of these groups will enable them to attract more participants and will also encourage them to take more alert and forceful positions on social issues of concern to the membership. The Haryou-Act project in New York's Harlem tries to do this by subcontracting many of its programs, with the idea that program resources can thus serve in building local organizations.

3. A short-term approach to the problem of scarce leadership resources in the community is the engagement of professional staff in community organization activity. This is, of course, not a new role for social workers. Whether the engagement of professionals in this role is indeed merely an interim solution depends on success in the development of local leadership.

Potential leadership is sought among local people. Efforts are made to interest persons who seem to show leadership qualities in organizing activity and to educate these persons about issues considered critical to low-income people. These individuals may be paid as a kind of "community worker," or they may be coached and encouraged to perform actively as volunteers.

Some projects have actually developed "community action institutes" to train neighborhood people who will be employed as block workers or organizers.

4. The social contiguity provided by ethnic, religious, occupational, or residential groups is a natural basis for affiliation and therefore is a reference in organizing group activity. Residential groupings—the building or block association—and racial or ethnic groupings seem particularly important among the poor. Many projects are located in ghetto neighborhoods and therefore work only with a racially and ethnically homogenous client population. In a mixed community such as the Lower East Side of New York, however, groups are often formed according to the racial and ethnic lines along which people divide themselves.

5. Participation in social protest action is sometimes encouraged by staff assigned to local organizations. Facilities required to pursue such actions may also be provided to these organizations or even to formally unaffiliated individuals who seem to play a leader role. These protest actions may range from participation in nationwide or city-wide events to demonstrations over specific grievances involving perhaps only a few residents.[15]

## Barriers to Participation

Some early experience with these program strategies reveals persisting problems in overcoming barriers to low-income participation and influence in community affairs.

When concrete services are the incentive for initial participation they tend to remain the focus of activity. The extent of need for such service among the poor seems to overwhelm any less urgent activities and the provision of services consumes

---

[15] It should be noted that while protest actions by the poor have received wide interest and attention, they have not generally been risked by the community action projects. Mobilization For Youth in New York City and the Syracuse University training program for community organizers, inspired largely by Saul Alinsky, are two exceptions.

the energies of staff and recipients alike. Thus staff assigned to help with housing or welfare problems find that emergency housing violations or delayed welfare checks are so widespread and compelling as to require their direct and continuing efforts at obtaining service, deflecting them from organizational activities.

Existing low-income organizations are weak and seem often to be mere emblems of power for leaders whose personal ambition is tied, not to a low-income following that has little to offer them, but rather to the service organization. Thus these organizations may use facilities or funds they receive to acquire the furbishings of respectability: typewriters, furniture, and the like. And new resources can merely precipitate bickering among leaders, deflecting rather than impelling their attention to membership.

The role of professionals in community organization remain problematical. Local people tend to regard them with uneasiness, as strangers. The professionals themselves must accommodate a strain between the style and actions indicated by their role in low-income organizations, the dictates of their professional training, and the organizational requirements of the antipoverty project itself. Thus the professional worker is expected by the community group with whom he works to take clear and supportive positions on issues that arise. If instead he defers to directives from his supervisors or to the dictates of professional neutrality, he may lose the confidence of the community group.

Other problems seem to reside in the strategies for selecting and cultivating indigenous leadership. When these individuals are paid, in an effort to compensate for the absence of incentives for leadership in the low-income community, they tend to orient themselves predominantly to the organization that pays them. Volunteers, when they can be cultivated, come to expect similar compensation.

Social protest actions, because they offer simple and dramatic definitions of problems, may penetrate apathy and override the puzzled disengagement bred of lack of information. These actions also require less personal and economic stability than sustained organizational participation. It should be noted that urban renewal programs elicited protest action from local groups in response to the threats posed by renewal. Social protest is likely, however, to incur hostility and repressive reactions from other groups in the community and from public authorities. Low-income groups may in consequence be even further cut off from channels to influence and also from the services that can serve as a basis for more stable organization. Experience with antipoverty programs testifies dramatically to this risk.

## Different Ways of Participating

The antipoverty project itself is a potential arena for resident participation. This has lately become something of a public issue and several different organizational forms of participation are being recommended.

1. Residents should participate on policy-making structures—ordinarily the board—either on the city-wide or local level. These residents are regarded as representatives of the resident population in the areas served. It is this kind of participation that has usually been associated with the legislative mandate for "maximum feasible participation of residents." A certain proportion of the seats on these structures are allocated to residents, with different schemes—elections, appointments, or conventions—for selecting them. These arrangements have often been the occasion for tugging and hauling among various groups, local and city-wide, for controlling influence.

2. Residents should participate as staff. These programs generally referred to as the employment of indigenous or nonprofessional workers, are among the most widely used of the poverty program strategies.[16]

---

[16] They are often interpreted in terms of other goals than resident participation, however; they provide employment for local people, for example,

3. Residents should be formed into active constituent groups. These groups are sometimes recommended as a program resource for professional staff, providing feedback for program evaluation, or they can be regarded as pressure groups that properly influence the project in its activities.

The "neighborhood boards" of Haryou-Act, planned also by the Youth-In-Action project in Brooklyn, are organizational devices intended to provide for all three of the foregoing forms of participation. These boards are supposed to be independent of the parent project—though funded by it—and governed by neighborhood people.

The boards are supposed to develop service functions and will presumably make policy in that regard (at least within the limitations set by the terms of their contracts with the parent project and within the overall limitations set by the city's poverty structure). The boards will employ local people in service-giving functions. And, finally, since the boards are composed of independent groups of residents they are potentially active constituents for the parent project.

These proposals can be reviewed for problems and potentialities in the light of the foregoing characterization of low-income urban life:

1. Persons from the resident community who are selected to participate in policy-making structures will, if they are to be effective, ordinarily be distinguished by superior abilities or resources. To this extent their representative character is qualified. Moreover, what has been said about the scarce resources for control of leaders in the low-income community applies to the control of these representatives as well. The community has little in the way of an alert and able citizenry or organizational resources to review, control, and direct what its ostensible spokesmen do. The antipoverty program, on the other hand, and the organizations with which it is af-

or intermediaries to bridge the cultural and organizational gap between clients and service bureaucracies.

filiated constitute an active source of pressure and inducement to the presumed representatives.

2. To some extent these problems also pertain when residents are employed as staff. Their sense of themselves as employees, however—facilitated by unionization—may create something of a bulwark enhancing resident identity. The tendency of supervising professionals to become overly protective and directing with resident staff, usually in the name of professional guidance and training, may also strain against the goals of participation and influence. This may be mitigated if the resident staff are organizing in cadres enhancing their resident identity and providing group support.

3. When constituent groups are restricted to "feedback" participation there may be little incentive for their continuing viability. Feedback in the form of more active pressure and influence by these groups, in the course of which the project could deliver incentives for continued engagement, might be more successful. This requires organizational arrangements that try to insure the project's responsiveness to constituent groups. For example, local public hearings can be held on various program practices provided these practices are deemed appropriately reviewed and changed in resonse to constituent groups.

## Conclusions

Whatever patterns are developed in the antipoverty projects for resident participation will reflect answers to two sets of questions:

1. Who should participate? In what actions should they participate? Where should this participation be located in the organizational structure? What conditions should govern this action?

2. How can participation by the specified groups, and in the prescribed forms, be elicited and maintained; i.e., what are the effectuating mechanisms for the forms of participation prescribed by the answers to the first set of questions above?

Decisions made in antipoverty programs will initiate patterns of participation and influence, and these questions should be confronted. Decisions pertaining to program activities designed to foster resident participation in community life generally will imply answers that properly vary with the kinds of participation considered and the institutional contexts of participation. The full scope of such decisions will reflect the political philosophy of the antipoverty program, as well as a range of assumptions regarding the conditions of social action. Insofar as these decisions pertain to participation in the project themselves they will imply answers that describe the antipoverty program as a political subsystem and the place of residents of the local community in this political subsystem.

The answers to these questions must reflect some of the fundamental ambiguities of our political values and must take account of the fluidity of social and political arrangements. Moreover, they require knowledge of processes of social and political change that does not yet exist. For these reasons, the questions will not be answered entirely explicitly or comprehensively.

The essential dilemma in gaining participation, however, and the problem that underlies many of the difficulties detailed here, is that participation and influence depend on a range of social and economic capabilities. Strategies intended specifically to induce participation may set directions. Sustained and effective participation, however, will finally depend on the allocation to these communities of the social and economic benefits that are the resources for participation and influence in a complex society.

# The Voice of the People*

## PETER MARRIS and MARTIN REIN

... Both the Ford Foundation and the President's Committee had already devised safeguards against the abuse of their aims—through the criteria by which grants were approved, control of development funds, the requirement of rigorous preliminary planning. But these sanctions, which relied on money and expertise, appealed to principles of rationality rather than democracy, and could be challenged as intellectually or politically presumptuous. The reformers believed that the people of the slums, too, must have a voice in any programme of their behalf. The grey area projects were to "plan with people, not for people," and the President's Committee insisted upon "evidence that individuals and organizations in the target community recognize in the project a legitimate force for change. Part of such evidence will be their involvement in the project's planning process."[1] Thus the programmes were not only to be dispassionately rational, and endorsed by community leaders, but also an authentic expression of the wishes of the programme's constituents.

To draw the institutions of a community together in a concerted plan of action, without compromising intellectual integrity, was arduous enough. But this further principle compounded the difficulties. The participation of the residents in the neighborhoods to be served was likely to inter-

* Reproduced by special permission from the authors and the publisher, from *Dilemmas of Social Reform*. N.Y.: Atherton Press, 1967. Pp. 164-190.
[1] Policy Guides to the Presentation of Proposals for Funding under Public Law 87-274, September 1963.

fere as much with the rational priorities of the funding agencies, as with the more political interests of institutions. The reformers believed that programmes had failed in the past for lack of co-ordination, consistent effort, and thorough analysis of the nature of the problems. Their own thinking was intellectually sophisticated and disinterestedly experimental. The leaderless, ill-educated, dispirited people of a city slum, if they could find their voice, would hardly speak to the brief of a nationally-minded elite of university professors and foundation executives. Research, planning, co-ordination, must seem remote answers to a rat-infested tenement, the inquisitorial harassment of a welfare inspector, debts and the weary futility of killing time on the streets. Yet, at least in principle, the reformers were ready to jeopardize their carefully laid strategy for the sake of this grass-roots participation.

Perhaps only in America would this have seemed so self-evidently right. The funders' mistrust of their own authority as an intellectual elite, and faith in the power of spontaneous, local democracy, reflect a peculiarly American tradition. "No sooner do you set foot upon American ground than you are stunned by a kind of tumult," observed de Tocqueville, over a century ago, "a confused clamour is heard on every side, and a thousand simultaneous voices demand the satisfaction of their social wants."

... The reformers in the Foundation and the President's Committee were attacking just those features of American life which de Tocqueville saw as the liabilities of a democratic creed—the gross social neglect, inconsequential policies, uncoordinated effort, carelessness of skilled application—and yet they were deeply committed to it. To Paul Ylvisaker the grandeur was indeed not in the public administration—nor in any philanthropic administration—but in what was done without it or outside of it. The strategy of reform was somehow to accommodate both the analytic precision of a carefully staged experiment, and the extension to its furthest limit of democratic participation. Neither, without the other, could have proved the fundamental assumption upon which the strategy was based: that a talented elite, with enough authority to deploy seed money, could generate a self-sustaining, democratic impulse towards reform.

But how was the principle of citizen participation to be interpreted in practice? Who truly represented the people of the neighborhod to be served by the programmes—the ward leaders of the political parties, civil rights groups, pastors, settlement houses? Anyone who enjoyed an identifiable status was already, for that very reason, partly assimilated to middle-class American society. Anyone who could hold his own in a committee of public officials, business leaders, the mayor and project directors, was unlikely to be still poor and un-educated. "Most efforts to organize lower class people attract individuals on their way up the social-class ladder," observed the prospectus for Mobilization for Youth. "Persons who are relatively responsible about participation, articulate, and successful at managing organizational 'forms' are identified as lower-class leaders, rather than those who actually reflect the values of lower-class groups." Mobilization proposed to encourage instead more truly indigenous leaders. But this alternative has paradoxical implications, as the Assistant Secretary of Labour rather unkindly pointed out to a conference on poverty: "Note what is to be remedied: instead of getting hold of local people who are 'relatively responsible about participation, articulate, and successful at managing organizational "forms," ' Mobilization for Youth is going to get hold of a lower level of true and genuine leaders who are —what?—inarticulate, irresponsible, and relatively unsuccess-ful? I am sorry, but I suspect that proposition. I was raised on the West Side of New York, and I must report that those are not the principles on which Tammany Hall, the International Longshoremen's Association, or the New York Yankees recruited indigenous leadership."[2]

[2] Address by Daniel Patrick Moynihan to the Conference on Poverty in America, Berkeley, California, February 26-28, 1965.

The formal organization through which the projects authorized their decisions inevitably precluded the effective participation of unsophisticated people. Faced with the inherent contradiction of vesting a joint authority of leadership in those you perceive as leaderless and alienated, the project boards do not, in fact, seem to have included a single poor man or woman. Only the Office of Economic Opportunity, in the more recent projects promoted under the poverty programme, has seriously considered the formal representation of the poor. It proposes that several board members— even a majority—might be directly elected by the people of the neighborhoods served.[3] But the difficulty remains that if these representatives can make their influence effective in so formal a setting, they may lose their understanding with their constituents. By achieving influence itself, such a representative of the poor loses many of the characteristics which identify him as one with those he represents.

If it was impracticable to invest the beneficiaries of the programme with the same kind of authority as a board of directors, the projects looked then for other means of keeping the board and its executives responsive to the demands of those it served. It was assumed that in any neighbourhood, however, disrupted and demoralized, potential leaders could be found to articulate needs, and organize the expression of local feeling. But the projects would themselves have to identify these leaders, and encourage them to rouse their neighbours to make their influence felt. Participation presupposed some programme of community organization, by which the process of democratic consultation could extend its reach.

It proved, however, very difficult to establish and sustain an unambiguous purpose for community organization. It could mean the polite formality of block committees, deliberating by Roberts' rules of order, or the clamour of protest marches on city hall, rubbing raw the sores of discontent. The intention was to distribute power—to extend to the people of the

[3] OEO's policy is discussed more fully in Chapter IX.

neighbourhoods a measure of control over the projects which served them. But since they were not organized to assume such power, control remained with the project staff, as a responsibility to foster whatever organization seemed appropriate. And as the devolution of authority was postponed, more paternalistic aims of community organization began to intrude: to promote self-help and social control through social cohesion, to facilitate the assimilation of middle-class values, to disseminate understanding of project policy. At the same time, in reaction to this insidious manipulation, organization might turn towards a more militant, but equally manipulative strategy of protest against established institutions.

Community organization could, then, be interpreted with a very different emphasis, according to the standpoint of the organizer. It could be used to encourage the residents of a neighbourhood to come to terms with the demands of a wider society, or conversely to force the institutions of that society to adapt more sympathetically to the special needs of a neighbourhood. Or it could be seen rather as a form of therapy, to treat apathy and social disintegration. And it might take an individual bias—promoting the social mobility of potential leaders, championing cases of personal injustice —or a communal bias more concerned with the neighbourhood as a mutually supportive community. To a redevelopment administrator like Edward Logue, community organization meant, essentially, a way of persuading a neighbourhood to understand and accept a redevelopment programme, and contribute constructively to it. To the settlement houses, it meant an education in the conventions of democratic participation, as middle-class society practiced them, more for its own sake than for any particular purpose. To the social theorist, it meant the reintegration of those informal community functions which in the past had mediated the assimilation of urban newcomers. To the reformers, it meant above all, a new source of power to reinforce their pressure for institutional change.

... The projects were, then, committed by the funding agencies to a democratic ideal of citizen participation, but were left with little guidance as to the form it should take, or even its essential purpose. They were found to be held responsible for the consequences of any movement they stimulated, yet they were not, in principle, to defeat their own democratic idealism by controlling the direction which the movement chose. How the projects would come out, if the people of the neighbourhood were drawn into conflict with civic leadership, remained obscure. Pledged to both sides, they could only hope to be allowed a benevolent neutrality. In practice, the three projects which had, by 1964, attempted some form of community organization, each experienced a serious crisis, and each resolved it differently. CPI accepted the limitations of its loyalty to the Mayor of New Haven; Mobilization for Youth was drawn into alignment with the people against institutions; and ABCD largely withdrew from the risks of neighbourhood movements.[4]

The crisis in New Haven arose out of a programme of legal aid, rather than neighbourhood organization itself; but legal protection, broadly interpreted, merges with the ideals of democratic participation. Both seek to assert the rights of the least privileged against richer, more powerful, and better organized interests. Court actions may serve as demonstrations of protest, just as marches, boycotts, or petitions may serve as an alternative to legal redress. The law lends itself impartially to manipulation by militant radicals or repressive conservatives. The interpretation of a legal service in a poor neighbourhood is therefore controversial, and in New Haven it brought CPI to near disaster.

In its original programme, CPI proposed that "a plan be

[4] The Oakland Inter-Agency Project, perhaps because it was organized within city government, never seriously experimented with citizen participation, though its programmes included support for conventional community organization through the Urban League and the Council of Social Planning. The other projects are too recently funded to have had much experience of action by the end of 1964.

worked out, with the co-operation of the New Haven County Bar Association, to provide legal assistance at the community schools. Lawyers would look at all legal problems of the family, would provide legal advice on simple matters, and would make referals on more complex cases." The intention was certainly not radical, and the lawyer's task intended to be merely advisory. One of the two lawyers hired was Jean Cahn, a young Negro graduate of Swarthmore, married to a Yale law student. Both the Cahns were deeply committed to the cause of civil rights, and to their sense of a lawyer's responsibility in that struggle. From the outset, she interpreted the legal adviser's role more positively than Mitchell Sviridoff, Director of CPI, thought was prudent, given CPI's dependence on the Mayor, and the Mayor's dependence on a broad consensus of support within the City. She also felt that, as a lawyer, her first duty was to the furtherance of justice, not the interests of her employer. The issue came to a head over a case, of all cases most emotionally charged: in February 1963, three young Negroes were accused of brutally assaulting and raping a white nurse.

. . . Meanwhile Mitchell Sviridoff became alarmed at the risks to CPI in Jean Cahn's involvement, and insisted she withdraw. He also strongly discouraged his staff from attending the meetings in the Negro community, where the question of injustice was being raised with growing concern. Jean Cahn refused and three of his staff persisted. Principle would not yield to prudence.

But Sviridoff was equally convinced than he should not jeopardize the future of CPI for a doubtful case. The Mayor was being harassed by anonymous letters and abusive telephone calls. If this public outrage found its target in CPI, his whole programme was in danger. . . . Though its neighbourhood lawyers had not been intended to provide more than advice, Jean Cahn's insistence on a lawyer's overriding duty to his client precipitated an issue which could not then be evaded by pleading the programme's limited aims. Could CPI at once champion the disadvantaged, in the face of public outrage and the embarrassment of its political allies, and maintain the coalition of institutional support on which its programmes depended? Mitchell Sviridoff believed not. Forced to choose, he sacrificed quixotic idealism to the practical politics of effective reform. Jean Cahn resigned, and the legal programme was temporarily laid aside.

... As CPI strove to establish itself, self-protection and internal cohesion threatened to displace its original aims. The Cahns were not alone in questioning the way in which it had, by its energy and self-confidence, pre-empted the initiative in social reform. So able an instrument of executive authority seemed by its nature unsympathetic to any independent expression of community demands. How long, then, would it remain responsive to those demands, in the face of other, more articulate claims?

In a semi-official reply to the Cahn's paper, a member of CPI's staff challenged—besides their specific criticisms—the whole philosophy of citizen participation. As a "partisan defender of the 'faith' of Community Progress," he claimed that the search for such participation rested on a misunderstanding of the realities of leadership in a complex society:

There is a dangerous tendency for middle-class persons to overestimate the potentiality for leadership in the poverty group. In areas of deep poverty, such as public housing projects, the potential for leadership is minimal.

... At the same time, the writer recognized that CPI could not represent the interests of the poor, without also being sensitive to the counter-pressures. "In essence, Community Progress Inc. is a *public* programme with, for the most part, *public* funds to spend on a programme to relieve poverty. The programme depends upon the co-operation of *public* officials ... It is not the Civil Rights Movement, and to confuse the two, or to judge one another by a common standard, would be disservice to both. Since Community Progress Inc. must be responsive to the whole community, it must balance community claims."[5]

This defence alligns CPI unequivocally with the enlightened self-interest of established power. So frank a scepticism towards grassroots democracy made the New Haven project, for all its accomplishments, widely mistrusted as a model of community action. Yet given its political commitments, and the nature of effective action in a highly structured society, Mitchell Sviridoff may well have followed the only practicable policy. The fate of Mobilization for Youth suggests what might have happened if he had chosen otherwise.

The Mobilization for Youth conception of community organization evolved, over five years, from a conformist tradition to a radical challenge.

...At this time, Mobilization was more concerned with encouraging and training genuine local leaders, than with defining issues. It proposed—like CPI—to recruit these leaders as full or parttime workers in its programme, but unlike CPI left them free to take part in community affairs as independent citizens. In this way, it hoped to promote organization, without over-influencing the organization's aims. But in the event, the stimulation of leadership, and the issues about which leadership might develop proved inseparable, and Mobilization was driven to take a political initiative. Organization needed a purpose, and Mobilization began to take up causes which might be served by collective action, as they appeared from the problems which people brought to the agency. It hired the team for a voter registration drive, organized a local contingent of the March on Washington, encouraged rent strikes, and—as we have seen—supported Mobilization of Mothers in their protest against a local school principal. At the same time, it developed a legal aid programme, through which the people of the Lower East Side

[5] Richard Oliver Brooks, in an open letter to Mr. James O. Freedman, circulated by CPI, July 1964.

could defend more effectively their rights—challenging, for
instance, the legality of adverse decisions of the State Welfare
Department.

Mobilization never committed itself unambiguously to the
issues it had helped to raise through its community organization programme. Pressure from militant neighbourhood
groups might help promote institutional changes in which
Mobilization itself was interested, but the support of protest
was also justified on more neutral grounds. "We believe that
the personal sense of powerlessness felt by low income people
is a major cause of their isolation and apathy," explained
George Brager, the programme director. "... To encourage
education and social learnings, therefore, it is necessary to
decrease the sense of powerlessness. To achieve this end requires the organization of isolated individuals and unaffiliated
groups to take action. It means that MFY must give assistance
to Lower East Side residents who feel, justified or otherwise,
that their rights are being violated.[6] The phrase "justified or
otherwise" seems to disclaim Mobilization's ultimate responsibility for the actions taken—and in principle, unless the
sponsors of community organization surrender control of
the organization they promote, they defeat their own purpose.

Unfortunately, the targets of popular protest seldom dis-
criminate between the sponsor and the actions taken by the
movements he encourages. As George Brager admitted, "This
programmatic direction has caused strain in MFY's relations
with important persons and institutions." The campaign of a
small group of Puerto Rican mothers against a school principal provoked, as we saw, a counterattack which went far beyond the immediate issue to impugn the motives of Mobilization itself. As a whole, Mobilization was not a militant radical organization, but an experimental application of a theoretical analysis of the roots of delinquency. It never attached
crucial importance to its programme of militant self-assertion,
which was small scale and doubtfully effective. More concerned

[6] Director's First Annual Report to the Staff, October 1963.

with the economic than political deprivation, it invested most
of its resources in youth employment and training. Yet Mobilization became the victim of a sustained and powerful pros-
ecution which all but destroyed it, and which would probably
never have arisen, if important persons had not been ruffled
by its encouragement of protest.

... Mobilization's experience of community organization
suggests that when institutions are provoked by community
protests, they will react against the sponsoring agency, rather
than meet the protest on its own terms. And since an agency
like Mobilization for Youth inevitably arouses jealousy
amongst other agencies whose function it has displaced, or
upon whose jurisdiction it has intruded, the reaction will
find willing allies. All the community action projects rested
upon a delicate balance of power. Even though their administration might be less vulnerable to criticism, probably none
could have withstood the kind of attack to which Mobilization was subjected. It seems, then, that Mobilzation's conception of community organization could only withstand the
opposition it must arouse if it were wholly independent of
resources under the control of such opposition. As Lloyd
Ohlin has recognized at the outset, the fate of community organization is inseparable from the nature of its sponsorship.
The Boston programme foundered on the same issue.

Since Edward Logue, Administrator of the Boston Redevelopment Authority, had initiated the plans for a grey area
project in Boston, ABCD's conception of community organization was at first closely related to urban renewal. Each
neighbourhood was to be encouraged to take an active part
in the planning of its own redevelopment. Through this participation, the proposals could be refined more sensitively to
the resident's needs, and the resources of the community
mustered to meet the social problems raised by physical reorganization, And since ABCD had committed itself to work
wherever possible through existing agencies, this community
organization programme was implemented through settle-

ment houses and voluntary councils, to which ABCD assigned its own professional staff. In this way, the programme acquired three sponsors—the Redevelopment Authority, the settlement houses, and ABCD itself—whose interests were not compatible. The Redevelopment Authority was seeking a constructive contribution to its plans, hoping above all that community organization would promote a local leadership committed to the Authority's aims, and influential enough to swing opinion in the neighbourhood behind them. ABCD was groping for a relationship with the people it served, through which they could articulate their needs, and share responsibility for programmes ABCD was planning. The settlement houses were more concerned to encourage the procedures of democratic organization than to guide it towards any issue. The confusion might not have mattered, if urban renewal had been popular. In the event, the community organizers not only failed to achieve a consensus of local support for the renewal plans, but hardened opposition. When a public meeting was called in Charlestown to discuss its redevelopment, the spokesmen of the Redevelopment Authority were shouted down.

From the standpoint of traditional community organization, the outcome was a successful demonstration of democratic self-assertion. To Ed Logue, it was a betrayal of the whole purpose of the programme. ABCD was caught in an uncomfortable conflict of loyalties. It could not keep the confidence of the people it served if it identified itself with renewal plans which they had rejected, and which they believed would contribute to the social hardships ABCD had been created to relieve. Nor could it openly challenge the Redevelopment Administrator, who had done so much to promote it, and who enjoyed, as much as ABCD and Mayor's confidence. ABCD therefore extricated itself as best it could, shifting the emphasis of its approach to the education and employment programmes in which the Ford Foundation and the President's Committee were chiefly interested.

... Each of the projects was forced to choose between its institutional alliances, and its sponsorship of a challenging redistribution of power within the City. Only Mobilization for Youth dared to risk antagonizing public agencies, and disastrously miscalculated their power to exact retribution. It seems unlikely that any programme of community action, so dependent upon a consensus of established leadership and public funds, could be at the same time an effective champion of radical democracy. If the sponsors of community organization cannot disclaim responsibility for the organization they create, and if at the same time they defeat their own purpose in seeking to control it, only a sponsor free from other commitments can afford to support his organization in whatever course it chooses.

But even had the projects been at liberty to risk the consequences of aligning themselves with the poor, was it practicable for a sophisticated professional staff to work out programmes in equal partnership with the people they served? Planning with people raised a conflict of intellectual as well as political loyalties.

... In retrospect, it seems evident that the projects could wholeheartedly share responsibility for their programmes with the people they served: they had too many other commitments to both theory and practice. They recognized that their manner of reform needed democratic safeguards, but in trying to build these safeguards into their own organization, they assumed an impossible harmony between different means to the same fundamental end. The competence of each citizen to uphold his liberty depends upon political, legal, economic and psychological resources which no one organization can secure. The means to each require a different emphasis, a different alignment of interests, a different perception of the problem.

The poor can be seen, firstly, as an interest group which like any other must compete for attention against rival lobbies. The neglect of their interests arises from their failure to organize and assert their potential influence. Their economic power is collectively considerable, despite their poverty, as bus boycotts, consumer boycotts and rent strikes demonstrate. And their political power is greater than their voting strength, because they can appeal both to an uneasy middle class conscience and a general fear of open conflict. But to be poor is not itself a status which defines a common political interest. It is, rather, a humiliating condition which most people are ashamed to acknowledge, and from which anyone with the ability to lead has also the ability to escape. Hence the organization of the poor has to centre upon more specific interests which concern them especially, but not them alone—rack-renting, racial discrimination, education. As tenants, members of a racial minority, parents, beneficiaries of social services, the poor can act in their own defence without the stigma of inferiority, and their case has a universal relevance.

But in a highly structured democracy, where every interest tends to institutionalize its representation, these characteristic concerns of the poor need to recruit comparable resources of organization and leadership. Spontaneous protest is too sporadic: soon discouraged by frustration, it lacks the power of sustained bargaining. If the poor are to attract the able organizers they need, the defence of their interests must offer a career which rewards the ambitious with growing prestige and power. Community organization falters because it cannot offer any future to the neighbourhood leaders it promotes but a lifetime of parochial effort. The real leaders are the professional community organizers, who alone have the incentive of a career with widening opportunities. No one can fairly be expected to put the best of his energies, year after year, into the affairs of his neighbourhood without recognition or reward. Political parties understand this: they distrribute patronage, curry local favour, and above all, hold out to every ward leader the opportunity of promotion.

Nor does the neighbourhood provide a natural focus of organization, except for those concerns which arise from the immediate environment—garbage collection, police protection, redevelopment plans. Community organization seems to assume that those who live near each other share a community of interest, which ought to find expression in a generalized social cohesion. But unemployment, discriminatin, punitive welfare regulations, even the denial of educational opportunity are not neighbourhood issues, and only accidentally unite the residents of the same block. Community organization, since it provides no hierarchy of affiliation from local to national levels, trivializes major interests by its parochial bias. The pressure for reform becomes fragmented, unsure of itself, and easily patronized.

Only the Civil Rights Movement seems to command the present resources to act as the lobby of the poor.[7] It has a hierarchy of organization from national to local groups, and professional leadership. As it broadens its concern from overt discrimination to the subtler economic and social barriers, it champions the cause of all victims of injustice, whatever their colour. And it acts from a principle of equal rights which does not stigmatize its following.

Community action projects will not find the Civil Rights Movement a comfortable ally. Vulnerable by their commitments to public agencies and political accommodation, they will be amongst the first targets of attack. But the power of the Civil Rights Movement will determine how radical are the

[7] Or, from a rather different standpoint, organized labour. Moynihan, in his Berkeley address, (op. cit.), remarked: 'Our social insurance system is unfinished. Our wage system is unbalanced and incomplete. Our employment nexus is frighteningly inadequate. These are fundamental political issues, and there does not yet exist a consensus that they should be resolved. Trying to cure poverty without attending to these matters is treating symptoms. The only force in American society—or any other industrial democratic society that I know of—that is capable of providing the mass citizen support for solving these fundamental problems, and for sustaining such efforts over long periods of time, is the trade union movement. The trade union movement was the original anti-poverty movement in this nation, and it remains incomparably the most significant one...' (Though some of its practices—such as restricting apprenticeships—seem now to contribute to the frustrations of the poor.)

reforms which the projects can press upon their institutional colleagues. The projects cannot themselves redistribute power since—dependent upon the consensus of established leadership which created them—the power is not theirs to give away. But they are commandingly placed to exploit the practical opportunities for change which open with every shift in the balance of forces. So long as they do not manoeuvre to weaken militant leadership, even when it attacks them, they can use it as a powerful incentive to authentic reform.

But to mobilize the sanctions which lie within the grasp of the poor, and redistribute power through political action, may not immediately help the individual to secure his rights. The poor are at a disadvantage, not only because their interests are collectively unprotected, but because they are individually less equipped to protect them. They lack money and knowledge to seek redress. The projects tried to meet this need through programmes of legal aid, and despite the New Haven experience, were certainly less vulnerable than in their attempts at community organization.

... The theory of a poverty cycle emphasized the oppression of spirit, the apathy and social disintegration which robbed the poor of any power of initiative in their own interest. The programmes had not only to provide opportunities, but regenerate a will to respond to them. In part, then, community organization was a form of treatment for collective depression. Discussion, participation, the devolution of responsibility, the self-analysis of community problems imitated the techniques of group therapy. This conception grew out of a fundamental faith in individual autonomy. But its expression in terms of social health was partly misleading.

The therapeutic analogy breaks down, because the projects approached the community with a preconceived diagnosis, while a doctor waits for a patient to present his symptoms, and can be dismissed at will. A community cannot, like an individual patient, ask for treatment and describe its symptoms. Hence it cannot initiate and ultimately control the relationship with its helper. Social therapy, therefore, tends towards a paternalism which undermines the very qualities it is seeking to promote: self-confidence and self-respect. A concept such as Leonard Cottrell's "doctor of community deficiencies" risks being self-defeating, unless the deficiencies are first in some way acknowledged and presented by the community itself. The dilemma arises whenever the restoration of individual dignity is taken as a psychological problem, inherent in those who are demoralized, rather than as a moral problem, inherent in the society which humiliates them. We derive our sense of worth from the whole context of relationships which define a social being. To restore dignity, you must above all treat people as deserving of respect. The poor cannot respect themselves until the employers, social workers, teachers, doctors, policemen, politicians, and public officials who relate them to the values of society at large respect them. And this means not only politeness and humility, but an honesty of purpose which does not seek to disguise the shortcomings of the services offered. Though community self-help can be useful and satisfying, the projects could probably best meet the psychological need of reassurance and acceptance by their influence on institutional attitudes, and especially by the integrity with which they presented their own programmes of service.

The organization of interests, the defence of individual rights, and the rehabilitation of self-confidence is each a means to the redistribution of power. But each is a distinct purpose, which leads towards, but cannot contain the others. And none can be effectively pursued within an organization primarily concerned to foster enlightened co-operation within the power structure.

In its reply to the Cahn's paper, CPI did not refute their analysis of the pressures to which it bowed. Nor, conversely, did the investigation of Mobilization for Youth challenge the right of protest. From their very different standpoints, both attacks exposed the conflict of loyalties to which the projects were vulnerable, and forced them to accept their limitations. But, as the projects realized, the self-assertion of the poor and the uncompromising defence of their rights were as much a part of the strategy of reform as institutional co-operation and professional understanding. They were only wrong to think they could hold them all together under one command.

# SECTION IV

# Alinsky

# Introduction

"Alinsky" is more than a well-known expert in community organization. He veritably incarnates an ideology for Americans knowledgable about community action. For a number of decades he has stood unflinchingly for the organizing of poor people into a powerful political force. Long before "black power," or "the new left," or even "maximum feasible participation of the poor" became fashionable parlance, Saul Alinsky preached and acted upon his controversial convictions. His impact on a number of social movements is undeniable, as is his impact on the armchair dialogue about social change agentry.

In a volume devoted to concepts and issues in citizen participation, logic impelled the inclusion of writings about Alinsky, and not merely those that make passing reference to one or another of his highly visible phrases such as "rubbing raw the sores of resentment," which are often taken out of context. The first selection turns to the man himself. More than 20 years ago, Alinsky wrote *Reveille for Radicals* from which this excerpt is reprinted. The following two articles are criticisms of Alinsky and his work. The first, by Stephen Rose, is essentially sympathetic; the second, by Thomas Sherrard and Richard Murray, raises some fundamental doubts about Alinsky's approach.

# Native Leadership*

SAUL ALINSKY

The building of a People's Organization can be done only by the people themselves. The only way that people can express themselves is through their leaders. By *their* leaders we mean those persons whom the local people define and look up to as leaders. Native or indigenous leadership is of fundamental importance in the attempt to build a People's Organization, for without the support and co-operative efforts of native leaders any such venture is doomed to failure in the very beginning.

These indigenous leaders are in a very true sense the real representatives of the people of the community. They have earned their position of leadership among their people and are accepted as leaders. A People's Organization must be rooted in the people themselves: if a People's Organization were to be thought of as a tree, the indigenous leaders would be the roots and the people themselves the soil. To rest on the soil and be nourished by the soil, the tree must be supported by its roots.

To organize the people means to talk with them, to get them together so that they can talk with each other and arrive at a common agreement. But it is obviously impossible to get all of the people to talk with each other. The only way that you can reach people is through their own representatives or their own leaders. You talk to people through their leaders and if you do not know the leaders you are in the same position as a per-

* Reproduced by special permission from the author and from Random House as holder of the copyright. From *Reveille for Radicals*. Chicago: Univer. of Chicago Press, 1946. Pp. 87-98.

son trying to telephone another party without knowing his telephone number. Knowing the identity of these natural leaders is knowing the telephone number of the people. Talking with these natural leaders is talking with the people. Working with them is working with the people, and building with them is the building of a People's Organization.

Most attempts at community organization have foundered on the rock of native leadership. The conventional community council of the past has evinced little knowledge or understanding of the significance of indigenous leadership. Such organizations have largely confined themselves to co-ordinating professional, formal agencies which are first superimposed upon the community and subsequently never play more than a superficial role in the life of the community. It is rare today to discover a community organization in which the indigenous interest groups and action groups of the community not only participate but play a fundamental role.

Practically all of these community organizations which talk of native leadership think in terms of token representation by community leaders. Even in their token representation one finds residents of the local community but very few if any of its leaders. The fact is that almost none of the professional or formal outside agencies that have been active in the field of community organization have any realistic appreciation of the meaning of indigenous leadership. They talk glibly of it but understand and practice little of it. If they have accepted local representation they have generally *selected* persons whom they defined as leaders rather than those persons whom the people have defined and accepted as leaders.

To a certain extent this is a natural, expected reaction. Formal agency representatives that have started community activities have usually regarded themselves as of the "leadership" type. It is the natural egotism of most people to think of themselves in those terms. Therefore when the workers of formal organizations enter a community and search for indigenous leadership they look for persons as similar to themselves as possible. That is one reason why so many of these little organizations known as neighborhood civic committees, community councils, or neighborhood leagues include local people who are of the professional class—doctors, dentists, lawyers, social workers, businessmen, and bankers. These types of neighborhood people, usually by virtue of educational background and personal manners, have much more in common with the representatives of the formal agencies than do the rank and file of the area. The organizers themselves feel much more at home with these people, and find them more articulate and talking in those terms and values that they readily understand.

Substantially what it amounts to is that the formal agencies' representatives, conceiving of themselves as leaders, hunt for those community persons with whom they can most readily identify themselves. But with rare exception those professional or business local people who are selected by the formal agencies as community leaders may possess a legitimate claim to being native to the community but no valid claim to being a leader. As to being native to the community, it will often be found that most of them are only halftime natives in that they work within the community and live outside in a more desirable residential area. Furthermore, having very little real relationship with the people (not being part of the people themselves), the actual extent of their being "native" to the community really boils down to their being physically native, whereas on the basis of their thoughts, their aspirations, their hopes, their desires, their sharing the tragedies of the people, these physically native professional and business people are as foreign to the local residents as are outside formal agencies. They have not only never been accepted by the people as leaders but have never even been thought of in those terms. They possess no following to speak of and a community council made up of ten of them would in actuality be an organization of ten people, and that is all. It wouldn't even be ten generals and no army, because they are generals only by self-appointment.

Thus it becomes obvious why these alleged community councils very shortly deteriorate into monthly social get-to-gethers for a small group of professional people who wallow in their egos as self-anointed saviors of the people and commiserate with each other on the poor benighted people of the neighborhood who don't have sufficient intelligence to know what is good for them, and ignore this proffered leadership. These community councils soon shrivel up and disappear.

The understanding of what constitutes a genuine native, indigenous leader is rarely found among conventional social do-gooders. The latter are to be found either in professional positions working with various outside agencies or else on the boards of typical community houses. A vivid demonstration of the wide gap separating definitions of leadership between the community people and these outside do-gooders was found in a conference between some of the representatives of the board of a community center and the leaders of the neighborhood People's Organization. The board representatives consisted of economically comfortable persons residing in a good residential section who devoted one evening a month to meeting in the center where they reviewed all of the purported good that they were doing in the community. This center was represented by a building and nothing more. It did not participate in the life of the community and was not recognized as a neighborhood factor by any of the significant neighborhood groups.

During one discussion some of the leaders of the People's Organization were trying to explain what they meant by native leadership, and they pointed out that those persons holding positions of leadership on the board of the local community center knew very little of the problems of the community and had less real interest in their solution. From the point of view of the People's Organization these outside board members were unknown to the local community, their services were unsolicited, their interest was questionable, and generally their method of doing things *for* rather than *with* the people was resented. So the leaders of the People's Organization inquired as to just what place these outsiders had within the community. (It cannot be too strongly emphasized that by "outsiders" the People's Organization thought much more in terms of persons whose interests and objectives were outside the community than in terms of geographical location.) At this stage a board member of the local center, a rather young academician specializing in education and personal pompousness, declared, "You people are really isolationists. You don't understand when you talk about leadership or representation just what we represent. We represent the City of Chicago."

This statement convinced the leaders of the People's Organization of the futility of continuing the meeting. Immediately after the meeting they discussed the professor's views:

"Now that professor says that he and the other guys with him represent the City of Chicago. What the hell are they talking about? When we talk about representing men we really mean representing them. I don't know what they mean by their words. Now take John here [a local labor leader]. When he goes into a factory and organizes the people into his union he says he represents them. He can bargain for them. The employer knows that if John feels that the workers should go out on strike, they will go out on strike—and that if John says they ought to end the strike, they'll go back to work. The boss knows that John really represents those people, but this professor who says he represents Chicago— if he even got into a fight with anybody, who else, outside of his second cousin and maybe a couple of friends of his, would get behind him? Who does he represent? He says 'the City of Chicago.' What the hell is he talking about? The poor guy, maybe he really believes it. He doesn't mean wrong, he's just nuts!"

Since representatives of formal agencies judge leadership according to *their own* criteria, evaluate what is good or bad in the community according to *their own* standards, and understand life in the community only when interpreted ac-

cording to *their own* code or standards—it is crystal clear
that they don't know the meaning of indigenous leadership,
let alone the identities of these natural leaders.

A graphic illustration of natural leadership is to be found
in the records of a criminological study made in a slum community. The sociologist making the survey became engaged
in conversation with an eleven-year-old newsboy in a slum
community in Chicago. This newsboy had seen the sociologist around the neighborhood a good deal and accepted
him as somebody living in the community.

*Sociologist:* What do you ever expect to amount to when
you grow up?

*Newsboy:* What ya mean?

*Sociologist:* Aw, you know, do you want to be a big business
man?

*Newsboy:* Naw.

*Sociologist:* Do you want to be a big lawyer?

*Newsboy:* Nix.

*Sociologist:* Do you want to be a banker?

*Newsboy:* Why do I want to be a banker?

*Sociologist:* Do you want to be a college professor?

*Newsboy* (in angry tone): Now look here, fella, what do
you take me for?

*Sociologist:* All I'm trying to do is get an idea of just what
you expect to be—do you want to be President of the United
States?

*Newsboy:* Naw, I want to be a big shot like Big Butch
[notorious leader of a large gang in the community], and
have people look up to me and really be a number-one guy.

[Further discussion with the youngster revealed attitudes
along this same line.]

*Newsboy:* Who is the President of the United States any-
ways? Some guy that Big Butch made President by getting
out the vote and paying a buck here and two bucks there. Besides, the President lives some place in Washington and I
don't know the guy. He talks about things like—

*Sociologist:* Like tariffs, foreign policy—

*Newsboy:* Yeah, stuff like that. Now Big Butch—he talks our language.

An inquiry among the residents of the community revealed different reasons why Big Butch was regarded as a natural leader. Many of these people were recipients of personal services, financial and other kinds of aid from the conventional social agencies. When discussing these agencies their remarks threw considerable light on why Big Butch was a natural leader.

"Take my family. If we need dough we go to Big Butch. Tell him about it and he gives over a double sawbuck and no questions asked. It's enough for him to know that we are in trouble. But you go to the Welfare and what happens? They start with how many times a day you part your hair and a hell of a lot of other questions that ain't nobody's business. There are the Smiths down the street. Well, Dottie, who you may have seen here—she's that twenty-year-old good-looking blonde—well, Dottie got into trouble with some guy in the city and the family really needed help. They went to the Welfare but before they could get the help they had to tell them that Dottie was getting a kid. Now, you know it ain't decent for other people to ask those kind of questions. If somebody is in trouble, they ought to be helped. Well, Big Butch would never think of poking his nose into anything like that."

When asked the difference as to the amount of actual help given by both the Welfare and Big Butch it developed that the Welfare had given the family about $150 while Big Butch had contributed $5.00. The Sociologist brought this point up. His companion looked at him with surprise and then snorted:

"You don't seem to understand. It isn't what you give that's so damn important, it's how you give it. They got that fin from Big Butch not just without a single snoop but with a pat on the back and real sympathy. When you go to Butch

you're a human being. When you go to the Welfare, you're
a—, a—. Well, they got a word for it—you're called a 'case.' "
William Whyte, in a penetrating analysis of an eastern
slum community reports:

> *In Cornerville the racketeers are known as free spenders and liberal*
> *patrons of local enterprises. They spend money in local stores. They*
> *patronize the activities of the corner boys with purchases of blocks*
> *of tickets to dances and with other contributions.*
>
> *One young man in a legitimate business said of T. S. and his*
> *associates: "These gangsters are the finest fellows you want to meet.*
> *They'll do a lot for you, Bill. You go up to them and say, 'I haven't*
> *eaten for four days, and I haven't got a place to sleep,' and they'll*
> *give you something. Now you go up to a businessman, one of the*
> *respected members of the community, and ask him. He throws you*
> *right out of the office."*[1]

It is apparent that the primary and most difficult job con-
fronting an organizer is the actual identification of the local
leadership. With few exceptions, the real local leaders are
completely unknown outside of the community. Outsiders
may know the names of the top local labor leader or banker
or businessman, but they rarely know the names of the many
little natural leaders who possess a following of twenty or
thirty people. Furthermore, ignorance of the identity of the
natural leaders of a community is not confined to the outside. Frequently the professional and business people inside
the community are not aware of the actual identity of these
neighborhood leaders.

The job of locating the individual native leaders is not
the kind that lends itself to a formal approach such as questionnaire methods or interviews. It can be done only through
a search that requires infinite patience. It means participating in countless informal situations and being constantly
alert to every word or gesture which both identifies and ap-
praises the role of certain individuals within the commu-

[1] William Foote Whyte. *Street Corner Society*. Chicago: University of
Chicago Press, p. 142.

nity. It means the closest of observation and constant testing of each clue. The most fruitful setting for the discovery of local leadership is often bar-room conversations, poker games, and all other informal get-togethers where the spirit of informality prevails over suspicion and reticence. It means intimate association with particular interest groups within the community—religious, business, social, labor, fraternal, and all others. It means working through these interest groups to discover the real leaders. In many cases these leaders will not be the officially elected officers, but rather the power behind the scenes. They will be the little Jim Farleys and Bob Hannegans.

> ...I found that in each group I met there was one man who directed the activities of his fellows and whose word carrried authority. Without his support, I was excluded from the group; with his support, I was accepted.[2]

Just as people have a variety of interests, so they have a variety of leaders. The problem of identifying native leadership is as baffling and complicated as the problem of understanding the forces, interests, and myriads of elements that make up the life of a community. A man belongs to a church, a religious society, a fraternal group, a labor union, a social club, a recreational club, a social or political group, and a host of other interest groups. Investigation will disclose that that man looks up to a particular person as a leader, one whose judgment he has confidence in, in political matters, but when he is confronted with a problem of finances he will turn to one of his associates in his fraternal society. And so on down the line. He may have in his orbit of activities five or six individuals to whom he will turn on different matters.

It is obvious then that one rarely stumbles across what might be defined as a complete leader—a person who has a following of forty or fifty people in every sphere of activity.

[2] *Ibid,* p. vi.

Let us look at it this way. Joe Dokes, a labor steward, may have a following of thirty or forty people who regard his decisions on labor as final. Ten of them, however, if confronted with a financial problem, will look to Robert Rowe, who is in an entirely different kind of employment and whom they know through their fraternal society. Ten others may look to John Doe, who is a bartender, for financial advice. Of the twenty last mentioned, thirteen may look to Sidney Smith for political leadership; Sidney is a police officer.

And so the question of determining who is a leader involves a large number of partial leaders or leaders of small groups and particularized aspects of their life. These natural leaders therefore run into considerable numbers. It is as true in that community as it is in any other segment of the population, including that of the reader. These natural leaders—the "Little Joes"—may, it is clear, occupy the most humble roles in the community. A window trimmer may be the president of the Holy Name Society. Or your "Little Joe" may be a garage mechanic, a bartender, an elevator operator, a streetcar conductor. These are the common people and in them are to be found the small natural leaders of the natural groups which are present among all people.

One of the most important tasks of the organizer, in addition to identifying these natural leaders and working with them, is working for their actual development so that they become recognized by their following as leaders in more than one limited sphere. This expansion of leadership from a partial role to a more complete one is a natural development that goes hand in hand with the growth of the People's Organization.

A partial leader soon finds that if he is to retain his leadership in a People's Organization he must become informed and prove his ability in many of the other phases that make up the people's program. As we have seen, the program of a People's Organization is all-inclusive and embraces every problem in the life of the people. A leader in such a broad program must of necessity demonstrate broad abilities and capabilities instead of the limited qualifications which suffice for a narrow following.

That is what is meant by the development of local leadership. It does not mean what so many people think, that there is no leadership among the rank and file. There is leadership, but it is of the partial variety, and its development is the development of partial leaders into well-rounded leaders of their people.

Even the best outside organizer, one who has democratic convictions and practices them, who has complete faith in the people and their leadership, cannot build a People's Organization to a complete structure. He can serve as a stimulus, a catalytic agent, and render invaluable service in the initial stages of organization. He can lead in the laying down of the foundations—*but only the people and their own leaders can build a People's Organization.*

Outside formal agencies who think in terms of going into a community and organizing "democratic" people's movements are doomed to failure simply because, as their own actions indicate, they fail to grasp the simplest elements of democracy. On the contrary, their thinking and actions demonstrate the very antithesis of democracy. In the last analysis their approach and their philosophy represent an anti-democratic intrusion into a democratic community. Gardner Howland Shaw, former Assistant Secretary of State and an outstanding exponent of domestic democracy who has devoted a good part of his life to the building of People's Organizations, stated the issue clearly:

> *There is nothing in our past or present experience which suggests that we outsiders can effectively organize . . . a community to which we do not now and never have belonged. And should a time ever come when it is possible to effect such an organization, then the character of American life will have so radically changed as to have ceased to be American. In a large measure it will have become totalitarian.*

*To be sure, we have established and we can continue to establish in the underprivileged community a variety of agencies which we have decided should be of benefit to that community; and undoubtedly some if not all of these agencies will benefit to a certain degree some of the members of that community . . . We can also establish these agencies in haphazard and competitive fashion, as we have often done in the past, or we can plan for their effective utilization with as much intelligence as possible through some sort of procedure or co-ordination as we have done on occasions more recently. But, whether the agencies are established or not established, and whether they compete with each other or are co-ordinated, the fact remains that the community is not being really organized either by us or by the people living within its confines. Essentially what we are doing is to decide what is good for the underprivileged area without any real participation by, or even sustained consultation with, the people of that area; we are trying to do something to rather than with it. In the last analysis, our approach is fundamentally authoritarian, fundamentally undemocratic.*[3]

[3] Gardner Howland Shaw. *Fighting Delinquency from Within.* Address delivered before the New York State Conference of Social Work, Rochester, New York, November 16, 1944. Published by the Welfare Council of New York City.

# Saul Alinsky and His Critics*

STEPHEN C. ROSE

Chicago is regarded as a great natural laboratory of the social sciences. Graham Hutton once declared, "Chicago has the best human virtues and the worst vices. It is, therefore, more truly human than any city, and it tells more about humanity." This opposition of best and worst is *the* literary approach to this "city of the big shoulders." G. W. Steevens called Chicago "the queen and guttersnipe of cities, cynosure and cesspool of the world."

One thinks of Al Capone *and* Jane Addams. The achievements of its great universities are set against all-Negro public schools whose valedictorians are thrust into remedial reading classes in college. An unseen force forbids unambiguous judgments, and one delves into the stuff of the laboratory, hoping for whatever truth ambiguity will yield.

Chicago is the center of an emerging crucial debate among custodians of public and private welfare enterprises as they seek to forge what President Johnson is calling the Great Society. The debate is basically about who calls the shots in urban development, and it involves the future of democracy in the metropolis, the basic structure of the social work endeavor, the place of the Church in the city and the nature of voluntarism within a pluralistic society.

The protagonist in the debate is a well-publicized, outspoken community organizer named Saul D. Alinsky, who heads the Chicago-based Industrial Areas Foundation (IAF).

* Reproduced by special permission from the author and the publisher. Copyright by *Christianity and Crisis*, Vol. XXIV, No. 13, July 20, 1964.

A prominent antagonist is *Christian Century* Editor Harold Fey, who has pinned a Marxist label on Alinsky and all his house. Alinsky's house includes the nation's largest Roman Catholic Archdiocese and the United Presbyterian Church in the U. S. A.

Lutheran planner and church executive Walter Kloezli emerges as the *advocatus diaboli* in proceedings that would either canonize Alinsky as the one true guide to urban church strategy or vilify him as a Machiavelli who has turned Luther's doctrine of the two realms upside down, casting the radiant light of theological approval upon a series of contemporary Peasants' Revolts.

An occasion for noting the debate is the recent publication of *Fortune* Editor Charles Silberman's book *Crisis in Black and White* (Random House, $5.95). Alinsky emerges as Silberman's hero, as the man who offers the best hope to the apathetic, poverty-stricken urban Negro whose greatest need is a sense that he has some control over his destiny. "The only difference between Alinsky and his enemies," says Silberman, "is that Alinsky really believes in democracy." Meanwhile Dr. Fey says that Alinsky's concept of community organization, in which power and the creative use of conflict are prime ingredients, is a "totalitarian" implementation of "class war" techniques.

## Strategic Cultivation of Bull Connors

To date Alinsky and the IAF have organized four communities in Chicago, not to mention others across the country, including effective coalitions of migrant workers in California. At least two further communities in Chicago are slated for possible organizational efforts.

The object of Harold Fey's charges is a greying, largish man in his mid-fifties whose office perches above Chicago's Lake Michigan. Louis Sullivan once said that the lake and the prairie enfold Chicago "as a wistful mother holds a subnormal child." Saul Alinsky believes that the hope of democracy, and of the city, lies in a rejection of the "subnormal child" image of the poor and disinherited. "I do believe in the democratic faith," says Alinsky. "If not, I have nothing left to believe in."

One visits Alinsky's IAF office half expecting to hear an elaborate political and economic thesis, a sort of mid-century *Weltanschauung*. Instead he finds a man who despises dogmas of any sort and insists there are no panaceas. One looks for radical solutions to automation and all the other "ations" that are replacing the "isms" and finds instead a man whose vision is an almost sentimental picture of a mountain path paved with external threats. Man's faltering climb to the top may someday be completed. He may vanquish the externals of hunger, inadequate housing, economic and racial injustice. Alinsky's world is centered upon the climbing of the mountain. On the ultimate question, the question of life's meaning, he professes only an inability to answer. A friend calls him an existentialist in the true sense of the term.

His basic perceptions are of the imminence and finality of death (the product of personal tragedies in his own life) and of injustice. He professes an almost instinctive siding with the underdog. His anger at injustice becomes somewhat wistful when it crops up in an organization he helped to create.

Perhaps a self-portrait emerges when he describes the way he chooses community organizers to work with IAF. Recruiting begins "when we hear of a guy who is mad and organizing on his own. . . . We ask, 'What kind of anger is it? Is it a neurotic anger that could be cleared up by eliminating some personal cause? Or is it an anger at injustice that will stay with him? . . . Then we see whether he will take advice, whether he has a passion for anonymity, and whether he wants to learn." The organizer must combine the Old Testament's prophetic anger with the cool detachment of the Greeks. Alinsky feels that Saul of Tarsus ("your Paul") fits this description: Saul . . . the organizer.

Under Alinsky's tutelage—he sees himself as a teacher—the recruit begins to see "the opposition" as an integral element of the organizing strategy. Example, Bull Connor was a great asset to Birmingham Negroes. Alinsky believes in the strategic cultivation of Bull Connors.

The IAF organizers—the number varies with the number of communities being organized—are "all prima donnas in their own way," says Alinsky. "The only way I manage to keep their respect is that they know I can go out and out-organize them." Alinsky normally spends only a week each year in actual grass roots operations. The rest of the time is spent consulting various IAF-organized projects. Now, with Silberman's book, about three-fourths of his time is devoted to explaining his work to reporters ranging from national magazine staffers to German TV documentary personnel.

Alinsky's detractors accuse him of running a well-oiled publicity machine. He responds that his most useful publicity is provided by his critics. A series of derogatory editorials in *The Christian Century* apparently inspired a number of Protestants to investigate the IAF and to see for themselves that "the charges just weren't true."

The range and diversity of Alinsky's personal associations is somewhat amazing. He has been a friend and informal consultant to Michigan's Governor Romney. At the urging of his long-time acquaintance Jacques Maritain, Alinsky had several cordial sessions with the Archbishop of Milan before he became Pope Paul. He advised the Archbishop on means by which the Church might combat Milan's strong Communist party. Alinsky's financial support comes from liberals and conservatives; IAF's Board of Directors includes Presbyterian executives, the president of a major life insurance company and an official of the Southern Christian Leadership Conference. His dinner guests may be partisans or friendly critics like the University of Chicago's urban expert Dr. Philip Hauser.

Alinsky's first organizing effort was in the neighborhood Upton Sinclair described as *The Jungle*. There in 1938 he welded together antagonistic national Catholic groups and packing house workers into what is now the powerful Back of

the Yards Neighborhood Council. A Chicago Building Department official calls the work of the council in community
upkeep "consistently tremendous." Recently this neighborhood has shown considerable resistance to the possibility of
residential integration. Alinsky hopes various IAF-spawned
community groups may be able to negotiate the orderly movement of Negroes into such allwhite areas. If not, he says he is
willing to organize a community to fight Back of the Yards on
the integration issue.

## Creating Self-respect . . . or Animosity?

Accusations are made that Alinsky organizes communities on
a basis of fear and hostility that can ultimately lead to the
polarization of neighborhoods and the destruction of patterns of metropolitan consensus. Alinsky insists, however, that
what is seen as apathy and dependency in depressed urban
areas is really the suppression of deep resentment over a sense
of impotence. The mobilization of community pride and of
the impulse to self-help involves arousing these resentments
and providing through a mass organization, the instrument
by which bad conditions can be changed.

In a 1962 speech he outlined the basic characteristics of an
effective community organization. These constitute his personal acknowledgment of what IAF strives for in its own
efforts.

• The organization must attract and involve most of the groups in
the community.
• Its program should be "specific, immediate and feasible" in order
to create self-respect through success.
• The organization should see power for what it is, and use it. "The
power concept must be seen nakedly, without the sordid raiment
which serve more as disguises for our own inability or unwillingness
or timidity to get involved in controversy in which we may get
smeared or hurt."
• "An action group . . . has two primary considerations in selecting
a means for operation towards an end. First, what means are avail-

able and, second, what means are most effective? . . . Any so-called organization which spends a great deal of its time discussing means and ends always winds up on its ends without any means!" (It should be pointed out that the tactics of Alinsky organizations have never gone beyond occasional instances of civil disobedience. Most tactics have combined clever "symbolic" demonstrations with the threat of economic or political coercion.)

• "Controversy has always been the seed of creation." No vital community organization can exist without it. In an organization of "have nots" it is inevitable that resentment will focus on the "prevailing dominant interests of the status quo," particularly when these interests inhibit the self-determination of the organization.

• The organization must recognize self-interest as its basic *raison d'etre* to be effective it must aim at a multiplicity of goals. This will insure a broad base of support. "In effect," says Alinsky, "everybody makes a deal: You support me in this, and I'll support you in that."

IAF's enemies charge that these organizing principles result in the creation of totalitarian super-organizations, controlled from the outside, and dedicated to such varied motives as keeping Negroes out, keeping Negroes in, fronting for Roman Catholicism's vested interests, and even, according to Dr. Fey, splicing together enough IAF-organized neighborhoods to gain control of a whole city. Silberman, in *Crisis in Black and White,* has made a thorough investigation of such charges, and he also points to the need for more detailed study of Alinsky's . . . efforts in community organization. Unfortunately, IAF's critics, particularly within the Protestant Church, have made little effort to substantiate their allegations. Opinion has superseded reporting.

One of the most emotion-laden charges against Alinsky is that IAF organizations are dominated by and subservient to Roman Catholic interests. There is no question that the Roman Catholic Church has supported IAF, nor is there reason to believe that it has not benefited from IAF's efforts.

The most direct challenge to Catholic motivation has been that of the Rev. Walter Kloetzli in his book *The Church and the Urban Challenge* (Muhlenberg Press). Writing in 1961,

Kloetzli suggested that the Chicago Archdiocese was using IAF to "freeze" neighborhoods—to halt migration from areas of Catholic strength and to limit the migration of Negroes into these areas. He also criticized the Catholic Church for espousing Alinsky's organizing techniques and offered some alternative principles of organization that are critical of the power concept and "the tactic of deliberately stirring up community animosities." The same observations have appeared in a number of *Christian Century* editorials.

## Neither Protestants Nor Catholics Alone

The man who will respond to these charges if given the chance is Msgr. John Egan, head of the Office of Urban Affairs of Chicago's Archdiocese. "If *that* [racial containment] was our policy, we sure have failed," he said recently. Monsignor Egan's willingness to speak openly and at length about the relationship between the Archdiocese and IAF places the burden of proof squarely on the shoulders of the critics.

Alinsky first met Monsignor Egan in 1954 at the behest of Jacques Maritain. Shortly thereafter the Archdiocese became involved in an effort to develop a self-help program among Puerto Rican newcomers to Chicago's Woodlawn area. Monsignor John O'Grady, then the executive director of the National Conference of Catholic Charities, suggested that Monsignor Egan and others consult with Alinsky about the new program.

Subsequently Alinsky was asked by the late Cardinal Stritch to study conditions affecting Puerto Ricans on the city's North Side. The satisfaction of the Archdiocese with this study gave rise to yet another request, this time for a survey of the effects of the large scale relocation of Negroes made necessary by the clearing of Chicago's Lake Meadows area for middle-income housing. Monsignor Egan was freed to work with Alinsky, and during the summer of 1957 he tramped through the all-Negro area south of Lake Meadows. "I really

got to know the effects of poverty and discrimination in this
town," he recalls.

The report concluded that relocation had resulted in an
aggravation of slum conditions in the study area. Monsignor
Egan remembers that Cardinal Stritch was "terribly upset"
by the findings.

During 1958-59, the Archdiocese was critical of the first
major urban renewal plan to be implemented in Chicago,
the Hyde Park-Kenwood Project. Monsignor Egan recalls
that some 22,000 persons of both races were slated for "urban
removal." The brunt of the relocation was upon the poor
Negroes of the area. Today Hyde Park-Kenwood bills itself
as a liberal-minded, integrated area, but this has been achieved
at the expense of low-income Negroes. A hopeful sign in recent months has been the willingness of Hyde Park residents
to endorse the construction of low-rise, small-density public
housing in the community.

Monsignor Egan states that three basic convictions came to
him during this period. First, the need throughout the City
of Chicago for community organizations that were "strong
and tough." "We had lots of weak organizations that were
avoiding or afraid of controversy." Secondly, "any organization had to represent and serve all the people." Finally, "if
urban renewal programs were going to succeed in reflecting
the mind of the people, we needed community organizations
as a strong voice to supplement and speak to the political arm."
Monsignor Egan adds that he "felt the political organization
in Chicago was not using tools to give people enough voice in
the democratic process."

And so, in the wake of the Hyde Park-Kenwood dispute, the
Archdiocese became involved with Alinsky, the organizer
(Monsignor Egan stresses that Alinsky "had absolutely nothing
to do with our entry into the Hyde Park-Kenwood fight"). In
1959-60 a coalition of Protestants, priests and businessmen
called IAF in to organize a large area of Chicago's Southwest

Side. Although the Archdiocese kept informed about the development of the Organization for the Southwest Community (OSC), Monsignor Egan says that all financial support of the organization came from parishes within the community.

In a thorough report on OSC in November 1961, the Rev. Robert Christ, then pastor of the Seventh Presbyterian Church of Chicago, made the following observations:

• Neither Protestants alone or Catholics alone could have established OSC; the necessity for joint action has resulted in a corporate effort by 25 Protestant congregations and 11 Roman parishes. . . . The coalition of churchmen has been largely responsible for the structure, policy and success of the organization.
• It was the combined church voice that secured non-gerrymandered boundaries (thereby including areas of Negro residence). The presence of priests and ministers on the membership committee secured the admission of Negro institutions at the organizing community congress.
• The novelty of the Protestant-Catholic coalition explains part of its effectiveness; opponents have not yet learned to respond when both . . . stand together on issues. The still tenuous nature of the coalition provides a built-in safeguard which will prevent the coalition from over-extending itself and abusing its power in the city.

Christ's report is persuasive on two points. Both Protestant and Catholic clergy took the lead (sometimes at considerable cost) in affirming a racially inclusive community. Checks and balances were provided to insure that neither group would dominate the organization and that the two groups acting together could not dominate it. Christ also points to the genuine ecumenical sense that emerged among Catholic and Protestant participants. The same observation has been made by numerous particpants in IAF-spawned organizations. The range and diversity of OSC is indicated by an enumeration of its various program committees: Real Estate Practices, Home Loan, Home Modernization, Law Enforcement and Safety, Education, Health and Welfare, Traffic and Transportation, Community Relations, and so on.

This seems to confirm that Monsignor Egan is justified in his assertion that Catholic Involvement is based on the recognition of the need for strong grass-roots organizations whose main objective is to create self-determination in a given neighborhood. One can generalize that Catholics are as sinful as Protestants when it comes to self-interest. Surely one of the motivating forces in Catholic participation in the Northwest Community Organization, IAF's latest effort in Chicago, was the desire to stem migration from an area served by 22 Roman Catholic parishes. But the success of NCO will involve restoring community pride and better living conditions to an area that otherwise might have continued downhill. This is a desirable goal since continued out-migration of middle-class elements will only sharpen the evident rift between city and suburb. Finally, it seems rather inconsistent to fault Catholicism merely because it, unlike Protestantism, elected long ago to remain in the inner city.

Kloetzli has also criticized the Chicago Archdiocese for its implicit acceptance of IAF's organizing technique. "I'm not saying Alinsky is the only organizer," says Monsignor Egan, "but I don't know of another. . . . If I'm going to build a building, I'll hire a professional contractor." Alinsky's credentials are those of performance. He adds: "It is peculiar that people will accuse Alinsky of using power, and then use power themselves. In order to achieve peace and tranquility and order, you may have to go through certain conflicts. But in my ten years' association with Alinsky, I have never seen him violate the moral law or advocate the violation of it."

Some observers dismiss Dr. Fey's charge that IAF embodies "totalitarian" principles and "class war techniques" as "just plain silly." Julian Levi, who directs urban renewal efforts for the University of Chicago and who has done battle with the IAF-organized Woodlawn Organization, says he "would not go as far as that." Dr. Franklin Littell, Chicago Theological Seminary professor and lecturer on totalitarian ideology, feels Dr. Fey's fears stem from a "basic misunderstanding of the nature of freedom." Dr. Littell sees adequate checks and balances existing in Alinsky-style community organizations and suggests that merely because they are highly disciplined is not adequate grounds for charges of dictatorship.

Totalitarianism involves a sinister effort to gain control of the masses. It is dangerous to charge that any institution or person espouses totalitarian principles without documentation. And all the evidence suggests that IAF lacks both the cynicism and the means to implement such an approach. In the first place, it is IAF practice to pull its organizers out of a community as soon as possible and sever all financial ties to the organizations it helps create. In the case of OSC, the IAF withdrew after nine months.

The structure of IAF-founded organizations provides for wide community participation in the decision-making process. After the initial organizing period a constitutional convention is held at which each member group is represented on a proportional basis. The constitution is debated clause by clause before it is approved.

A similar congress is held annually at which a program committee presents resolutions that will determine the work of the organization for the coming year. Alinsky calls this annual congress "the House of Representatives." The "Senate" is an executive board made up of one representative of each group. This board divides into various smaller groups with responsibility for implementing program. The annual meeting is the final authority in all matters of program and policy. Officers are elected yearly, and the number of permissible consecutive terms is determined by the constitution.

At this year's convention, The Woodlawn Organization turned down a proposal that would have thrown support to Negro candidates for public office only. This significant vote was generally acknowledged by all present, including Dr. Fey, to be an example of the democratic process at work. The only difference is that Dr. Fey clung to the reasoning that the proposal's defeat stemmed from the failure of the "ruling clique" to "brainwash" a majority of TWO's constituency.

The accusation that IAF used "class war" techniques involves one in semantics. If the notion of the class war is accompanied by visions of Bolshevist insurrection and the dictatorship of the proletariat, the specter of IAF becomes one of sheer fantasy. Alinsky has never professed or implemented the ideas necessary to a notion of class war. If, however, the concept of class war is liberated from its militaristic imagery and seen as part of the continuing effort of American "outs" to become "ins," Alinsky and the facts would confirm the proposition. Such a notion is not foreign to democratic soil, and the rationale for conflict of this sort is found in such documents as the *Federalist Papers* and Reinhold Niebuhr's *Moral Man and Immoral Society*.

What Alinsky's severest critics have done is to magnify the old American town-grown conflict (TWO vs. the University of Chicago) into a class war. They might better focus their fears on the Black Muslim Temple located in Hyde Park or the John Birch Society, which is explicitly totalitarian in concept.

The American underdog has always tended to elevate the class concept only for the purpose of obliterating class barriers. Today it is the rare union member who would sing the militant (and eminently class conscious) labor songs of the Thirties. And if there is any criticism to be made on this score, it is that IAF's organizations may (as in the case of Back of the Yards) grow away from sympathy with the underdog as they attain a greater measure of affluence and "middle-class" status.

## Woodlawn: A Case Study

The unsubstantiated charges of Catholic domination, totalitarianism, and the like, should not be permitted to obscure a number of genuinely important questions. Some observers have suggested that the IAF approach is overrated in terms of actual results; also that it is possible to upgrade depressed communities without cultivating hostility toward the "dominant interests of the *status quo*."

It is both the nemesis and the salvation of the social welfare community to be forced to consider results. Unfortunately neither the journalistic nor academic method of determining results is entirely satisfactory. Nevertheless, let us examine the results of IAF's organization in a Chicago community. In 1960 IAF organizers entered the Woodlawn area, directly south of the University of Chicago.

Woodlawn is practically all Negro. It is one of those neighborhoods in which old, middle-class homes have been sliced up to accommodate part of the vast migration from the South that may ultimately provide Chicago with a Negro majority. Slum landlords have been among the few beneficiaries of the pervasive myth that the Northern city would provide a vastly more abundant life than might be eked from Southern soil. Rents for comparable units are about 50 per cent higher for Negroes. Woodlawn has everything one would need to create a macabre picture of slum life: high school dropouts, crime, unemployment and a high percentage of welfare recipients. And like most similar areas, Woodlawn has a number of institutions, including more than 30 churches, that have tried with limited success to stem the tide of slum culture.

IAF entered Woodlawn after receiving a formal invitation from a group of local clergymen. The organizing effort was supported by the Emil Schwarzhaupt Foundation, the Roman Catholic Archdiocese and the United Presbyterian Board of National Missions. To date the total financial outlay for The Woodlawn Organization has been $177,500. Of this amount $27,000 was raised within Woodlawn. The Schwartzhaupt Foundation contributed $74,000, the Archdiocese $50,000, with the remainder coming from the Presbyterians. Alinsky says that IAF will probably withdraw by the end of 1964 and

TWO will operate on an annual budget of $30-40,000, all of it raised within the community.

IAF's policy of withdrawing after the organizing phase has the effect of forcing indigenous support of the organization, thus assuring self-determination. The total allocation for TWO over a four-year period is about half the annual budget of the Church Federation of Greater Chicago and one-third the annual budget of the Chicago City Missionary Society. By any standards, particularly those of institutions working in slum areas, the IAF dollar has gone a long way in Woodlawn. (Alinsky speculated recently about what the IAF could do with $5 million. With such resources, he said IAF could organize depressed areas in five large cities and have enough left over for Harlem. It is doubtful that Alinsky, who says the Founding Fathers would have had rough going with the Ford Foundation, will ever get his five million.)

The history of the organizing effort in Woodlawn is fully recounted in Silberman's book. In brief the organizers had little difficulty in locating community resentments. Residents were embittered over the high-handed aplomb with which Chicago School Superintendent Benjamin Willis has consistently disregarded the pleas of the Negro community. They were aroused against some local merchants who gave short weights and overcharged. Merchants and residents alike were fearful that the University of Chicago's stated plan to extend its campus southward would be carried out with no regard for the people.

Then too, the organizing of the community coincided with the great upheaval that we have come to call the Negro Revolution. This was an unquestionable asset in community mobilization, but it should be pointed out that TWO became a spearhead of the Chicago protest movement well in advance of the catalytic events in Birmingham and Mississippi. The IAF approach here was completely free-wheeling in terms of strategy. The emergent Woodlawn Organization had no suburban board of directors urging it to go slow or to eschew direct action. It was an institution financed by the *status quo* in order to fight the *status quo*.

The initial organizing was not without conflict, and there were elements in the community that responded negatively to what must have been considerable initial pressure to join. The West Woodlawn Council of Block Clubs and the Student Woodlawn Area Project (sponsored by the University of Chicago) are among the groups that chose to work independently. This reflects some criticism of TWO from within the community, but it also dispels the notion that the organization is an all-powerful monolith. Despite Dr. Fey's fears, it is not THE Woodlawn organization.

Early in TWO's history five pastors withdrew from the Greater Woodlawn Pastor's Alliance, criticizing the alliance for endorsing tactics "based on the cultivation of fear, hatred, and useful antagonisms." A flurry of charges and counter-charges followed. One of the pastors, the Rev. C. Kenneth Proefrock, wrote that the alternative to IAF was an insistence upon careful planning, orderly change and legal processes."

In order to determine the extent of church support of TWO today, the writer made contact with 19 of the 36 churches in the community. Of the 17 churches not contacted, four had no phone, five no longer existed and eight did not answer after three days of repeated calling. Each church was asked its reaction to TWO and the extent of its participation in the organization.

Of the 19 churches contacted, 11 indicated a positive response to TWO and the active support of church members; three respondents indicated opposition; two were inactive in the organization but favorable toward its aims; one minister said his church "just sits back and watches"; one church was inactive but expressed awareness of what TWO "has been and can be"; and, finally, with the noise of a midweek Pentecostal service in the background, one respondent said that he had "never heard of it." Most of the favorable responses echoed the belief that TWO's program was consistent with the aims of justice and that association in the ministerial alliance had been a spur to ecumenicity.

## TWO's "Power"

Initial programs of TWO included rent strikes and a march on local merchants accused of short weights. What Alinsky calls "our entrance into the community of atomic powers" took place on Saturday, August 26, 1961 when more than 2,000 Woodlawn residents rode in a cavalcade of buses to Chicago's City Hall to register to vote. The demonstration had a tremendous effect on community morale, and observers say that even the least articulate Woodlawn residents gained a feeling of participation. Incidentally, the only election in which TWO has participated vigorously resulted in a three-to-one victory for a TWO-backed white alderman over a Negro lawyer who ran with the backing of the Democratic machine.

Today TWO, thorugh its representative membership, claims to speak for some 30,000 Woodlawn residents. In a time when the illusion of power (created largely by extended news media coverage) seems almost as determinative as actual power, TWO can rightfully contend that it has power. The *Chicago Daily News* once ran an ad promoting a series of favorable articles on TWO that included a picture of the former president, the Rev. Arthur M. Brazier. The headline-sized caption read, "This man has POWER." The ad went on to indicate that Brazier could, by his leadership, dictate the future course of urban renewal in the Woodlawn-University area.

The claim may have been extravagant but it underlines a fundamental precept of IAF-style organization: the creation of a strong, indigenous leader (Brazier is minister of a Pentecostal church in Woodlawn but doesn't live there). One observer suggests that a prime achievement of TWO has been, through emphasis on leadership, to restore the image of the strong, purposeful male within the matriarchal Negro community.

What has TWO's "power" yielded in terms of tangibles? There is no question that TWO was able to force the university to negotiate its proposal to move into the north edge of Woodlawn. By an agreement forged in Mayor Daley's office last summer, the university will not begin demolition of the area until housing has been built to accommodate relocated residents.

A fortuitous circumstance was the recent agreement of TWO and the Kate Maremont Foundation to sponsor jointly the construction of 762 units of middle-income housing in Woodlawn. Rents in these units will be very modest and a TWO spokesman claims that persons relocated from the university clearance area will have first choice of the new units. Almost 2,000 units of housing will be demolished, however, and some observers wonder what will happen to the remaining relocatees.

The city will not pass the ordinance designating the proposed middle income housing site until a pending study proves that there is no urgent need for public housing in the same area. TWO has set itself against the construction of public housing adjacent to the proposed middle-income housing. The Rev. Lynwood Stevenson, currently president of TWO, says his organization is not opposed to public housing *per se,* but would prefer that additional low-rise public-housing units be scattered throughout Woodlawn to accommodate relocatees who can neither afford nor otherwise qualify to live in the proposed middle-income housing.

This emphasis on middle-income housing has led some, including a local paper, *The Woodlawn Booster,* to suggest that the organization is reneging on its commitment to the low-income residents of the area. The paper holds that TWO is growing more and more middle class in its outlook and that its object is to create "another Hyde Park."

It is undoubtedly true that, with success, an institution will begin to assert the self-interest of its most powerful elements at the expense of the less powerful. Indeed, in this writer's opinion, the acid test of TWO's considerable and commendable success in gaining a strong voice in urban renewal policy will be the extent to which it lives up to its original determination to serve *all* of its constituency. It would be a tragedy if Woodlawn were to become another Hyde Park at the expense of its low-income residents.

Today, TWO members seem justified in scoffing at such speculations. Practically every observer of Woodlawn acknowledges that TWO has implemented grass-roots democracy in the area. Dr. Edgar H. S. Chandler, executive vice president of the Church Federation and an acknowledged leader in the ecumenical movement, says this year's TWO convention was a remarkable successor to the town meetings he knew in his New England boyhood. In addition to its success in combating the university, slum landlords and unfair merchants, TWO can rightfully claim the following laurels.

• City-wide influence in the struggle for integrated, higher-quality schools. TWO was instrumental in inaugurating an important court case in this area.
• The relaxation of employment barriers in several stores.
• The creation of a better understanding of welfare problems through meetings with public aid officials and cooperation with the local welfare office.
• The creation of an ecumenical spirit within the community and on a city-wide level through interfaith contacts.
• The formation of a strong citizens group to watch over future urban renewal programs in Woodlawn—with a majority of the representation from TWO.

## IAF's Cardinal Sin—Impoliteness

Woodlawn, through TWO, will soon be the beneficiary of what may prove a more significant venture than the University of Chicago fight. The Federal government has given

TWO a grant of $76,000 and a big challenge. Can TWO, with its indigenous base, select, counsel and provide training for the indigent unemployed? Similar programs have foundered on the rocks of paternalism and poor communication. TWO claims that it can use the grant to turn unemployables into employables. Success in this venture would be a powerful argument against welfare colonialism and in favor of the indigenous, self-determination approach of TWO.

TWO members acknowlege that there is much more to be done in Woodlawn. It is still a slum, but as Silberman suggests, a slum with hope. If Woodlawn's achievements have been overrated, it is only because they stand in such stark contrast to the failures of other similar communities, where millions of dollars have been spent to get slum dwellers to confirm the stereotype that they are somehow unable to control their own future if given the chance.

The tactics of TWO have included everything from sit-ins at the office of Mayor Daley to pre-arranged mass walk-outs at School Board meetings. Unquestionably there are well-intentioned persons—ministers, social workers and citizens of Woodlawn—who have been deeply hurt by the raucous and rude attitude of those who advance TWO as the ultimate savior of the community. Nothing is more upsetting than to be told that for 30 years your method was wrong. At times the disciplined anger of TWO organizers has erupted in personal assaults on critics which, whether justified or not, merely proves that mixture of motives that Reinhold Niebuhr has so often and ably perceived.

And yet there is a spirit to the operation and to Alinsky that leads one to conclude that IAF's cardinal sin has been that of impoliteness, a quality that most Americans are attracted to only in secret. Indeed, what may alarm the critics most of all is IAF's elevation of impoliteness to the policy level. In a facetious memorandum, Alinsky recently advised his staff to cease referring to slums as slums and to call them "grey areas."

## Unresolved Questions

The controversy over Alinsky has created a number of important issues within the church and the social welfare community. One of these, raised by some Protestant clergy, is whether a local congregation is justified in joining an IAF organization as a congregation. Some churches that are quite active in TWO have not joined officially in order to maintain their priestly function as a mediator in conflict situations. It can be argued that TWO is a political instrument and that, for this reason, a church should refrain from identification. Most persons who hold this position, however, endorse the enthusiastic participation of laity and ministers through other institutional structures, such as the block club or the ministerial alliance.

Another theological issue for some is the reconciliation of Christian ethics with the use of self-seeking power. It seems to me that the Christian citizen must judge the points at which power benefits only the one who seeks it and speak out against the perversion of power solely for personal gain. IAF organizations seem less susceptible to this perversion of power because they are organized around a multiplicity of goals. The perils of power, however, do not justify the avoidance of power when the end is just.

This concept of power is tied in with the revitalization of voluntarism implied in IAF's organizing policy. Because these organizations lack police power, nothing prevents their dissolution save the will of their members. It strikes me that most of the organizations that we call voluntary (including the church) are really involuntary. We lack clear reasons for joining; we perceive little differences in our lives whether we are in or out; and in many so-called voluntary organizations the structure that might encourage controversy and debate is corroded by the pervasive sense that controversy is a bit more sinful than change.

One could begin a diatribe on the loss of national purpose, the frustration we are beginning to feel at cybernation (one of the few big words that is existentially understood by the rank and file), and the general breakdown of responsibility implied in last spring's knifing in Queens when neighbors, fearing involvement, did nothing. The basic point is that IAF's insistence on power in the context of a democratic organization has given people some sense that they matter. Alinsky says he would never be able to organize the leisure class. I suspect that the future of democracy, however, is somehow dependent on infusing the affluent society with the sense of purpose that emerges when one is forced to make clear-cut decisions. Is not the good psychiatrist's role to release in his patient the capacity to exercise the will?

The tyranny of the minority in America will be made possible only by what James Reston has called "the indifference of the majority."

Another issue involves the nature of urban government. Dr. Fey feels that IAF organizations are a judgment on the urban power structure for its failure to provide the education and tools for democratic decision making. He contends with justification that Chicago is a city without a plan (although the City Fathers say there *is* a plan) and that, in this setting, the squeaking wheel gets the grease. TWO squeaks loudly, gets headlines and gains a victory, while some docile communities accept their lot. The judgment has merit. Even those who condemn TWO indicate that Chicago's urban renewal authorities have failed miserably in providing a voice for those who are to be affected by the bulldozer. Unless the city realizes this, urban renewal programs are destined to failure.

Meanwhile the urban renewal officials cite the ease and extent of citizen participation in stable Hyde Park. Which means that urban renewal has benefited the articulate at the expense of the "have nots." Which is precisely the point at which IAF entered Woodlawn. It is true that other cities have developed less controversial programs of citizen involvement, but controversy can become consensus only when there is genuine partnership between the administrators and the community.

TWO is not, as some have claimed, anti-urban renewal. But it does demand a voice in it.

## A Holden Caulfield Age

Two brief observations in conclusion.

First, the social work community must put up with IAF's rudeness long enough to consider the tremendous implications of the theories of power and self-determination in the renewal of slum culture. In a provocative speech to the Child Welfare League of America in 1962, David R. Hunter provided a masterful analysis of the basic problem faced by every agency from the smallest community service to the largest welfare operation:

Somehow today it is hard to escape a feeling of powerlessness and ineffectuality. The big things are getting away from us. We seem to be occupying ourselves in the recesses and eddies of the main stream. [Social work] has shopped too exclusively at the stores of the psychic sciences and too rarely dropped in at the supermarket to select from the sociology, political science, anthropology and economics shelves. The public is entitled to know what can't be accomplished by present methods. . . .

Finally, it seems to this writer that IAF's achievements ought to be studied thoroughly and dispassionately, particularly within the Christian community, to see whether they do not offer a way by which churches might better express their mission in the city. There are many pitfalls, and it cannot be doubted that some of IAF's more sophisticated partisans have seized on it as a means of proving to themselves that they have a righteous cause, or to solve identity problems. But this is understandable in an age when Holden Caulfields are more prevalent than Saul Alinskys.

# The Church and Neighborhood Community Organization*

THOMAS D. SHERRARD and
RICHARD C. MURRAY

Compelled by obedience to its Lord, the church has gone out into the life of people and discovered that it can become an architect rather than a victim of the city. By sharing in the life of its neighborhood, the church has been shown a path which leads to the renewal of community life and the renewal of the church itself.... Because (participation in community organization) has made the church's faith relevant and immediately applicable, involvement in community has resulted in growth in the faith for numerous laymen and ministers.... Churchmen involved have declared, "Now the church is getting down to business; at last I know what it is to serve God...."[1]

This is only one of many recent statements from churchmen and church groups. The present upsurge of interest and activity on the part of the churches is most heartening—even if it is startling. Only a few years ago it was the rare priest, minister, or rabbi who could find the time to become deeply involved in community organization. The extent of this interest, the reasons for it, the methods being employed, and the results being achieved are, of course, of great interest to those social workers engaged or interested in community organiza-

* Reproduced by special permission from the authors and the publisher, *Social Work, 10* (3), July 1965.

[1] Robert Christ, "The Local Church in a Community Organization" (New York: Board of National Missions, United Presbyterian Church in the U.S.A., 1965), pp. 10 and 14. (Mimeographed.)

tion practice. There are, in addition, important implications for the entire welfare system and professional social work as a whole—not to mention political ramifications. If social work remains aloof from the major currents and conflicts of our time, it risks being forever behind.

Not only does this trend of church involvement represent a large-scale readjustment of a major institutional force in our society, it also has been undertaken with a militancy that is unprecedented in recent times. It has been accompanied by sharp criticism of the social welfare establishment and social workers in general. "Red Feather bosses" and "welfare colonialism" have become popular expressions, which reflect—or may presage—less publicized shifts in national church organization budget allocations from social service departments to departments concerned with urban policy, politics, civil rights, and community organization.[2]

The churches have always engaged in charitable activities. Throughout the ages they have fed the hungry, clothed the naked, taught the ignorant, cared for the sick, and provided solace and counsel for the troubled. These activities have been expressions of Christian love, services provided to the faithful or designed to reach new converts. Dedication to community organization as a fulfillment of good works is new.

[2] For more extended discussion of the churches and their role in community organization in urban areas, see *The City Church*, Vol. 14, No. 4 (September-October 1963), which is devoted to church social action and community organization in Chicago; Colin W. Williams, *Where in the World* (New York: National Council of Churches, 1963), chap. 4; Gayraud S. Wilmore, *The Secular Relevance of the Church* (Philadelphia: Westminster Press, 1962), chap. 4; Lyle E. Schaller, *Conflict, Reconciliation and Community Organization*, manuscript in preparation, 1965; Dan W. Dodson, "Power as a Dimension of Education," *Journal of Educational Sociology*, Vol. 35, No. 5 (November 1961), pp. 203-215; Wayne A. R. Leys, "Machiavelli in Modern Dress," *Christian Century*, Vol. 76, No. 45 (November 11, 1959), pp. 1308-1309; Editorial, "Justice and Beyond Justice," *Christian Century*, Vol. 82, No. 8 (February 24, 1965), *Social Action*, Vol. 31, No. 6 (February 1965), entitled "Strategy for Community Change," is a full issue devoted to community organization in relation to the churches, with articles by Robert N. Davidson, William Biddle, and Dan W. Dodson.

In recent years, however, many of these church social service activities have become increasingly professionalized, run by social workers and co-opted by government; from the standpoint of the clergy, they are impersonalized, secularized, and distant from the church organization, even when they have retained their religious support. They have not provided the kind of bridge required by the churchmen who are anxious to reach alienated, inner-city populations in a meaningful way. Therefore, as an alternative, the churches have recently begun to encourage, sponsor, and in many instances finance with substantial sums of money, secular organizations of people with the frank objective of effecting social and political change.

It is hard to assess the extent of these developments with certainty, but in many large northern cities—in Chicago, New York, Detroit, Cleveland, Rochester, Syracuse, Buffalo, Kansas City, and elsewhere—large-scale community organization activities sponsored by church groups are either under way or contemplated. In these and many other cities, related activities sponsored by urban church groups, city missionary societies, councils of churches, as well as by individual inner-city churches and the home missions departments of several denominations, are going on at an accelerated pace. In few instances are they being carried on in co-operation with social welfare institutions, and in even fewer instances are they manned by social work personnel. The reasons for the widening gap between these institutional forces with so much in common deserves serious attention.

## Why the Trend?

The dynamics of the trend toward community organization by the churches—which has engaged labor unions and student groups, as well—are difficult to analyze. There are many forces loose in the land that have contributed to it. Most immediate is the civil rights movement and the profound impact it has had upon all American religious bodies. Even though in the beginning most institutional churches responded hesitantly or with grave misgivings to the stirrings of protest against racism, at present church involvement and commitment to civil rights and related causes are widespread. Undoubtedly there still exists among many clergymen a sense of guilt and impatience over the fact that "mainline" churches, and especially their active laity, remain vehicles for maintaining middle-class values, prejudices, and privileges. Community organization provides the means for both bypassing the conservative and involving the timid church members.

Many of the younger clergy particularly have experienced a sense of guilt and frustration after exposure to the realities of brutal injustice against minorities and other lower-class groups, and it is this that has been transformed into a profound discontent and impatience with their own churches. Many of the men coming out of the seminaries have turned away from the parish ministry and are looking for other institutional forms through which to carry out their mission. They have found their way to the expanding and experimenting urban church departments, the home missions departments of the various denominations, or councils of churches.

In a time of profound social change and doubt such as the present—epitomized in the civil rights movement but manifested also in direct action by students on the nation's college campuses and in large-scale peace movements—redefinition of leadership within institutions is to be expected. Established leadership searches for new symbols, slogans, and programs to retain shifting allegiances; new leadership comes to the front as unusual opportunities present themselves to attract followers.

Another factor has been the role of the government and the politician. In response to this social unrest, the first half of the current decade has witnessed unusual activity by government after the quiet of the late fifties. The present climate of crisis makes it politically feasible and necessary for government to move ahead on many fronts. The attack on the problem of delinquency has become a community campaign and

a national effort; long-standing economic and social dispari-
ties have become dramatized in the national War on Poverty;
such diverse issues as population control, capital punishment,
exploitation of migrant workers, water and air pollution, and
conservation have come alive again. Because they depend on
personal commitment, voter enthusiasm, and dedicated volunteer activity and involvement, political organizations must
either try to rise to the spirit of the times or find attractive
substitutes if party loyalty and voter enthusiasm are to be
maintained.

It is not always so clearly seen that religious organizations
have a corresponding dependence for their continuing vitality
on the active involvement of a broad constituency in secular
affairs. Since the Reformation, centuries of a conservative
or other-worldly disregard for social and political events
(punctuated by occasional nonconformist religious movements) have ill-prepared mid-twentieth-century Americans
for the current shifts by religious institutions in response to
the internal crises and other generalized threats to Western
European society.

## High Membership But Low Influence

Clergymen are further troubled by an apparent paradox.
Church membership—especially in the suburbs—has been
growing to the point where it is at an all-time high, and
churches are sharing in the general affluence. At the same
time, they sense a diminution of effective religious influence
in our society. In fact, it may be precisely these opportunities
they see in the social movement atmosphere that make them
impatient. Instead, as urban transition has taken place, they
have become conscious of the inability of established churches
to maintain effective relationships with the rapidly growing,
alienated, low-income populations of the inner-cities or assume moral leadership on acute social issues.

The liberal theological spokesmen and the young emerging church leadership have clearly perceived that in order

to maintain or to recapture a position of influence for the churches in the midst of present-day social movements, religious bodies must provide vigorous leadership in the fight for social justice. In a very real sense, the churches are engaged in a competition for the loyalties, the commitment, and the engagement of the residents of the large northern urban centers, particularly the inner-city residents of deprived neighborhoods, Negro and white. In some instances, this may take the form of interchurch rivalry. Often it seems to take the form of aggressive ecumenicism and solidarity against certain local secular forces. It is expressed as a war on City Hall, on petty corruption or economic abuse (such as in Chicago, Cleveland, and Detroit), and in the seeking of support from federal or state government in battles for social issues.

The declining numbers of parishioners and the declining strength of the inner-city churches in the face of population shifts have strongly motivated these churches, both Protestant and Catholic, to look to a broader constituency. They attempt to build a platform or construct an arena, based on the neighborhood, in which the influence of the church can be more effectively applied.

One explanation for these phenomena in the inner-city churches has been in terms of economic losses of real estate owned by both Protestants and Catholics, particularly the ethnic Catholic parishes, their churches, schools, and social services. The same problem has already faced universities, hospitals, and other institutions, both commercial and non-profit, which have had to make the difficult choice of whether to flee to more felicitous surroundings or to face urban deterioration. When the latter choice has been elected, often the institution has become the focal point around which local forces have become mobilized, often with the help of urban renewal and other governmental aids to arrest urban blight and to spur redevelopment. No doubt this same dynamic is at work in the case of the churches, and in many instances the problem is heightened and the choice narrowed by the flight to the suburbs at great distance of entire congregations. But for those churches that have a commitment, not only to a potentially mobile congregation but also to a geographic parish, the problem is intensified.

## Crisis in the Church

Closer examination suggests that such economic determinants are only contributing factors. The commitment of these new voices among the clergy appears to go much deeper than mere economic consideration or sentimental attachment to a geographic area and traditional buildings. In fact, in only a few instances—in Chicago for example—has strong church organization tied to strong community organization been able to withstand the forces of urban deterioration and racial succession. One such example is in the Back-of-the-Yards neighborhood, which was tightly organized during the 1930's and has remained so ever since, successfully resisting the break-up of first- and second-generation Catholic parishes.

Urban missionary activities are, of course, nothing new in the history of organized religion, although often frowned on and ignored, or at the most grudgingly supported by the church establishment. Whether Nonconformist, Methodist, Evangelical, Christian Socialist, the Social Gospel Movement, Labour Chapels, or the Salvation Army, each in its time reached out to the poor and the dispossessed. They went outside the buildings, formalities, and conventions of the established churches and into the streets, the slums, the saloons, or brought new services to the poor with only a minimum of religious rituals. The National Council of Churches of Christ in America has had its home missions department and most denominations have a similar department, but it is perhaps a measure of the deep alienation of modern urban low-income population from established churches that the clergy of the inner-city have been unable to establish a truly productive relationship to slum populations through older mission methods. Instead, they have launched into what is in fact organized political and social reform as a basis for establishing rapport. These clergy have set out to prove the "relevance of the church" by creating a new earthly society.

There is, however, a still deeper crisis within churches over what it is these institutions and their clergy actually should do and should be. The moral crises of the two world wars, threats of atomic destruction, and the postwar rise of Eastern European and Asian Communist nations and non-Christian developing countries have severely shaken the security of the Christian churches—just as it has shaken the general security of America in ways that have yet to be appreciated. The ecumenical movement and reforms in the Catholic church testify that these currents of change are truly different in quality and quantity from previous pressures in recent centuries.

Thus, when urban clergymen in apparent desperation throw their energies into community organization, civil rights, and urban politics, seemingly in disregard of their traditional duties and goals, something more is afoot than a few men attempting to get their churches out of debt or seeking to enhance their careers. These men are searching for a new meaning of "church" in urban society. For many of them, the traditional role of church pastor has lost its meaning.

Nor should this be looked on as a "rump" movement within the churches that will soon pass away. The movement is now being supported at the highest levels in the larger church administrative bodies. Large sums of money have been allocated for this organizational activity, even in the face of obvious political risks. Churchmen are looking to community organization as a means of capturing leadership in one of the most significant social movements of the day as the Social Gospel movement supported labor unions fifty years ago.

It is fairly obvious that use of the Catholic and Protestant churches as instruments of social change presents problems to clergy who were trained in the use of a somewhat different technology. They have looked for technical assistance and have found willing help from the Industrial Areas Foundation, which has been providing organizational assistance in Chicago for the past half-dozen years. The IAF is now moving with the encouragement of the National Council of Churches and the national offices of several of the denominations to other northern cities to do likewise.

## Saul Alinsky

The authors have been observing informally during the last six years, and more systematically during the last two, the activities of these church-sponsored community organizations in Chicago. As in all northern urban centers, there are many community organizations sponsored, or participated in, by churches, as well as organizations sponsored by foundations, social agencies, and business groups. However, the concern in this discussion is with those organized under church sponsorship, with the help of organizers from the IAF under the direction of Saul Alinsky, a familiar figure on the community organization scene since the mid-thirties, when the already mentioned Back-of-the-Yards Council was formed under Catholic auspices. He and his organization were subsequently active in a number of places across the country, but achieved no great claim on public attention until they joined forces with the urban church movement already described.[3]

[3] For discussion of the IAF and its method by the staff and various observers and critics, both pro and con, see Saul D. Alinsky, *Reveille for Radicals* (Chicago: University of Chicago Press, 1945); Alinsky, "The Urban Immigrant," in T. T. McAvoy, Ed., *Roman Catholicism and the American Way of Life* (Notre Dame, Ind.: University of Notre Dame Press, 1960); Alinsky, "Citizen Participation and Community Organization in Planning and Urban Renewal," address to National Association of Housing and Redevelopment Officials, Chicago, January 1962; Nicholas von Hoffman, "Reorganization in the Casbah," *Social Progress*, Vol. 52, No. 6 (April 1962); V. B. Blakely and C. T. Leber, Jr., "Woodlawn Begins to Flex its Muscles," *Presbyterian Life* (September 15, 1962), pp. 12-15, 41-42; Charles E. Silberman, *Crisis in Black and White* (New York: Random House, 1964), chap. 10 (this is essentially the same as "Up from Apathy—The Woodlawn Experiment," *Commentary*, Vol. 37, No. 5 [May 1964]); Stephen C. Rose, "Saul Alinsky and his Critics," *Christianity and Crisis* (July 20, 1964). See in *Christian Century*: Editorials in the issues of May 12 and June 7, 1961, July

There are four such organizations (including the Back-of-the-Yards) in the city of Chicago. They operate in different parts of the city in different types of communities, with widely differing populations, and therefore differ correspondingly in many important respects. However, in addition to the fact that their instigation and major support has been derived from the Catholic church (and in two cases also from Presbyterian churches), they have other important characteristics in common.

## Organizational Characteristics

Alinsky's organizations primarily seek to impose a monopoly of control over limited areas in the city—either neighborhoods, groups of contiguous neighborhoods, or community areas, as they are often called in Chicago. They differ from more conventional or traditional community organizations in that this attempt to gain monopolistic control over affairs in the area takes precedence over the development of social services. It appears to take priority also over other common goals, such as improved housing, sanitation, law enforcement, and education. These latter matters, however, often constitute the subject matter for mounting campaigns for developing interests and providing an agenda for action, in order to attain the primary objective of organizational control. In this sense, then, they may be said to have basically political objectives.

The organizations are like labor unions in trying to maintain their status as sole bargaining agents. Typically they represent themselves as spokesmen for all the citizenry and all the interests in the area. They purport to speak for the citizen, the parent, the voter, the businessman, the taxpayer, the

18 and August 22, 1962; E. C. Parker, "How Chelsea Was Torn Apart" (February 3, 1960), p. 130; Letters to Editor, February 12 and April 7, 1965. See also Walter Kloetzli, *The Church and the Urban Challenge* (Philadelphia: Muhlenberg Press, 1961), chap. 4; Harold E. Fey, "The Industrial Areas Foundation: An Interpretation" (Chicago: National Lutheran Council, 1964) (mimeographed); Philip Hauser, "Conflict vs. Consensus," *Chicago Sun-Times*, December 13, 1964, Sect. II, pp. 1-3.

tenant, the home owner, and—in order to do so with any degree of reality—they must necessarily dispute the legitimacy of any other group wishing to represent either "the people" or significant interests in the community. When internal conflicts exist, they tend to represent the more powerful in order to maximize their strength.

These are organizations of organizations, built from the top down with a core of committed local clergy at the center. Other groups, such as local businessmen's organizations, PTA's, service groups, block clubs, and so on, are added as rapidly as they can be attracted, co-opted, overcome, or digested. As might be expected, this behavior has brought them into conflict with other agencies and organizations.

Another characteristic of Alinsky's organizations is their ready recourse to direct action techniques, such as picketing, rent strikes, demonstrations, sit-ins, and the like, but these direct action methods no longer guarantee certain results. Civil rightists, students, teachers, political activists of all hues, and many other groups have taken to the streets also to achieve their goals. Even the students and faculty of the art school at the local art museum in Chicago hit the streets with placards recently to air obscure differences with their patrons. But a half-dozen years ago these methods were profoundly disconcerting to the Establishment, helped to delineate issues, and guaranteed a wealth of publicity, which is an indispensable commodity for organizations of this sort. Now, however, an inflation in direct action has occurred. What fifty pickets could accomplish in front of City Hall now takes five hundred, and it still may not be effective. After two massive school boycotts and large-scale school demonstrations, smaller local organizations are hard put to find impressive means to register dissatisfaction with schools as easily as The Woodlawn Organization (TWO, the IAF's only Negro community organization) did with a partial boycott of a single school in 1962. Direct action against private individuals such as landlords continues to be effective.

A somewhat related characteristic is the use of conflict as organizational cement. The creation of conflict situations is quite openly espoused as the best means of gaining public attention, attracting adherents, and overcoming the existing apathy of the residents of lower-class communities. Scapegoats are carefully chosen for their availability and vulnerability, and causes for complaint chosen for ready comprehensibility, mass appeal, and potential for dramatic exploitation.

It follows, then, that organizations which depend primarily on a turnout of demonstrations, pickets and other signs of irate mass support in order to expose, threaten to expose, or compel others to act require a continuous stance of militancy and righteous anger that can readily be directed at those who hesitate to comply. The rationale for this goes beyond the efficacy of coercion and compulsion. It is perhaps assumed that this stance of righteous anger attracts and holds certain kinds of people who seem to require more compelling and intensive involvement than they get by attending meetings and engaging in community problem-solving. A militant stance of this sort may also encourage the timid who have legitimate complaints and have suffered and been exploited to come forward and air their grievances. It is also assumed that aggression is a natural way for people who have been oppressed, mistreated, exploited, or neglected to respond to those who have misused them, and that this mode of organization will, therefore, overcome apathy and sustain participation among those who would not otherwise be willing to expend their energies on any social enterprise.

This activity may indeed be therapeutic, if by acting out and giving vent to their hostilities these deprived individuals and groups attain subsequently a more stable and realistic relationship to their institutional environment. However, unless there is accompanying change in their environment such activity may disrupt and further present the participants from making a new social adjustment. Any "therapy" must, above all, be realistic and honest at the same time that it raises aspiration and motivation—admittedly a difficult balance to achieve. It is yet to be proved that conflict organization is indeed therapeutic.

Finally, and perhaps most important of all, is what appears in these organizations to be an almost paranoid preoccupation with power. It follows, of course, that if one is to carry out successfully a strategy of conflict and to attempt to coerce and compel others, one has to move from a position of power. There is constant talk of "naked" power, even of "revolutionary" power, and every organizational move is designed primarily to enhance the power of the organization and its bargaining position. The argument is a clear and simple one, that the residents of low-income neighborhoods (most residents of the city for that matter, but particularly lower socioeconomic groups) suffer from a pervasive sense of powerlessness, which in large part accounts for civic apathy. This, in turn, accounts for the persistence of conditions that prevail in the slums of the large cities—bad housing, lack of medical care, delinquency, crime, drug addiction, segregation and discrimination, inadequate education, and related conditions associated with poverty.

There is also the assumption that the "power structure"— or to use the more all-embracing and currently popular term, "the Establishment" (which presumably includes all those who in some way gain, or think they do, from maintenance of the status quo)—opposes substantial social reform. Nor will the Establishment permit any concessions, it is maintained, except those that are forced by the exercise of power. The only recourse for the people is to establish "power-based mass organizations" designed to wrest concessions from the powers-that-be. This envisions a perpetual contest of the weak against the strong as the essence of democracy.

Some time ago, Alinsky addressed the annual meeting of the Association of Community Councils in Chicago. Among many provocative and challenging remarks were what he identified as three principles, or "propositions," that presumably contain the kernel of his thinking about community organization. Based on observations of his current actions and utterances, there seems to be no reason to assume that he has substantially altered his position during the last eight years.

I would like to state my first proposition: *The first function of community organization is community disorganization.* Disorganization of the accepted circumstances and the status quo of the arrangements under which they live—these circumstances and arrangements must be disorganized if they are to be displaced with changing patterns, providing the opportunities and means for citizen participation. All change means disorganization of the old and organization of the new. . .

This brings us to the second proposition: *The character of the means or tools through which change can be effected must be clearly understood by the people of all times—it is power through organization.* . . No individual or organization can negotiate without the power to compel negotiation. . . This in essence is the function of the community organizer. Anything otherwise is wishful non-thinking. To attempt to operate on good will rather than on a power basis would be to attempt something which the world has not yet experienced. This brings us to our third proposition: *Prevailing arrangements, or power patterns, can only be altered by power.* Here it is important that we pause and examine the words which are being used in this discussion. This is a prime issue if we are to achieve any understanding of points of view. It was obvious earlier in this presentation that such terms as "agitation," "to rub raw the resentments," "to stir up dissatisfaction and discontent," "create conflict"—that these were harsh words, grating and jarring on many ears, which prefer phrases such as "stimulating citizen participation." This is a critical point where our tongues trap our minds."[4]

## Appeal to the Clergy

Such hard-hitting, off-the-cuff remarks, coupled with a gift for polemics, have endeared Alinsky to the urban clergy.[5]

[4] Saul Alinsky. "From Citizen Apathy to Participation." Paper presented at the Association of Community Councils of Chicago, October 1957, pp. 4 and 6. (Mimeographed.)

[5] See, for instance, Dolores McCahill, "Controversy Necessary Ministers Told," *Chicago Sun-Times*, September 29, 1964.

This is exciting stuff, heady talk—phrases such as "naked power," "revolution," "guerilla warfare" are bandied about freely. The impression is given by Alinsky and his workers that "gut" issues are being dealt with, that the participants are at last coming to grips with some of the central social issues of our time. Here finally is the relevant church, the meaningful mission! At long last in the smoke-filled room of the storefront organizational headquarters, exciting, behind-the-scenes decisions are made and political manipulations managed. At last the young clergy are in the thick of battle, exerting their influence on the course of events. At mass meetings the pastors on the platform give public evidence of their commitment to the cause. In the conflict atmosphere of Alinsky's organizations they can give full vent to their sense of frustration over the church's failure in the past to provide adequate leadership to the social movement of the day.

One may well speculate why these noisy and seemingly radical activities in the inner city have not attracted more attention from the conservative sectors of the sponsoring churches and why some strong counteraction has not developed within church circles. The communication gap between the city and the suburbs may be just another measure of the alienation in our society, what William Wheaton referred to as the "two cultures"—the affluent and the deprived.[6] It may be that many of the suburban laity are unaware of what is going on in the inner-city, and feel so remote that they do not even care. However, the suburban clergy cannot be wholly unaware.

Curiously enough, there also may be a certain kind of quiet satisfaction in the suburbs in the fact that the target of much of the protest and the challenge of these militant organizations is City Hall. Even though, as in Chicago, big business has by and large made its peace, at least temporarily, with the Democratic political machine, there is widespread contempt and

[6] William L. C. Wheaton. "The Two Cultures and the Urban Revolution." Paper presented at the National Conference on Urban Life, Washington, D.C., March 1962. (Mimeographed.)

distaste in the suburbs for the machine politics of the inner-city, which is associated with sin, graft, corruption, crime, and squalor. Viewed in this light, these new community organizations may in some respects be the successors to the middle-class civic reform movements, whose supporters are now commuters rather than voters in the city. There may well be a tacit agreement to let the political pot boil and even encourage the gadflies. But though they may be annoying to the Democratic office holders and city administrators, there is little evidence of the building of an effective political structure—in Chicago at any rate—that can challenge the machine in the near future.

One of the young analysts from the New Left has described these organizations as devoid of ideology and maintains that the claims to radicalism and all the "revolutionary" talk simply satisfy some angry people but fail to come to grips with basic issues.

Alinsky is an independent operator who gets his money from private institutions, particularly the Catholic and Presbyterian churches. Alinsky eschews ideology and program, seeking only to develop lower class protest movements which he has faith will evolve their own program (as if in some mystical way lower class people will gain the technical and ideological means to fathom the larger implications of specific city policies which currently affect them). But despite his contempt for official agencies, Alinsky remains an organizer from the top. . .

Despite the fact that he employs mass power to win limited objectives, Alinsky seems to have no over-all philosophy of political power, nor does he espouse the need for alternative politics to achieve broader social change. . .

He is true to the American pragmatic tradition which exalts action and denies the practical value of theory. With these perspectives, Alinsky-organized movements are bound to lead to frustration because they cannot transcend the immediate object of oppression towards an understanding of the larger economic and political forces which lie behind the grievance.[7]

[7] Stanley Aronovitz, "Poverty, Politics and Community Organization," *Studies on the Left*, Vol. 4, No. 3 (Summer 1964), p. 104.

Arthur Hillman, a long-time observer of the IAF, suggests a parallel with the Goldwater movement—"protest without a program."[8] Perhaps what is in the making is a potential conservative alliance against the so-called liberal establishment.

## Evaluating the Chicago Experience

Making any objective evaluation of the success of these organizations is difficult. What are to be the criteria for measurement? If success is to be rated by high visibility, local notoriety, nationwide newspaper and periodical coverage, reluctant attention paid by local officials, and respectful attention by federal officials and congressmen, then these organizations, particularly The Woodlawn Organization (TWO), have been very successful.

Without any doubt the hostile and aggressive stance of the organization stalled for three years the expansion of the University of Chicago through the use of urban renewal legislation and dissuaded the city from attempting to develop the large-scale federally financed anti-juvenile delinquency program in the neighborhood that was later unsuccessfully begun on the Near North Side. If one regards urban renewal as "Negro removal," and if one considers "welfare colonialism" to be a major threat, then these results can be viewed as positives rather than negatives.

Another criterion of success might be the successful involvement of people and the development of leadership. This, too, is difficult to assess because there are many levels and qualities of "involvement." The value and significance of involvement must be defined in terms of purposes and results. TWO can turn out several hundred or more people for large public meetings occasionally, and probably attains a higher level of continuous participation than most other organizations of this kind. Anyone who has worked in such communities knows

[8] Arthur Hillman, Memorandum, January 15, 1965, and Letter to Editor, December 28, 1964. See also Alvin L. Schorr, "The New Radicals, Manqués," *Social Work*, Vol. 9, No. 4 (October 1964), p. 113.

how difficult it is to keep participation at a high level. Thus, because of their high visibility, both inside and outside the community, IAF organizations in Chicago and especially TWO can be considered quite successful.

However, the claim to have reached the most deprived segment of the community would be most difficult to support.[9] To what extent the large mass of residents really feel represented, are even aware of or affected by the existence and activities of these organizations is moot and could only be assessed, if at all, with an elaborate research effort. Only then could claims for the therapeutic effect of conflict organization be judged.

These church-sponsored organizations have introduced a number of persons into political and city-wide prominence but they have not become city-wide leaders. Organization preoccupation with local self-interest and hostility toward city-wide institutions severely limits their municipal leadership potential while continuing the behind-the-scenes control more suggestive of leadership management than leadership development.

But to refer to these organizational activities in Chicago as "community development" programs, as many of their supporters have done, raises serious questions.[10] Community development, particularly as practiced in the developing countries overseas, has been judged by some critics to be one of the most significant social inventions of our time. A cherished objective of community workers has been to find out whether

[9] To refer to these as "mass organizations," as is constantly done by IAF supporters, is an exaggeration. Nicholas von Hoffman, the principal organizer in Woodlawn for the IAF, wrote recently, after he had left the organization: "It is an organization of perhaps two per cent of the people. Those who talk about organizing 'all the people,' or 'the masses,' or 'the great majority of the people,' are talking unrealizable balderdash." "Finding and Making Leaders" (Ann Arbor, Mich.: Students for Democratic Society, 1964), p. 9.

[10] John C. Bennett. "The Church and Power Conflicts," *Christianity and Crisis, A Christian Journal of Opinion,* March 22, 1965.

these methods and techniques can be adapted to conditions in industrialized Western countries.

The criteria for community development have become fairly well established in the literature.[11] The most important component is, of course, significant involvement and local direction at the grass roots. As has often been noted, however, there is another and equally important criterion for such programs—they must be more than mere local bootstrap self-help operations. They must be carried on in the context of over-all national—or, at the very least, regional—social planning, with the economic, social, and political developmental goals spelled out and clearly understood at all levels. This is not just an academic or doctrinaire distinction. It may actually determine the difference between solid accomplishment and mere organizational thrashing about. There is some evidence of the latter in Chicago.

It is perhaps understandable, because of church sponsorship, that the activities of these four organizations in Chicago have tended to be somewhat parochial. Instead of finding ways to relate themselves effectively to governmental or even to large voluntary planning units, they have in most instances adopted an aggressively hostile and even contemptuous stance toward them, making co-operation in planning extremely difficult, if not impossible.

In this connection one additional aspect of the TWO program should perhaps be mentioned. It was, of course, the neighboring University of Chicago that bore the full brunt of aggressively hostile, organizational attention at the outset.

[11] For example, see Lloyd Ohlin, "Urban Community Development," paper presented at the Conference on Socially Handicapped Families, UNESCO, Paris, France, February 1964, pp. 15 and 16 (mimeographed); Arthur Dunham, "Some Principles of Community Development," *International Review of Community Development*, No. 11 (Columbia: Department of Community Development, University of Missouri, 1963); Thomas D. Sherrard, "Community Organization and Community Development, Similarities and Differences," *The Report of the United States Committee to the Eleventh International Conference of Social Work, 1962* (reprinted in *Community Development Review*, AID, Department of State, 1962).

The university, as an awkward Leviathan playing its role in urban renewal and institutional expansion, was chosen as the organizational scapegoat—a characteristic technique of IAF organizations. "If you could bite the university so it would howl, if it would deign to take angry notice of you, then you had it made," is the colorful way one organizer put it.

With a demonstration of forbearance, a group of university faculty explored, initiated with TWO, and finally persuaded the U. S. Department of Labor through the federal manpower program to give a substantial demonstration manpower training grant to the organization.[12] Although there is a research and evaluation provision in the grant, results of the project are not yet available at this writing. Preliminary information available to the writers indicates that the project results rank above average among similar training experiments. The existence of this project and similar concessions suggest improved relations with the University of Chicago in the future. However, sensitive public officials may not be so forgiving, especially if they have been bitterly, and in part unfairly, attacked on both local and national platforms.

## Social Work and Social Change

It would be unwise for the profession to dismiss these organizational activities as emanations of a disaffection and frustration, or to assume that the movement will soon dissipate itself. The serious intentions of leaders in high church circles are unquestionable, and the strength and potency of this movement and its enduring effects should not be underestimated.

Church leadership, clerical and lay, needs to be trained in new and radical methods of initiating action and in guiding low status groups

[12] It should be noted that the manpower program was financed through a direct contract with the federal government and that local officials had no part in its negotiation. The writers have the distinct impression that even state officials were either carefully neutral or very cool to the whole idea.

based on developing indigenous leadership; helping people identify their own concerns; developing mutual associations varied in form to help people help themselves; and encouraging participation in the larger community.[13]

Many social workers could also subscribe wholeheartedly to this statement, but to what extent can the social work profession demonstrate that it has of late been devoting major resources to effect large-scale social change in lower-class communities? To what extent has social work been receptive to radical ideas, much less to actively developing radical new methods? In recent years the profession has not been notably successful in helping and guiding low-status groups. As one of the authors noted last year:

We are obviously at our weakest when facing the need for basic changes in the societal system in lower-class communities. Numerous efforts to apply the same time-tested techniques in such situations have been notably less than successful. Obviously some differential approaches are in order.[14]

It becomes increasingly evident that not only are new approaches required, but also a new commitment, a rededication to some of the basic purposes and values of social work.

As Bremner has described, social work had its roots in and drew its earliest inspiration from organized religion. In many respects religion and social work have maintained these connections over the years, although estrangements and tensions have occurred from time to time, some serious and some not so serious. Social work gained its original impetus, not from the churches as a whole, but from movements within the church designed, as Bremner quotes, to counteract

the tendency of organized Protestantism to seek "comfort and ease in

[13] "The Churches and Persistent Pockets of Poverty in the U.S.A.," *Town and Country Church, 1963*. Report of a Joint Consultation of the Division of Home Missions and the Division of Christian Life and Work, National Council of Churches, January 1962.

[14] Thomas D. Sherrard. "Planned Community Change," *Social Welfare Forum, 1964* (New York: Columbia University Press, 1964), pp. 107-109.

the society of the rich." He (the Reverend Rainsford) charged that as a result of indifference to the urban working class, the Protestant churches had lost the initiative in the years between 1830 and 1890.[15]

This is not unlike many of the complaints and warnings being sounded by some of the clergy today.

It must also be recognized, however, that any new co-operation with the churches cannot be based on nineteenth-century concepts of charity and service to the poor. They must be compatible with bold desires to change conditions that produce poverty and deprivation in the urban slums.

While the government—a secular force—is now, and will increasingly become, the major protagonist with which the social work profession must deal, organized religion will continue to have a stake in social affairs. They are potential allies. This objective might help to reduce the distance between the staid stance of social workers and the much more socially and politically involved role of the clergy.

The institutionalization and the transformation of the civil rights movement into more political channels will create problems for both social workers and churchmen as they accommodate themselves more to changing institutions and less to changing hearts of men caught up in active social movements. They may then be able and willing to join together again to intercede for the weak and forgotten individuals who are unable to keep up with the swift current of social forces, and to break down antiquated barriers that freed those forces.

[15] Robert H. Bremner. *From the Depths* (New York: New York University Press, 1964), p. 57.

# SECTION V

# Implications for Community Decision Making

# Introduction

The tenets of "participatory democracy" have particularly telling implications for the process of making decisions through the formal and informal structures of the community. What are some of these implications? How can citizen participation function best to produce creative decisions? Indeed, can maximal citizen participation be seen as an inhibition to stimulating social change? In terms of the production of communal decisions, how should "citizen participation" be judged?

These are the questions to which the contributors in this section address themselves. The Cahns present a tightly reasoned statement of the values of participation. "Citizen participation is a nuisance," they state. "It is costly; it is time-consuming; it is frustrating; but we cannot dispense with it . . ."

The very title of Harold Edelston and Ferne Kolodner's paper cross-cuts a series of considerations to arrive at a basic question, "Are the Poor Capable of Planning for Themselves?" No armchair theoreticians, they describe an empirical study in community organization as a way of grappling with the issue so provocatively posed in their title.

Robert Crain and Donald Rosenthal compile and interpret selected group data as part of a study of criticial socio-political relationships on community decision making. Their conclusions challenge the simplistic notion that greater citizen participation increases the likelihood for constructive social change.

The final selection is derived from a governmental hearing, representing the sometimes-heated dialogue among a U.S. Senator, an economist, an urban affairs consultant, and a social scientist concerned with public policy. This debate reflects a variety of value-orientations as it highlights the pressing questions posed by citizen participation on neighborhood and community decision making. It is, we think, a fitting conclusion to this volume since it symbolizes conceptual dissonance rather than artificially induced agreement.

# Citizen Participation[*]

EDGAR S. and JEAN CAMPER CAHN

*A few chiefs have no right to barter away hunting
grounds that belong to all the Indians, for a few
paltry presents or a keg or two of whiskey. . . . It
requires all to make a bargain for all.*
——Chief Tecumseh at Vincennes, 1810

## Part I.  Two Cardinal Fallacies of Democracy

### A.  The Genetic Fallacy

The concept of Citizen Participation has
spawned its own doctrinal version of Original Sin. Arising in
the context of the War on Poverty and the notorious mandate of "maximum feasible participation," officials have
properly required that the poor be involved in the planning of
local programs—only to find themselves faced with the question: Are the poor to be involved in planning *how* the poor
are to be involved in the planning? And this infinite regress
can readily be converted to an indictment of any effort, any
program or any institution as paternalistic, manipulative, unilateral, elitist, and undemocratic. For regardless of the point
in the evolution of a program or a concept where the poor are
involved, it is always possible to point to an earlier point at
which they were not involved. And from that it is easy to charge
that the entire undertaking is tainted with the poverty program's
version of Original Sin.

[*] This material was prepared for the Center for Community Planning,
Office of the Secretary, Department of Health, Education and Welfare.

The skepticism and distrust implied in this line of reasoning is not without firm basis in historical experience. The manipulative, after-the-fact, consultation with community groups that characterized urban renewal was perhaps the most egregious example of how a requirement of community involvement could be converted into a ritual plebiscite with approval in fact constituting involuntary *ex post facto* ratification. Typically, the mode of presentation carefully excluded the variety of policy alternatives discarded in the course of shaping the overall renewal plan.

Nonetheless, there is a fallacy lurking in this infinite sequence of demands—and those who are sincere about citizen participation have too often been the victim of illogical attacks on their sincerity and integrity based on what we term the Genetic Fallacy.

The essential fallacy here lies with the assumption that the accident of *origin* of a program necessarily defines the *nature* of the program. An institution is what it is—either responsive or unresponsive, faithful or unfaithful to its mission, effective or ineffective.

The test is not merely one of how it began—but rather, at any given point, were choices removed irrevocably from public scrutiny and reappraisal—and were those decisions conducive to meaningful democratic participation in the functioning of the institution.

We shall discuss later the dimensions of that participation. For the time being, though, it is all-important to clear away the genetic fallacy which has been given great currency and which often intimidates officials from making any beginning at all toward securing meaningful community participation.

The appropriate question must be framed in terms of objectively verifiable concerns:

1.  Were choices foreclosed?
2.  What were the actual consequences (not the intended consequences or hoped-for consequences) of those choices that have been made?

Democracy's cause would be well served by a generous application of Occam's razor to notions of intent, motive, and first cause.

Without apology, we must recognize that there is a necessity to start somewhere—and that whoever takes the initiative is in some sense acting unilaterally, even when he acts to consult others. The call for a Constitutional Convention in 1787 was viewed by many as high-handed, aristocratic, dictatorial, and antidemocratic. And it may well have been. However, the process of perfecting democracy is an unending one; but, nonetheless, it must be begun. And whether the beginning is made by a poor person, a rich person, a professional, or a lay person, the beginning is intrinsically nondemocratic. The fallacy lies in converting that necessity—the necessity of beginning—into an indictment of the fruits of those endeavors.

Laying this fallacy to rest still leaves the more difficult question: Is there some minimal requirement of involvement, some minimal investment in consultation, discussion, and dialogue which should go into the process of defining and creating a public institution? The answer, we believe, is yes— though the nature of that minimal requirement will vary depending upon the points at which alternative approaches become both irrevocably discarded and totally lost from view.

In planning an institution, there is one threshold question which cannot be treated entirely unilaterally, but which must be subjected, in some measure, to broadly based scrutiny, namely, the extent of the resources which will be devoted to the democratic process during the first period of operations.

Democracy is expensive. It costs money to hold meetings, to consult people. It takes time, staff, and resources. And a commitment to democracy must necessarily be reflected, not only in organization charts, but in budgets and timetables and allocation of energies. But just as we believe that the citizen —rich or poor—can make a rational and informed decision in allocating resources among competing priorities and competing demands, so too we believe that the citizen is capable of making an informed decision as to the portion of resources which he thinks should be committed to the democratic process—to scrutiny, to surveillance, to review, and to effective control. It is conceivable that the citizenry wants results, not conferences—changes and performance rather than meetings. And if put clearly, we have seen groups knowledgably accede to what amounts to a grace period when a higher amount of unchecked discretionary decisions will be permitted without scrutiny simply for the sake of getting the show on the road.

Nonetheless, we think that this decision—this initial rough allocation on the dollars to be spent on the democratic process—must be made in concert with those who are supposed to be served by the institution. Those choices must be put not simply in terms of dollars and percentages—but most specifically, in terms of what those dollars will buy: how many meetings, how many reports, what kinds of disclosure, how many phone calls, how many publications, what kind of accounting with what kind of detail and specificity, and what kind of participation in the review of the first year's performance and the construction of the next period of operations when there is a record of performance to judge and review.

Some initial investment, during the planning period, must be made to consult and confer as best one can in whatever way one can. For the most part, even a private enterprise about to launch a new product would invest in market research to the extent possible. In the field of social institutions, the product is in part the democratic—or undemocratic—nature of the institution itself.

The question must be put: Does the consumer want meetings about the nature of the institution; or does he want actual programs and actual performance; or does he want periodic reports by special technicians in lieu of meetings—or what mixture of these does he want? That mixture may well change as time goes on and increasing concern arises as to whether the institution has retained fidelity to its original mission. It is our belief and our experience that all citizens including specifically the poor, the underprivileged, the minority ethnic groups most discriminated against, are capable of saying democratically "We want a job done." They will also demand to be in a position to determine whether the best possible job is being done for the least amount of money—and whether some of these jobs could not be performed by them as well for the same amount of money or less.

However, the right to scrutinize involves the right to decline to scrutinize—and that threshold determination is the minimal democratic mandate. In short, in a democracy, the question "Who will watch the watchers, who will watch those entrusted with keeping the program honest and responsive?" is answered by the people. And the people have the right to say "No one need watch the watchers right now, so long as they retain the right, later on, to change their minds."

We will deal later with the practical implications of putting this minimal mandate—the option to scrutinize or not to scrutinize—into effect. But before we do so, it is necessary to deal with a polar fallacy. There are those who distrust the originators of a program and press for infinite regress of the democratic process into the prenatal stage of an institution and beyond. But there also those charged with the design, creation, and administration of an institution who tend to distrust the capacity of the citizenry to function competently, to judge wisely in the governance of an institution. This fallacy too has been given great currency in the War on Poverty by well-intentioned and dedicated professionals who feel themselves inundated by the demands and pressures placed upon them by their clientele. Those pressures have been given form and articulation in what we call The Fallacy of the Monolithic Man.

## B. The Fallacy of the Monolithic Man

The Fallacy of the Monolithic Man underlies the professional argument for elitist control of institutions. But the poor are not monolithic; they are composite, capable of speaking and deliberating in a variety of modes. They are composite as a group, although they have a community of interest of common grievances and common needs which may transcend their individual differences. And the poor are composite as individuals. The very individual who asks for help is quite capable, in the context of a community meeting or group discussion, of saying that resources should not be totally devoted to providing service in crisis situations. Despite his awareness of the pressing nature of individual needs, that very person is capable of insisting that substantial resources be diverted in effecting significant social change.

The fallacy is summed up in three simple propositions:

(a) The poor tell us what they want when they ask for help.
(b) If professionals devoted 100 per cent of their efforts to responding to the demands of the poor, they would never get to the significant underlying causes but would deal only with symptomatic, unending crisis demands.
(c) Therefore, the poor cannot be permitted to control institutions or to decide what professionals are to do if those institutions and those professionals are to achieve significant social change on behalf of the poor.

Thus, they conclude, the choice of priorities, the design of programs, the allocation of resources must necessarily be a matter for professional decision.

The fallacy is contained in the first proposition; that the poor tell us what they want when they ask for help. It assumes that a person is a monolithic person, capable of speaking in only one mode—and that a person asking for help is only capable of approaching the problem of allocating resources as he does when he is seeking assistance.

That is nonsense. When a person is asking for help, he is asking for help. He is not making a decision about the optimal allocation of resources. He is an advocate, his own advocate. He is not a judge, but that does not mean he is not capable of being one if that role were assigned to him. Professionals stand guilty of having structured a situation where the poor may speak only in one capacity—asking for help, acknowledging need and dependency. Having structured a process by which the poor may make demands on their resources, they then decry the irrationality of a system—their system which allocates resources by giving help to whoever comes in the door on a first-come, first-served basis.

Framed in economic terminology, the professional essentially is arguing that because the poor speak as consumers, they are incapable of making an allocation of resources between the production of consumer goods and long-range investments which promise to yield improved services, increased capacity, social reform, and an improved standard of living. So long as the poor are asked about the allocation of resources only in their capacity as consumers, they will respond "We want more consumer goods." People respond to the terms of the question put; none of us, asked what we would like to consume, would assume that we were, at this point, either allowed or expected to respond to an entirely different question: Do we think it is wise to consume at all from the point of view of the general good?

Yet the poor—as all of us acting in our capacity as citizens —are quite capable of sacrificing present consumption for capital formation and investment.

Until recently, there has been no attempt to create forums in which the poor have been asked to make decisions as composite human beings, as human beings who have something valid to say about the allocation of resources from the point of view of the entire community. Instead, they have been forced into the role of responding as selfish, dependent individuals. By confining the poor to speaking in that role, professionals purport to prove an incapacity to function responsibly in any other role.

Yet as a nation governed by a written Constitution, we should recognize that democracy, to function, requires the structuring of forums and institutions where important decisions can be reached by people perceiving themselves as deliberating issues of great weight and moment. We have created different forums and different modes of decision-making so that it will be more likely that people will approach an issue from the vantage point and in the role which is most likely to produce the necessary degree of considered deliberation. As an example, to amend the Constitution requires a more elaborate and lengthy process than to enact a piece of legislation. Similarly, certain administrative and policy decisions, executive orders and regulations are exempt from the lengthy and complex process of formal legislative enactment.

In brief, decisions of different fundamental weight and "irrevocability" require consideration in differently structured forums. To say this is not to undermine democracy, but rather to effectuate it—realizing that today's *democratic decision* can constitute tomorrow's *tyranny*—and the more firm the iron grip of the past is over the future, the more careful the consideration should be before such binding decisions are made. The issue becomes then not whether the citizenry can be trusted to make decisions—but rather, how can the decision-making process be structured so as to increase the likelihood that that decision will be reached in an appropriately deliberative, carefully considered, and rationally chosen fashion.

Between these two polar fallacies—the Genetic Fallacy and the Fallacy of the Monolithic Man—lies the great middle ground we must now explore. We ask then What does Citizen Participation mean—once freed of the compulsion to engage in some form of infinite regress; and equally disabused of the notion that citizens receiving assistance are thereby necessarily divested of their capacity to function as citizens?

## Part II.  The Values of Citizen Participation

Citizen participation is a nuisance. It is costly, it is time consuming, it is frustrating; but we cannot dispense with it for three fundamental reasons.

First, participation, in and of itself, constitutes affirmative activity—an exercise of the very initiative, the creativity, the self-reliance, the faith that specific programs such as education, job training, housing and urban renewal, health, consumer education, and others seek to instill. Participation is, in fact, the necessary concomitant of our faith in the dignity and worth of the individual. The denial of effective participation, including the opportunity to choose, to be heard, to discuss, to criticize, to protest, and to challenge decisions regarding the most fundamental conditions of existence is a denial of the individual's own worth and a confirmation of his impotency and subserviency. That message is read loud and clear. The exhortations—Stand on your own two feet; pull yourself up by the boot straps; become self-sufficient; you can do it—ring hollow when an official, by acting unilaterally, in effect officially states his lack of trust in the capacity, the instinctive reactions, the intelligence, and the sensitivity of the individual. In this context, protest must be viewed as a first affirmative step toward full citizenship for an electorate which before has spoken largely in the language of withdrawal and alienation—of crime, of violence, delinquency, and dependency—but which now seeks other, more positive forms of expression and involvement.

When a grown man is treated as a child, with respect to those very services being rendered him, he is unlikely to view those services as anything other than rituals of humiliation designed either to prove his incapacity to function or to keep him dependent and out of trouble.

Second, citizen participation, properly utilized, is a means of mobilizing the resources and energies of the poor—of converting the poor from passive consumers of the services of others into producers of those services. This can be a form of exploitation and manipulation—but it can equally be a way of subjecting demands of accreditation, testing, minimal educational requirements, to the test of performance. And we may find that we have unwittingly deprived ourselves of a vast manpower resource for the attainment of national goals by disfunctional and artificial barriers to participation and contribution. Citizen participation thus becomes a pressure toward mass production for mass consumption, an assault, so to speak, on the prevailing relationship between excellence and artificially induced scarcity.

Third, citizen participation constitutes a source of special insight, of information, of knowledge and experience which cannot be ignored by those concerned with whether their efforts are fulfilling their aims. Comprehensive action programs, devised by professionals and accepted by the dominant social, political, education, and economic institutions represent—from the empiricist's point of view—merely a consensus, a majority agreement on how to solve certain social problems. Citizen participation provides another and radically different perspective on those solutions—the consumer perspective, the perspective of the person who must live day to day with the end results of those efforts. We have paid in the past for failure to take into account this source of corrective knowledge concerning the defects, inequities, and false assumptions on which these programs are based. Token approval, acquiescence, and resignation eagerly have been equated with citizen participation. But in doing so, we as a society have deprived ourselves of the only form of validation yet devised for a majority consensus—critical scrutiny and dissent by those with a different perspective.

The need to avail ourselves systematically of the views of the consumer of these programs, of the intended beneficiary, to promote and provide for the articulation of their needs, concerns, and grievances, becomes all the more critical in the context of comprehensive planning where the commitment of resources is greater, the sources of dissent and criticism more readily muffled and ignored, and the scope of potential error increased many fold.

These are the three fundamental rationales for citizen participation:

1. The value of its acknowledgment and promotion of dignity and self-sufficiency;
2. The value of its by-product in the utilization of untapped manpower resources;
3. The value of the knowledge it affords: the criticism, corrective insight, and continuing validation of efforts which are at best informed hunches on how best to give content to broad national goals which can be attained only through the perilous process of trial and error, experimentation and assessment.

To these affirmative contributions, one negative or prophylactic function must be placed on citizen participation, one which makes clear that officials dispense with meaningful citizen participation at their peril.

The resources allotted to all programs are finite. And within the limitations of fiscal appropriations, priorities must be set, choices made, and desirable projects sacrificed. Officials bear the responsibility for making those choices, for setting those priorities, based upon research, documentation, and policy formulations. But while they bear the responsibility for making those choices, they do not have to bear the burden of living with those choices, of experiencing directly the consequences of those choices. Only the intended beneficiaries of those programs must live—directly, and ineluctably with scarcity—with the consequences of choices. People do not live happily with scarcity, with deprivations—but they reconcile themselves to those scarcities, those deprivations if they have had a say in choosing between X and Y, if the scarcity they live with is one of their own choosing. They may rail against those limitations, and in so doing free up other resources—but even when that is done, the total funds available are finite; choices must still be made—and people must live with those choices. Labor negotiations—the principle of collective bargaining, of union representation—is posited on the grounds that union members will settle for what they get, even though it is less than they want (and it always is), if they feel they have been fairly and adequately represented in a process where the terms of the contract are established by bargaining in good faith. The beneficiaries of social-services programs must also live with a contract which gives them less than they want—a social contract whose terms extend well beyond merely wages and hours and working conditions, whose terms comprehend the totality of opportunity, of education, of security and liberty and dignity for the individual and the group.

A willingness to abide by the terms of that contract will be founded upon whether those who negotiated that contract were viewed as genuine representatives who did their best and fought as best they could for the best terms they could get. Contracts negotiated by phony leaders, by sell-outs, by puppets, by Uncle Toms are not likely to be felt as mutually binding any more than union members are happy with company unions. We know what happens in the industrial order when people do not feel obliged to be bound by the terms of the contract. It is called a "wildcat" strike. In our major cities, we also see what happens when the terms of a social contract are imposed unilaterally and manipulatively—a wildcat strike not on the industrial order but on the entire social order. We call it a *riot*.

And citizen participation—real, genuine, meaningful, total —is probably the only guarantee, frail though it may be, that people will be willing to abide by the terms of today's social contract and have sufficient faith in the system to feel that it is in their best interest to wait for the next round of negotiations to press for still better terms within the framework of orderly dialogue and negotiation. Otherwise, the dialectic, the bargaining process shifts to the streets—and the barricades. And citizen participation takes on another and more sinister meaning: civil disorder. The participants term it *rebellion*.

## Part III. The Dimensions of Citizen Participation—in General

Recent efforts to implement the concept of citizen participation have taken two principal forms (though others, now emerging, will be noted subsequently).

The first has involved representation of the poor on boards of directors and advisory boards of local poverty programs. The second has taken the form of employment of members of the "group to be served" in the program. They are usually called indigenous workers, subprofessionals or nonprofessionals. (One Negro employee, asked which term he preferred, is reported to have answered: "I'd rather be white.")

Not only have the efforts been limited to these forms primarily—but more disturbingly, debate, discussion, and examination have been circumscribed by preoccupation with these two modes which at best are illustrative.

Democratic participation cannot be equated with mere representation on a board of directors, whatever the percentages involved. Nor can it be equated with efforts, of whatever scope, to provide for employment of impoverished citizens in new job categories.

Citizen participation does not mean the illusion of participation, the semblance of involvement, the opportunity to speak without being heard, the receipt of token benefits, or the enjoyment of stop-gap palliative measures. Participation means participation—in every dimension of life, of culture, or of our economy, our educational system, our political system, our decision-making processes. It means full enfranchisement with respect to the totality of society's activities.

And so, before attempting to make concrete recommendations for specific means to implement this general and indeed cosmic mandate, it would be well to step back and look at all the dimensions of participation—realizing that any single effort or set of efforts will necessarily fall short, but that they can at least be better designed if they begin—not from some piecemeal approach or gimmick—but from an appreciation of the many forms, aspects, and implications which participation actually entails for the more fortunate members of society.

We have chosen to approach the question of participation not in terms of specific models, single suggestions, or universal formats—but rather in terms of values and rights which attempts to implement participation should maximize. To us, seven dimensions of participation appear distinguishable. They are all obviously related, complementary, and to a certain extent, unavoidably overlapping. Yet we view each dimension, to the extent separable, as a distinct right, akin to those inalienable riches which stem from a commitment to the democratic credo. These include:

1. The right of effective speech
2. The right to be wrong
3. The right to be different
4. The right to influence decision making
5. The right to contribute
6. The right to consume—with dignity
7. The right to a continuing share in this society's burdens and benefits.

We present this overview because officials, in seeking to do all that they can, often lose sight of the totality of what needs doing, and so, in attempting to define what can be done, they begin constrained by a political awareness of what seems politically feasible, without checking to see how it relates to the total picture—and whether, in their preoccupation with today's slogans, battles, and frays, they have not overlooked certain possibilities and certain dimensions which lie outside the area of present debate and controversy and which can be effectuated pragmatically without being caught up in the rigid and often irrelevant terms of the ongoing political debate.

These dimensions are not only complementary; they are also necessarily overlapping in some degree. Nonetheless, we believe that something is gained by distinguishing these aspects of participation as individually distinctive. . . .

# Are the Poor Capable of
# Planning for Themselves?*

HAROLD C. EDELSTON and
FERNE K. KOLODNER

All the recent attention focused on "maximum feasible participation" of the poor in Federal programs designed for their benefit has failed to clarify the appropriate application of the principle to the planning of such programs. The performance of the major exponent of the principle, the Office of Economic Opportunity, has been particularly deficient in this regard. While professing that the concept extends to planning of programs as well as to their implementation, the OEO has produced in Washington major prepackaged programs which have apparently been conceived and planned by technicians alone. Furthermore, it has time and again set deadlines for the receipt in Washington of program proposals which afford no time in their preparation to hear from the groups to be served. Much of the blame must also be ascribed to Congress because of its hypocritical action on the Economic Opportunity Act, when amid its own clamor for more participation by the poor, it substantially reduced the potential for it by increasing the proportion of funds to be spent for designated programs at the expense of those to be locally conceived and planned.

These recriminations are in no way intended to detract from the substantial accomplishments in opening oppor-

* Reproduced by special permission of the authors. Delivered at the National Conference of Social Welfare, Dallas, Texas, May 1967.

tunities for the poor in functions other than the planning of programs. The literature abounds with testimony to the effective participation of the poor on policy-making boards, as staff members in newly created positions, and as activists in indigenous groups with social action goals. But this participation, for the most part, has come after the basic decisions on the nature of a program have been made in a prior planning process. Though participation on a policy-making body can influence the direction a program takes after its initial establishment, the fundamental purpose and administrative framework have already been established and maximum involvement of the poor cannot be claimed.

It was to afford such prior participation to the poor that the Community Action Agency (CAA) of Baltimore City, an agency of the city government, contracted with the Health and Welfare Council of the Baltimore Area to provide technical planning assistance to residents of the CAA's geographical jurisdiction, known as the "Action Area." The first assignment, which extended over a period of a year, generated the subject matter of this paper. It is conceded that a single experience cannot lay claim to an outcome which has broad implications for universal application. Nevertheless, this one has significance because of the issues it raised and the problems it evoked, few of which as yet have been accorded public cognizance by Federal officialdom. As will be demonstrated later, many of these issues and problems continue to be ignored by those Washington officials now setting administrative guidelines for citizen participation in new social planning programs authorized by recent Federal legislation.

The aforementioned planning experience was atypical with respect to the contractual arrangement between the CAA and the Health and Welfare Council (HWC). The elements of this relationship could in themselves constitute subject matter for a separate paper. But this aspect will not be treated herein. The administrative arrangement does not represent widespread practice, rendering any observation to be drawn from it of limited current interest. Consequently, an attempt has been made in dealing with the central theme of this article to exclude from consideration any variables attributable to the contractual relationship which might have affected the outcome.

The assignment given to the HWC stipulated that the latter would provide the techical planning assistance of its staff to Action Area residents who would be organized by the CAA staff to plan a "housing program." It is of particular significance that no mandate for the scope or content of the program was given; the assignment by the governing Commission of the CAA was completely open-ended. Whether the Commission would accept whatever end-product was presented to it was speculative; but it was clear that it was for the first time offering an opportunity to ghetto residents to design a program of their own choosing. It was further understood that the CAA would ultimately take responsibility for implementing the program.

To organize a representative group of Action Area residents, each of the 15 neighborhood centers then being operated by the Community Action Agency was asked to name two delegates to a planning committee. Though no formal ground rules were established, there was encouragement given to seek out individuals who had no prior history of community involvement so that the committee could be responsive to the unorganized residents of the area. No uniform election procedures were employed; representatives were selected by organized groups in those centers which had been organized, and were named by CAA staff in those which had not yet developed an internal organization. With only one exception, all residents among those so chosen undoubtedly could qualify as poor by OEO's economic criteria.

At least two-thirds of the committee members had no known prior history of active participation in community or neighborhood affairs and in only three instances was the prior participation of any significance. One of the three exceptions was a highly articulate leader of a militant civil rights organization

who dominated the early committee sessions but for some unknown reason later withdrew from active participation; his
withdrawal was followed almost immediately by participation
in the discussions by more of the heretofore inarticulate
members.

The committee elected its own officers, adopted the name
of Neighborhood Housing Action Committee (NHAC), and
decided upon its procedures.

The advisory role to be performed for NHAC by the HWC
staff member was intended to enable the committee to function in a self-determining manner but within the limits of its
planning purposes. The HWC staff person served as interpre-
ter of technical material, as liaison with established agencies,
as compiler of the program alternatives to be considered, and
as translator of committee ideas into technically acceptable
form.

The subject matter of the planning project could hardly
have been more technically difficult and politically volatile.
The housing programs of a deteriorated inner city like Baltimore's do not lend themselves to easy solution or any single
solution. Even to understand the intricacies of programs already available is no small feat for the layman. Yet the very
complexity of the problem has put to the hardest test possible
the feasibility of involving the poor in planning.

The objective at the outset was to facilitate a process in
which the residents could identify their housing needs as they
themselves perceived them, and select a program to meet these
needs from among all possible alternatives. An opportunity
was to be given to a representative group of the poor to enjoy
a decision-making experience which would presumably generate a high sense of commitment to the program among them
and their neighbors when it was implemented. A subsidiary
objective was to develop indigenous leadership among alienated persons to whom the experience would be unprecedented
in their own lives.

Though this experience is obviously not the first effort to involve the poor in planning, there is little evidence that the objectives ascribed to it have frequently been accomplished. From the sparse documentation which is available, as well as from personal observation, the conclusion seems reasonable that most involvement of the poor in planning has to date been relatively circumscribed. Examination of typical planning projects in which ghetto residents have allegedly been involved would probably reveal one or the other of the following processes:

(a) The poor are solicited for their perceptions of their needs. The method may be systematic survey research, not-so-systematic interviewing of selected individuals, or group discussions observed and recorded by a non-participant. The usual pattern does not include any decision making in which needs and problems are translated by the poor themselves into programs and solutions. It is the planning technician who makes the choices by exercising his judgment on which specific prescriptions are potentially the most effective solutions to the problems delineated.

(b) Another process, which may or may not be sequential to the foregoing, exposes the technician's choices to the review of citizens who at this point in time can only exercise a veto. Disapproval does not usually signify that the participating citizens perceive alternatives which are more desirable than the choices made by the technicians. Rejection more commonly represents a negative reaction to threats against immediate self-interest, such as the potential demolition of one's residence to make way for a public improvement; objection to proposed program auspices because of a negative personal experience, and so on. The objections raised do not usually lead to reconsideration of an entire plan, with the participating citizens enabled to make a different set of choices from among all possible alternatives. Instead, the more frequent result is mere modification of the original plans to meet expressed objections to particular details.

(c) A third process occurs when in the absence of any effective formal structure for citizen participation, planning technicians bow to the persuasion or threats of militant leaders of an inarticulate population. The influence may be exerted during visits by such leaders to the technicians' offices to make demands or to voice protests; or by the formers' statements in the public press. Often the response of technicians represents the effects of intimidation. The expressed or implied threats of public renunciation of the entire plan may be responsible for their decision, rather than the presentation of an alternative plan which the opponents have developed by a rational planning procedure. Furthermore, in such situations it is usually infeasible for the technicians to determine whether the representations being made by one or two activists reflect accurately the opinions and aspirations of the group which they claim to represent; assumptions that the poor have been heard from may be far from accurate.

All three of these processes fall short of meeting the objectives of the effort described herein; none represents a means of enabling poor people to select specific program components from among a variety of alternatives which they comprehend sufficiently to render their choices intelligent ones.

The objective for NHAC is not one to which all social planning authorities would subscribe. It repudiates, for example, a caveat offered by Roberta S. Sigel in a recently published article on citizen advisory committees:

"On some levels poor people can be utilized and should be utilized more fully—for the action, for implementation, and even perhaps for goal formulation. The least appropriate level is the one at which general goals have to be translated into technical and detailed blue-prints."[1]

Though the expectation that our effort could succeed might be considered naive, the professional staff involved had no illusions that the task would be an easy one. Nevertheless, there was conviction that there had been little opportunity heretofore to put to a test the thesis that poor people could have a role in planning which has more substance than merely defining needs or reacting to plans already formulated. Fur-thermore, we contend that their participation in planning is likely to be an empty gesture unless their role permits them to gain an understanding of what they are acting upon. Our ef-forts were initiated with the intention of determining whether poor people could be enabled to gain such understanding by participation in blue-printing a program. The major new ingredients were sufficient time and strong resolve.

The most obvious conclusion to be drawn from our expe-rience is that the road to reaching its stated objectives is strewn with practical obstacles. The first obstacle is the apathetic re-sponse of poor people to the opportunity to participate in an activity which, at least until the implementation stage is reached, is primarily an intellectual exercise in problem solv-ing. It raises the issue of whether the very attempt to promote their participation does not represent the imposition of the patronizing, paternalistic approach which the concept of "maximum feasible participation" is intended to eradicate. Our experience produced no evidence that the poor are con-sumed with desire to partake of planning. Prior claims by local civil rights leaders to the contrary were not borne out by the response to the efforts to organize a planning group repre-sentative of Action Area residents. The committee was organ-ized twice because of a declining interest among the original members whose apathy may have been due to a number of

[1] Sigel, Roberta S. Citizens Committees—Advice vs. Consent. *Trans-action,* *4* (6), May 1967; Washington University, St. Louis, Mo.

factors: lack of understanding of what the purpose of the committee was; disbelief in the sincerity of the sponsoring organizations; unwillingness to spend their time on an activity whose accomplishment at best was likely to be deferred to the indefinite future. Some original committee members were replaced, and the replacements functioned more actively not so much because they differed in any respect from the persons for whom they substituted, but rather because of the persistence of the HWC staff worker in urging and persuading them to attend meetings.

The problem is perhaps best illustrated by the recurring tendency of committee members to divert their efforts to immediate direct action on the housing problems which they identified in the first steps of the planning procedure. Even the name which they adopted, Neighborhood Housing *Action* Committee, is indicative of their initial orientation. Several times during the early deliberations suggestions were offered by members that the group organize a "rent strike" or a public demonstration to protest against current housing conditions. Rightly or wrongly, they were discouraged by the HWC staff advisor from such a course by her insistent reference to the purpose for which they had been convened. But intellectual comprehension of that purpose was lacking in all but a few among the group. The adventitious circumstance that the leadership was among the few who accepted the necessity for remaining on a planning course probably saved the day. Their willingness to defer direct action was conditioned by the understanding that direct action was not proscribed but merely deferred to the completion of a plan. If necessary to achieve implementation of that plan, a later resort to direct action of their own choosing would be possible and appropriate. The intervention of the worker, however, has raised the issue in some quarters as to whether the group actually was self-directed. Nevertheless, without such intervention, they would have diverted from their planning course, probably never to return again.

As the process is reviewed in retrospect, it becomes apparent that the content of the program plans produced by the Committee was determined to a great extent by the impatience of the participants and the consequent anxiety of their leaders and the staff advisor that interest could not be long sustained without some concrete achievement. Also responsible for the anxiety was fear that the end result would be rejected by the City Council, which would be called upon to provide the local share of funds; and by OEO, to which the plan would probably be directed. The result was encouragement by the staff that the group adopt program alternatives for which there were immediate funding possibilities and which could be realized immediately. Alternatives which would increase the supply of low-income housing were admittedly more basic solutions to the housing problem but less likely of immediate achievement. Consequently a program proposal resulted which provided services to make present housing accommodations more palatable. These services could be established relatively quickly and involved a minimum of technical complexities to defer tangible accomplishment. Even so, almost a year was required to produce a plan which planning technicians, unhampered by an unsophisticated group, might have produced in several weeks. We cannot candidly say that the group produced the best of all feasible plans. The important consideration, however, is whether their commitment to the plan which they produced does not compensate for its quality. The fact in this case is that the commitment was perhaps more intense than it should have been because it led to an unrealistic expectation of future results, as characterized by the chairman's statement, "If we can get this program, it's going to make our neighborhood a completely different place to live! People will start moving back in."

Another major obstacle proved to be the absence of a satisfactory relationship to the outside community, particularly to the agencies having a major impact in the housing field. The decision to abstain from extending invitations to outsiders was made by the group itself. They rejected repeated suggestions by the staff advisor that at least representatives of the major impact agencies be invited to attend some of their sessions. Their resistance to broadening the participation was clearly based on fear of domination by those who were more technically informed and articulate about housing matters. The group wanted an opportunity to educate themselves to the point where they could cope adequately with the vested interests. They felt that they needed to gain an understanding of program alternatives, which representatives of the housing establishment and middle-class persons already had or could acquire more quickly than they.

Though the homogeneous composition of the group violated the precepts for community organization practice to which the HWC staff ordinarily subscribes, there was valid reason for accepting intellectually the group's decision to remain non-representative. There was a realization that if two disparate levels of sophistication among participants were combined in one group, the poor would be left so far behind that they eventually would be unable to comprehend what was going on, rendering their participation meaningless. On the other hand, if the pace were geared to their slow learning rate, it would be difficult to maintain interest and participation of the others. These contentions seem to deny the many allegedly successful examples of involvement of the poor on governing boards, advisory bodies and the like which are broadly representative of the various economic and social strata. The writers' experience and the absence of reliable documentation on the processes involved leads them to disbelieve claims of effectiveness, especially when participation is by poor people for whom the experience is their first. When their participation is active on such representative bodies, we suspect that the poor are "representatives" of the poor, persons who may live in a designated ghetto and associate with their inarticulate and poor neighbors, but who have acquired a

sophistication in group participation which sets them apart.
They may or may not represent their neighbors, and in the
absence of any statutory election procedures, cannot be held
responsible if they don't. Thus the issue is whether meaningful
involvement in a group process can occur among the poor when
they are part of a more broadly composed group.

The unilateral planning procedure could also be justified
by the contention that the planning objectives did not pre-
clude the possibility of plans to bring about change in the
policies and practices of the housing agencies, property owners, and the rest of the establishment. To include representation of them on the committee might have been self-defeating
because of the opportunity it could afford to the vested interests for thwarting any plans to challenge the status quo.
Nevertheless, their omission creates obstructive conflict situations which have presumably led OEO itself to espouse broadly representative citizen committees for policy formulation.

One such situation confronted NHAC when there were
violent objections to the proposed housing program publicly
raised by groups who had felt rebuffed for being excluded
from the planning process. Implementation was substantially
delayed by these objections and at times it appeared that the
entire plan was in jeopardy. It turned out that the substance
of the plan had not generated the objections, but rather the
suspicions created by the "secret" deliberations of the group
which produced it. A dilemma is to be found in the paradox
that participation of the poor in planning is most meaningful
when they proceed alone at a pace which they themselves dictate, but meanwhile create a separation from the very groups
whose assistance may be needed in implementing their plans.
Repair of the separation was eventually sought in NHAC's
case by a strategy of informal interpretation by the staff member of why the unilateral process had been necessary. Fortunately in this instance it successfully overcame the earlier opposition of the public and private agencies whose willingness

to be reconciled may in some measure have been due to a desire to avoid being charged with opposing the poor. However, the property owners remained unpacified.

Another obstacle proved to be the self-serving tendencies of members of the group in decision making. A major motivating factor common to a number of the most vocal committee members was their own personal need for job-upgrading and their use of their participation in the planning process to achieve that end. The professional persons lending their support to the effort had proceeded in the faith that the group would act in the best interests of their peers, even if not necessarily in the best interests of the total community. That faith proved to be justified for the greater part of the process, in which the committee's approach was as objective as could be expected. The deviation from objectivity became apparent when program planning reached the point of defining the personnel provisions to be made in the proposed program. Pressures then arose from within the group to downgrade the educational and experience requirements of certain jobs. At the time the staff naively ascribed the phenomenon to a desire to create greater job opportunities for the low income population. But it later became apparent that certain members had personal motives, when they announced their candidacy for certain positions in which they had exhibited prior interest of a presumably impersonal nature. The potential damage to sound planning lay in the fact that it may have been for personal aggrandizement that certain members insisted on lowering the qualifications for certain positions, while professional staff were convinced that higher qualifications were needed to make the program work.

Some who have heard this story of a planning effort have charged that the participants were duped into believing they had freedom of choice, when in fact they were severely restricted. The restrictions, which are conceded, assumed several different forms. In the first place, there was the strong leadership exerted by the professional staff person assigned to provide "technical assistance." The staff person did not sit idly by merely to facilitate any decision of the group, but tried to exert influence to avoid unrealistic decisions and insure a successful result. She was being guided by a planning principle aptly expressed by Perlman and Jones:

". . . The question of what to do becomes a question of what can be done, for the choice of a policy for action must be realistic in the light of resistance to change that can be anticipated. The strategy to follow must be related to opportunities that are available in the real world of competing interests, if it is to be more than a Utopian dream."[2]

The opportunities available in this instance were the program options offered by Federal legislation. Though the staff worker several times discouraged certain courses of action that seemed impossible of accomplishment for the group, there was a sincere attempt to enable them to make choices from among promising alternative programs. Nevertheless, the available program options did impose restrictions and in this sense they were deprived of complete freedom of choice.

Another kind of restriction is inherent in the inability of the poor to comprehend theoretical formulations and to conceptualize well enough to gain a complete understanding of causative factors to which a program should be directed. The planning technician faces a communication barrier when he tries to provide help to them without seeming to be patronizing. When technical material is interpreted and translated into terms that they can understand, the process is exhaustingly time-consuming. The technical advisor can easily evoke the suspicion of the group if he pushes too hard through impatience with progress being made. In the writers' experience, for example, suspicion was aroused when the staff advisor handed out to NHAC a summarized version of the highly complex Federal Housing Act. This attempt to expedite the learning process was met with demands from the group that

[2] Perlman, Robert, & Jones, David. *Neighborhood Service Centers*. U.S. Dept. of Health, Education and Welfare, Office of Juvenile Delinquency and Youth Development. Washington, D.C., 1967.

they each be given a copy of the full act. The request was met, even though the staff worker knew few, if any, of the group would be able to understand the technical language of the legislation.

The inability of uneducated poor people to conceptualize and their tendency to individualize all problems cast doubt upon the likelihood that the process itself can produce innovative ideas. A careful analysis of the proceedings of NHAC would probably reveal few ideas which spontaneously arose from group discussions. All but one of the program ideas which were discussed were brought to the committee by the technician. Though some of the final program alternatives adopted by the group were modified through discussion from the form in which they were initially presented, their original conception did not arise spontaneously from within the group. Perhaps it is unrealistic to expect originality from such a group when citizen committees of middle-class sophisticates are not generally credited with creativity. However, it may be of greater importance to the objective of the process that the group adopt the ideas as their own, irrespective of their source. Such was the case with NHAC, for by the end of the process the members firmly believed that they had produced the program ideas. The very length of the process abetted this impression, because it was difficult over the course of so many sessions to remember who proposed what.

Fortunately, the story has a happy ending. The program was completed, accepted, and funded, but not without the necessity at a late stage to resort to direct action. Such action took the form of organizing a mass turnout of residents to attend a meeting of the City Council in support of the program, when it appeared that the City's legislative body was about to block implementation of the program proposal in response to pressure from organized "slumlords." Even the various news media were brought into the fray and responded with enthusiastic editorial support.

The major lesson to be learned is that meaningful participation of the poor in program planning requires substantial time and money. Neither has thus far been committed as a general policy of government at any level. Nor is there any evidence of intention to do so. The "demonstration cities" program, while calling for citizen participation which would include the poor, has established a time schedule for planning which guarantees that participation will be of the most perfunctory kind. The program began inauspiciously in this regard when less than three months was made available to cities for the filing of applications which represent basic prior planning decisions. Furthermore, the planning period to be allotted to successful applicants is far too short and the expected funding of planning activity far too niggardly to permit meaningful participation of poor people. Potentially explosive situations may be kept under control by involving on citizen advisory committees self-proclaimed representatives of the poor why may or may not in fact represent the unorganized poor, but who can offer a vent to the latters' frustrated emotions by means of periodic outbursts to oppose particular planning propositions.

The demand for action in all sectors of government militates against the kind of time-consuming process herein described. Congress voiced its impatience with the juvenile delinquency demonstration program because it took so much time for planning before any action was visible. The present national Administration itself has mouthed the desirability for sound local social planning by the poor but made it impossible to achieve by unrealistic administrative time deadlines. And the poor themselves have shown little disposition to divert their energies from coping with their own personal everyday problems to planning for alleviation of their community's ills.

In the face of such self-contradictions and obstacles, one might logically question whether such a planning process of the nature described here is necessary, feasible, or desirable. An ambivalence on the part of the writers may be detected throughout this presentation. But there is no wavering in our conviction that claims of involving the poor in planning are spurious when it is clear that the process has precluded an opportunity for them to comprehend what is happening. It seems to us that there are only two choices: either time, money and method must be available to facilitate a process which is more than perfunctory, or the pretense should be dropped altogether and program planning left to the technicians. Any course between is meaningless ritual.

# Community Status as a Dimension of Local Decision Making*

ROBERT L. CRAIN and
DONALD B. ROSENTHAL**

*We hypothesize that the higher the socioeconomic status of the population of a community, the greater the level of citizen participation in day-to-day community decision-making. The main effect of this seems to be to increase the power of the citizens vis-a-vis the local government and the elite; in turn, this leads to high levels of controversy, decentralization of decision-making power, and a tendency toward immobility on the part of the government. The relationship is curvilinear at the extreme upper end of the distribution; very high-status cities demonstrate a more tightly organized and more potent decision-making structure, similar to low-status cities. Data are used from national surveys of urban renewal, school desegregation, bond referenda, fluoridation controversies, political-party structures, Negro registration in*

* Reproduced by special permission from American Sociological Association as holder of the copyright, from *American Sociological Review,* Vol. 32, 1967, pp. 970-984.

** The authors wish to thank Amos Hawley and Donald Matthews for permitting secondary analysis of their data, and Bruce C. Straits and David H. Klassen for their able assistance.

*the South, election contests, and civil-rights movements.*

The study of community decision-making and city politics is at the present time a search for the basic relationships—the small number of correlations which are so large and so consistent as to be of prime consideration in any analysis. Thus, studies to date have concentrated on isolating the effects of such major factors as the impact of active and inactive civic elites,[1] of weak and strong party structures,[2] and of basic characteristics of the population.[3] In this paper, we advance one basic hypothesis dealing with the effect of the socioeconomic status of the population of the community upon the decision-making process.

## Community Socioeconomic Status

In the analysis of the political behavior if individuals, socio-economic status is an important variable; and it is hardly surprising that the average socioeconomic status of a community should be one of its most important characteristics. Given the differences in political values between

---

[1] The "power structure" literature is, of course, extensive. For a recent consideration of the polarization in American politics between the civil elite and the working-class (frequently ethnic) politicians, see David L. Westby, The Civic Sphere in the American City. *Social Forces, 45,* December 1966, pp. 161-169.

[2] Edward C. Banfield. *Political Influence.* New York: The Free Press of Glencoe, 1961; Edward C. Banfield and James Q. Wilson. *City Politics.* Cambridge: Harvard University Press and the M.I.T. Press, 1963; Charles R. Adrian. Some General Characteristics of Nonpartisan Elections. *American Political Science Review, 46,* September 1952, pp. 766-76. For our own consideration of this problem in the context of fluoridation outcomes, see Donald B. Rosenthal and Robert L. Crain, Structure and Values in Local Political Systems, in James Q. Wilson (Ed.) *City Politics and Public Policy,* (forthcoming).

[3] A summary of this literature and the development of a basis for distinguishing among local issues is available in Lewis A. Froman, An Analysis of Public Policies in Cities. *Journal of Politics, 29,* February 1967, pp. 94-108. The present analysis, however, runs somewhat contrary to the argument advanced by Froman.

higher- and lower-status persons, we might expect the distinguishing values held by local electorates to be the most important difference between high- and low-status communities. In contrast to low-status persons, we expect better educated and wealthier persons to endorse innovation and "progress," to be more liberal on civil-liberties issues, to be more "public-regarding" in their attitudes toward government, to support the development of "amenities" such as recreational or cultural facilities, and to favour "reform" in government.[4] These are important differences, but the evidence indicates that there is something more important about the high-status community which often produces a completely unexpected set of outcomes. Highly educated and higher-status citizens are more active in political roles and in their participation in politics,[5] and this has important consequences, regardless of what it is they want the government to do.

It seems to us that the "citizen"—persons who have no "special" political resources—influences government almost entirely through collective action. Thus, when we speak of citizen influence on government, we are thinking primarily of the action of organizations such as the PTA, the American Legion, neighborhood associations, fraternal societies, church groups, ethnic organizations, trade unions, amateur political clubs, and occupational associations, where the general membership does not have specialized political resources although individual members may. Among citizen-related groups, we are also including those *ad hoc* and informal groups organized to agitate concerning a particular decision. Thus, the county medical society is better thought of as an elite group, rather than a citizens' group because of the special status which flows

[4] Samuel A. Stouffer. *Communism, Conformity and Civil Liberties.* Garden City, N. Y.: Doubleday, 1955; S. M. Lipset. *Political Man.* Garden City, N.Y.: Doubleday, 1960; Banfield and Wilson, *op. cit.*

[5] Robert E. Lane. *Political Life,* Glencoe, Illinois: The Free Press, 1959, esp. pp. 220-34; Lester Milbrath. *Political Participation,* Chicago: Rand-McNally, 1965, pp. 114-128.

to the organization as a result of the expertise of those involved in it.

Well-educated persons, and high-status persons in general, are more interested in politics and better informed; they are more likely to hear about a new issue in local politics. They are also more likely to feel efficacious about their ability to influence decisions, and have the time, money, and skills to participate in an effort to influence those decisions.[6] Finally, they are more likely to be members of voluntary organizations which can play political roles. Furthermore, there is a multiplier effect; each person who becomes active in a voluntary organization is a resource who can be used to recruit others.

It follows that one major difference between high-status and low-status communities is the number of voluntary organizations, their size, and the number of people who can be mobilized in a campaign. We have only indirect evidence to support this proposition, but the point is nearly an obvious one. We suggest that this higher level of citizen participation in political activities, and in organizations which can become involved in local decision-making, has the following effects:

1. Opposition to the existing government and its policies is easier to mobilize. Granted, the middle-class electorate may have, on the whole, less to gripe about, but they can organize more effectively even around minor grievances.

2. Political campaigns will be more issue-oriented, since the organization of the middle-class community will often have special interests in particular issues, rather than reflecting generalized dissatisfactions; the groups will call attention to the issues, and also publicize the stands taken by the elected officials. If issues become more important, political leaders will be less able to depend on party or personal loyalty.

---

[6] Most measures of alienation find that working-class persons score more highly. This may be due to a variety of factors, but the relationship with feelings of inefficacy and estrangement are clear.

3. In all cities it seems likely that citizens' groups react to issues created by others, rather than introduce new issues of their own.[7] It is also easier to organize in opposition to a proposal than to organize in order to support it. The effect of these propositions is to create more opposition in middle-class cities to proposals advanced by the government (or by business or other groups) than in working-class communities.

4. Citizens who are interested and skilled in influencing government will apply pressures to break down the barriers which insulate the government from them; thus we would expect them to favor nonpartisanship, the referendum, and other "reform" measures.[8]

What are likely to be the effects of these processes upon the men in decision-making positions?

1. One main effect should be to make government officials more cautious, since they will be unable to predict how citizens will respond to anything that they do. They may often perceive the citizenry as more opposed to a particular program than it is in fact, since the opposition will be more easily organized.

2. It is likely that many politicians subscribe to the "what have you done for us lately?" theory; that issue-oriented voters are quicker to punish than to reward; if the public is more or less evenly divided on an issue, the politician will lose votes no matter which side he takes. This leads to additional pressures to remain neutral or to prevent issues from arising.

3. Elected officials will wish to conform to the values of citizen participation by holding public meetings, listening

[7] We would hypothesize that middle-class communities are more readily structured to encourage bureaucratic professionals to initiate policy than are working-class communities. The result would be the kind of policy initiation base discussed by Banfield, in his *Political Influence, op. cit.*

[8] Froman, *op. cit.*

attentively to petitioners, and permitting decisions to be made by referenda.

4. Since party loyalty is weaker, elected officials will themselves be less concerned with party loyalty; they are more likely to go to the mass media, or to publicize their position when it wins them votes, thereby increasing public discussion and controversy.

5. If an issue does arise and become controversial, the pressures on elected officials to remain neutral will increase; hence a controversial issue is more likely to result in nothing being done.

Taken together, this adds up to the following statement of relationship: Middle-class cities will have a less stable government, will be less willing to embark on controversial programs, and when they do attempt to innovate, there will be higher levels of community debate and hence higher levels of controversy and a greater possibility of stalemate. In contrast, in low-status cities, citizens are less readily able to mobilize to influence the decision-making process; this may result in either government by a traditional political machine, or in a government heavily influenced by the local economic elite; but in any case there should be less controversy, and few programs, once begun, will be sidetracked. The data to be presented below support this interpretation, but with one important deviation: the argument does not apply to the cities with the very highest level of education. We shall consider that problem after we have examined the data.

There is some support in the literature for the present viewpoint.[9] Amos Hawley advances essentially the same argument when he says that high-status cities have more difficulty implementing urban renewal plans because power is more decentralized.[10] Many of these points are related to

[9] Banfield and Wilson touch on this theme repeatedly in their works. In addition to *Political Influence* and *City Politics*, see James Q. Wilson, *The Amateur Democrat*. Chicago: University of Chicago Press, 1962.

[10] Amos H. Hawley. Community Power and Urban Renewal Success. *American Journal of Sociology, 68,* January 1963, pp. 422-431.

those advanced by Berelson, when he argues that apathy and seemingly blind party loyalty are functional for political stability.[11] Gusfield, in his critique of pluralist theories of democracy, points out the ways in which citizens' associations may serve to increase conflict and political extremism.[12] This does not mean that the mass society theory, as advanced by Kornhauser,[13] is directly in disagreement with our position; there is no disagreement with the proposition that unorganized mass participation can lend itself to extremism, but only concerning whether a large number of strong voluntary citizens' groups actually insulate the government and the voters from each other, as Kornhauser's pluralistic society model proposes.

In addition, David Greenstone and Paul Peterson find, in their current study of the poverty program in the four largest cities of the United States, that the weaker the political party organization, the slower the city is in obtaining federal funds; this supports our idea that such cities are likely to be "inefficient" in their decision-making process.[14]

## Urban Renewal

It seems clear that the "establishment" benefits from urban renewal. Businessmen concerned with saving the central business district, city fathers trying to keep the property tax base up, and developers looking for sites, all profit in obvious ways; both the elected public official and the government administrator are provided with a chance to demonstrate their ability in a highly visible way. Given the possible ways

[11] Bernard R. Berelson, Paul F. Lazarsfeld, and William N. McPhee. *Voting*. Chicago: University of Chicago Press, 1954.

[12] Joseph R. Gusfield, Mass. Society and Extremist Politics. *American Sociological Review*, 27, February 1962, pp. 19-30.

[13] William Kornhauser. *The Politics of Mass Society*. Glencoe, Illinois: The Free Press, 1957.

[14] J. David Greenstone and Paul Peterson. Reformers, Machines and the War on Poverty. In Wilson (Ed.) *City Politics and Public Policy*, (forthcoming).

that a city can provide matching funds, it also seems clear that, for many cities, the costs of an urban-renewal project can be nearly zero. It is harder to say who pays for all the benefits, other than the person who pays federal income tax; but certainly the slum dweller and the owner of a home in a conservation area may think he is coming out on the short end. In the low-status city, the government and various elites will be able to arrive at an acceptable program and push it through; but in the high-status city, we argue that citizens' groups will be organized—some to protest the dangers of integration, others to complain about the failure to allow for Negro relocation, still others to prevent demolition of their own neighborhood, and others to complain about creeping socialism. The government program will be in danger of sinking under the weight of controversy.

Amos Hawley has already made this argument, saying that high socioeconomic status implies a decentralization of power. Since his presentation of data has been criticized, it is worthwhile presenting his data in a slightly different way.[15] The problem raised involves the possibility of a spurious correlation; high-status cities probably have less need for urban renewal, since a high-status population is probably living in better housing. Since the Census of Housing does not provide a perfect indicator of need for urban renewal, it is difficult to decide whether the association between community status and urban renewal "success" is casual or spurious.

The data are based upon 763 cities, all over 15,000 in population, and all in states which had enabling legislature for urban renewal during the period of study. Educational attainment is measured by the percentage of the population with four years of college, grouped into five categories. Of the 763 cities, 308 officially entered the urban renewal program. However, by 1962 (when these data were gathered), only

[15] Hawley, op. cit.; Bruce C. Sraits, Community Adoption and Implementation of Urban Renewal. *American Journal of Sociology, 71,* July 1965, pp. 77-82.

62 percent of the 308 had completed their first urban renewal project; and 42 cities (14 percent) had withdrawn from the program. In terms of our argument (and Hawley's), these "dropout" cities are important, since it is here that the impact of community opposition was apparently most successful. However, it is also true that the inability of a city to complete its first urban renewal project by 1962 suggests some impediment in the decision-making process, and finally, some cities faced with citizen opposition may have chosen not to enter the program at all. Thus, all three indicators—entry, completion, and dropout—can be used as tests of our hypothesis.

As expected, well-educated cities are less likely to become involved in urban renewal; $y$ (entry, education) $= -.16$. Obviously, this could be because cities with well-educated populations simply have fewer slums or decaying business areas requiring renewal. Therefore, in order to test this alternative hypothesis, the size of the city and the age of its housing are introduced as "control" variables. Size of city reflects not only the opportunity to have slums, since there is more space, but also the presence of a city administration large enough to handle the task of submitting a proposal. Older and larger cities are more likely to have entered the program: $y$ (entry, housing age) $= +.32$; $y$ (entry, size) $= +0.58$. Thus, "educational attainment" might simply be a reflection of a factor like age of housing. However, when size and age of housing are used as controls,[16] the association between educational attainment and the probability of entering the urban-renewal program decreases only very slightly: $y$ (entry, education; size, housing age) $= -.15$. Thus, we argue that if education were merely a measure of *need* for urban renewal the partial association, when we control for another measure of need such as age of housing, would necessarily decrease more than it has in this case. We conclude that education measures not need, but ability to act.

[16] The partial gamma is computed by taking the weighted average of the $y$'s in the subtables, using the total number of cases as the weight in each case.

There are two other even more convincing approaches. First, if education is only a measure of need, it will have its most decisive impact on whether the city enters the program or not, not on what happens after that. To have entered the program at all asserts a need. But the data disagree; high education is more strongly associated with dropping out of the program, or with failing to complete the first project by 1962 than it is with entrance. The simple gammas are only $y$ (dropout, education) $= +0.07$ and $y$ (completion, education) $= -0.16$, but when we again enter size and age of housing as controls, the partial associations increase and are higher than the association with entrance to the program: $y$ (dropout, education; size, housing age) $= +0.21$, and $y$ (completion, education; size, housing age) $= -0.24$, both higher than $y$ (entry, education; size, housing age).

If, on the other hand, we read education as a measure of the degree of decision-making inefficiency and uncertainty introduced by citizen participation, then the associations behave approximately as expected, at least when size and age are controlled; the well-educated city shows some hesitancy in entering the program, but it is most different from other cities when the time comes to work out the details of a concrete proposal. Citizen participation in the planning process means more opposition, more issues to be negotiated with more people, more chance of failure.

## School Boards and School Desegregation in the North

In 1964 and 1965, graduate students were assigned the task of interviewing elites in eight northern cities and preparing case studies of the school desegregation issue.[17] With only eight case studies, and with only a limited amount of "hard" data, the material must be considered impressionistic at best. However, it seems to lend support to our argument, and, more

[17] The present section is based on a study reported in Robert L. Crain, *The Politics of School Desegregation*, (forthcoming).

important, it gives us some indication of the nature of the mechanism which links socioeconomic status to styles of decision-making. After a series of staff discussions, agreement was reached on a ranking of the eight cities in terms of three variables:

*Acquiescence* is the extent to which the school system met the demands of the civil rights movement, both symbolic and "real": the acquiesent school board was one which committed itself verbally to integration, treated the civil rights leaders with relatively little antagonism, and also adopted an integration program which numerically increased the number of students in integrated schools.

*School Board Cohesiveness* is the extent of agreement and cooperation among board members; it is based upon our knowledge of the public controversies, and upon the individual board member's response to sociometric questions, and his rating of how much agreement there is among the board members.

*Strength of Political Parties* is a measure of the ability of the parties' leadership to control party nominations for office; again it is measured impressionistically.

Why should cities with high-status populations be less likely to have school boards which acquiesce to the civil rights movement? Figure 1 presents the argument schematically. First, high-status cities tend to have weak political parties. (This rank correlation is −0.77; although it may be exaggerated because of the poor quality of our measure of party strength, the association is strong.) The city with weak political parties has a school board which is generally more heterogeneous in social background than that in a low-status city. The argument is simply that a weak political party deprives the government of freedom from public opinion—which may take the form of demanding ethnic representation, or anti-integration appointments, and which may change from one year to the next. Granted, a government which is insulated from the voters may use its freedom to appoint party hacks, but it may also

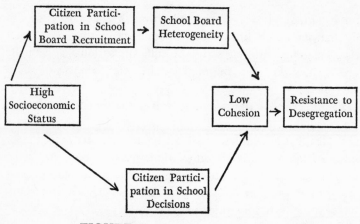

FIGURE 1.

Schematic Presentation of Relation of Community Socioeconomic Status to Outcome of School Desegregation Issues in Northern Cities

appoint civic leaders; whichever it does, it will at least appoint a homogeneous board whose members can work together. Thus the presence of weak political parties is associated with low levels of school board cohesion, although again, the rank-order correlation, $+ 0.90$, is likely to be exaggerated. In addition, a high-status and participative public encourages intra-board conflict, since there is a ready audience for the ambitious board member and a following available for any member who wishes to rebel. The correlation between socioeconomic status of the city and board cohesion is $-0.74$, but there is no association between the socioeconomic status of the city and the status of the school board.

To make the final link in the chain of causation, cohesive boards are much more acquiescent than boards with internal dissension. The main reason for this seems to be that the cohesive board can thrash out disagreement in the backroom rather than in public, and thus can avoid mobilizing the anti-integrationists. The cohesive board can ignore the wishes of the public. Granted it is possible for an extremely conservative but cohesive board to refuse to acquiesce, but it would be rare indeed for a school board to be more conservative than the average white citizen; all of the school boards studied were more liberal than whites in general, on comparable questionnaire items.[18] Although school board members' attitudes are more important than board cohesion in determining acquiescence, cohesion is strongly correlated with acquiescence: $r = +.71$. The least acquiescent boards have had histories of severe conflict on other issues and close votes on the appointment of superintendents.

## The Civil Rights Movement

The school desegregation study also collected information on the civil rights movement in each city. The civil rights movement is a special case of the mobilization of citizens to influence government. Our principal hypothesis is that the higher the status of the population, the more easily mobilized it is. This should result in a larger number of civil rights organizations, and more civil rights activity.

In general, the greater the competition between groups and individuals in the movement, the more militant the leadership—a completely unsurprising finding. The greatest competition seems to be in the two cities which have traditional political machines; the conflict is of course between the "establishment" and the direct action groups. If these two cities are excluded, a correlation ($r=0.61$) appears between the socioeconomic status of the Negro population and militancy, in the remaining six cities, apparently because of the higher level of competition between civil rights groups and leaders in the high-status cities. The high-status cities also have civil rights movements which are more symbol-oriented, and more

[18] For example, 91 percent of the school board members disagreed with the statement, "White people have the right to keep Negroes out of their neighborhood if they want to, and Negroes should respect that right," compared to only 43 percent of the national population. The last figure is from Donald J. Treiman, Status Discrepancy and Prejudice. *American Journal of Sociology, 69,* May 1966, pp. 651-64.

concerned with city-wide issues; this is consistent with our image of the high-status community as one which is more responsive to ideological appeals, and which is more easily mobilized in support of vague or abstract "public-regarding" goals. In the South, data were gathered on only six cities, and the differences between such cities as Montgomery, Alabama, and Miami, Florida, are so extreme as to make comparison difficult. However, it is true that high-status southern Negro communities tend to have more highly organized civil rights movements, more competition, a higher level of civil rights activity, and more ambitious goals—a pattern which is consistent with the northern data.

## Falling Between Two Stools

Whether a compromise is a happy medium or whether it falls between two stools, folk wisdom warns us that many relationships are curvilinear. The data to be presented in the remainder of this paper are consistent with those presented earlier, except that in almost every case there is a reversal at the extreme upper tail of the distribution. Can we argue that if we only increase the educational level and the level of citizen participation enough, it will at some point begin to strengthen the structure of government, rather than continue to make it more unstable and susceptible to public opinion? We think so, although the argument is not an obvious one.

Both William Kornhauser and James S. Coleman have argued that citizen participation in voluntary associations brings stability to government, and prevents rancorous conflict.[19] We would modify that proposition to read that citizen participation at a *high and stable level* in formal associations has this effect, while moderate and irregular participation has the unstabilizing consequence described in the earlier section of this paper. We further argue that a high and stable level of participation occurs in only very highly-educated communities.

[19] James S. Coleman. *Community Conflict*. Glencoe, Illinois: The Free Press, 1957.

Consider, for example, Rossi and Dentler's description of Hyde Park in Chicago, or William Whyte's description of Park Forest as examples of extremely high levels of education.[20] Citizen participation in these communities is very high—so high, in fact, that organizations which in other communities might have highly fluctuating memberships and a doubtful future at any time will be able to operate in a more permanent fashion. In addition, the number of organizations in the community should be greater. We think this has three important implications:

1. Channels of contact between the citizens and the government are regularized. Continued contact over a period of time between stable groups and the government tends to produce an accommodation between them: political leaders find it easy to check political actions out in advance with representatives of these groups, and the opportunity for negotiation and compromise is greater. Over a period of time, the general point of view, or values, of government officials will be closer to that of the population as a result of this contact.[21]

2. The response of the public will be predictable. The main reason for this is that, when a problem comes up, particular organizations already exist to take positions (few issues will require new organizations, although they may encourage the formation of groups representing coalitions between pre-existing groups); since groups are reasonably permanent, they have an established and relatively stable leadership and a partially articulated ideology which will determine their response. There are other reasons, as

[20] Peter H. Rossi, & Robert A. Dentler. *The Politics of Urban Renewal.* N. Y.: The Free Press of Glencoe, 1962; William S. Whyte. *The Organization Man.* N. Y.: Simon and Schuster, 1956.

[21] To some extent, this argument may appear to run counter to the view of those who suggest that issues each have their individual spheres of action and individual actors. However, we are merely indicating that, while arenas may or may not differ, participation across-the-board by the public is more important in high-status communities.

follows: (a) Since much of the population is already participating in local political organizations, there is less possibility of a revolt led by people who are relatively inactive in the community. Borrowing Kornhauser's and Coleman's words, the ratio of unattached but "available" people to those already attached is probably lower in very high status cities. It is more difficult to subvert existing organizations, and also harder to form new ones, since there are fewer organizational vacuums to fill. (b) The leadership is more stable, since it is more highly developed, has more permanent bases of support, and is generally better known in the community. (c) The existing organizations can be used to exert influence, and even discipline, on their own members and on the rest of the community; its leadership will have more political experience, and more skills in developing support for their position. (d) It is assumed in these communities that the position of the citizenry is known. People take it for granted that their city is liberal, pro-education, and anti-urban renewal. In fact a random sample of the population may not find much support for this conventional wisdom, but, if the participation level of the community has been high for a long period of time, it is likely that battles between opposing groups have been fought "to a finish" already, and the issue assumed settled.[22] (e) Existing organizations can be used by the government to communicate and exert influence on the citizens.

[22] At least in the few really high-status "participative" communities of the kind we are discussing here, it is likely that issues have not so much been suppressed as that the important parameters of the system have been regularly tested and that no elements capable of changing it have entered that system to cause its general reorientation. At lower levels of organization and education, problems of issue suppression described by Bachrach and Baratz, or Agger, Goldrich and Swanson, might arise. Peter Bachrach and Morton S. Baratz. Two Faces of Power. *American Political Science Review,* 56, December 1962, pp. 947-952; Robert E. Agger, Daniel Goldrich, and Bert E. Swanson. *The Rulers and the Ruled.* N. Y.: John Wiley, 1964.

None of these points is very original; several have been stated in different form by either Coleman or Kornhauser. Our point of departure from their argument is that these conditions hold only when the population is *highly mobilized*. If many people in the community are willing to participate, but there are not enough to maintain a rather complete set of permanent and stable organizations, then not all these conditions will hold. Instead, when a new issue comes up, an existing organization may find its membership suddenly becoming more active and new leaders coming forth; the ideological position of the group may be subject to change. Or a new group may be organized, making its claim to be the group to specialize in a particular area, and previously unknown persons may become important leaders. Furthermore it is more likely in these cities that the government will be out of touch with the population to a greater extent, and less able to use the structure of voluntary associations to develop support for its proposals. Of course, at the other extreme, the government of a very low-status community may take positions which are at variance with the population values but, if the community lacks the resources to organize in opposition, the government need not pay much attention.[23]

## Fluoridation Controversies

Fluoridation—the addition of small amounts of fluoride to the public drinking water to reduce tooth decay among children—is a good test of our thesis.[24] Almost universally endorsed by the medical profession, with the strong support of the federal government, and with few local government officials actually opposed to it, fluoridation has still had an

[23] This argument has ramifications for other levels of political systems as well, if we accept the general proposition that greater citizen participation and political differentiation results in unstable or conflict-prone political life.

[24] For a full report of that study see Robert L. Crain, Elihu Katz, and Donald B. Rosenthal. *The Politics of Community Conflict*. Indianapolis: Bobbs-Merrill, 1967.

unfortunate history of controversy and defeat. Apparently it is the sort of program which is expendable if there is public opposition.

TABLE 1.

Decisions on Fluoridation by Community Educational Level*

| | Median Educational Level | | | | |
| Decisions | 8 years or less | 9 years | 10 years | 11 years | 12 years or more |
|---|---|---|---|---|---|
| Percent of cities adopting fluoridation without referenda | 41 | 39 | 37 | 22 | 29 |
| (N) | (63) | (99) | (100) | (66) | (66) |
| Of all other cities, percent holding referenda | 29 | 26 | 38 | 46 | 32 |
| (N) | (37) | (60) | (73) | (51) | (47) |
| Percent of cities with mayors publicly supporting fluoridation | 61 | 64 | 57 | 45 | 57 |
| (N) | (63) | (88) | (95) | (61) | (52) |

* All data indirectly standardized (Stouffer's method)[25] by region.

The data were gathered by a mail survey of public health officers, city clerks, and newspaper publishers in 1,086 American cities of over 10,000 population. The health officers, when asked, almost never said that public officials declined to support fluoridation because of their uncertainty about its medical effects; they did claim that unfavorable officials were concerned about public opposition. This, then, is a good test of the influence of public opinion on the government. National surveys have shown that well-educated persons are considerably more favorable to fluoridation than persons with low levels of education; our theory was developed because we found that the correlation for communities runs exactly

[25] Samuel A. Stouffer. Standardization of Rates when Specific Rates are Unknown. In A. J. Jaffe (ed.), *Handbook of Statistical Methods for Demographers*, pp. 65-70.

counter to this, as shown in Table 1. In general, high-status cities are less likely to adopt fluoridation, and more likely to hold a referendum on the issue—except for the extreme upper group, which is more likely to adopt and less likely to hold a referendum. The data are standardized indirectly, to remove the differences between the four regions of the country—the South, East, Midwest, and West. Observe that, since the percentage of cities holding referenda is based only upon non-adopting cities, it is statistically independent of the adoption rate; thus the data represent two independent findings. The last line of the table indicates that the proportion of mayors favoring fluoridation follows the same curve, mayors becoming less favorable as education increases until we reach the top group. This should not be read as independent evidence, however, since the mayor's position is very strongly associated with the outcome.

## TABLE 2.
### Community Educational Level and Opposition Activity in Fluoridation Decisions

| | Educational Level | | | | | |
| | Referenda Campaigns | | | Governmental Decisions | | |
| | 9 years | | 11 years | 9 years | | 11 years |
| Opposition Activity | or less | 10 years | or more | or less | 10 years | or more |
|---|---|---|---|---|---|---|
| Percent of cities with opposition literature | 68 | 86 | 92 | 39 | 47 | 54 |
| (N) | (40) | (36) | (52) | (179) | (111) | (124) |
| Percent of cities with opposition speakers (of all cities with meetings) | 77 | 87 | 94 | 67 | 68 | 77 |
| (N) | (35) | (31) | (47) | (109) | (69) | (90) |
| Percent of cities with imported opposition speakers (of all cities with opposition speakers) | 56 | 56 | 71 | 55 | 62 | 64 |
| (N) | (27) | (27) | (44) | (73) | (47) | (69) |

We have some data to clarify the mechanism which translates high educational attainment into defeats for fluoridation. In Table 2, we see one reason why well-educated cities have more difficulty with fluoridation; they simply have more opposition. The data are based upon the reports of the health officer; the limited number of cases means that we cannot separate out the extreme upper tail in this table or the next one. Since the antifluoridation movement uses a national (indeed, international) network of spokesmen, the use of imported talent is a measure of the sophistication of the opposition, just as is the use of printed literature and of public speakers.

Not only are well-educated cities more likely to have opposition, the government is more responsive to the opposi-

TABLE 3.
Community Educational Level, Opposition Activity, and Fluoridation Outcome*

| | Percent of Cities Adopting Administratively | | |
| | Educational Level | | |
| Opposition Activity | 9 years or less | 10-11 years | 12 years or more |
|---|---|---|---|
| High | 23 | 19 | 17 |
| (N) | (70) | (109) | (44) |
| Low | 37 | 36 | 38 |
| (N) | (110) | (100) | (22) |
| Difference | −14 | −17 | −21 |

| | Percent of Cities Holding Referenda | | |
| | Educational Level | | |
| Opposition Activity | 9 years or less | 10-11 years | 12 years or more |
|---|---|---|---|
| High | 17 | 23 | 24 |
| (N) | (70) | (109) | (44) |
| Low | 11 | 10 | 6 |
| (N) | (110) | (100) | (22) |
| Difference | +8 | +13 | +18 |

* Data standardized by region.

tion. The three indicators of level of opposition in Table 2 are combined in Table 3 into a single dichotomy, and the effect of opposition in cities of varying levels of education is examined. Whether one considers the prevention of administrative adoption, or the precipitation of a referendum, opposition had its greatest impact in high-status cities, as reflected in the percentage differences in the last line of each half of the table. Thus, the data indicate that high-status cities have more citizen influence, are more responsive to that influence, and, in the case of fluoridation, the effect is strong enough to overcome the fact that high-status cities have populations which were initially more favorable to adoption.

TABLE 4.

Community Educational Level and Referenda Results*

| | Median Education | | | | |
|---|---|---|---|---|---|
| Referenda Results | 8 years or less | 9 years | 10 years | 11 years | 12 years or more |
| Percent of school board referenda receiving less than 60% "yes" vote | 62 | 44 | 54 | 50 | 45 |
| (N) | (32) | (26) | (45) | (29) | (30) |
| Percent of other bond referenda receiving less than 60% "yes" vote | 48 | 53 | 57 | 56 | 46 |
| (N) | (47) | (46) | (65) | (58) | (64) |
| Percent of fluoridation referenda resulting in defeat | 71 | 78 | 76 | 83 | 56 |
| (N) | (34) | (53) | (67) | (52) | (53) |

* Data standardized by region.

*Referenda Outcomes.* The theory of the impact of level of education can be extended to include referenda outcome as well. First, if fluoridation referenda are typical of all referenda, a referendum held after a political campaign is not simply a public opinion poll; the positions taken by govern-

ment officials and by various organizations are important to
the outcome. In addition, we would argue that the typical
voter responds to high levels of noise from his fellow citizens
in much the same way that the government official does—
namely, by becoming confused and hesitant to support something "controversial." The hypothesis was tested on three
types of referenda, as reported by city clerks in the fluoridation study; fluoridation votes, votes on school bonds or taxes,
and votes on the last other referendum for public improvements. As Table 4 indicates, the school bond results do not
fit the theory; they simply show that well-educated cities are
slightly more likely to support the schools. The other two
types of referenda do conform, with the very low- and very
high-status cities most likely to vote "yes."

## The Structure of Local Politics

Generally speaking, the high-status city is more likely to have
a "reformed" government with a city manager and with greater use of referenda, as shown in Table 5.[26] High-status cities
are also less likely to use the now unfashionable commission
form of government. However, if the high-status city has retained the mayor-council form, it is not more likely to have
non-partisan council elections. High-status cities also hold
more referenda. Again the data have been standardized to
remove the effect of region. We are more interested, however,
in the informal structure of government; here the curvilinear
relation reappears. In the fluoridation survey, the local newspaper publisher was asked, "How influential are political
parties in the elections for city council and mayor?" Looking
first at partisan mayor-council cities we see that the publisher
is more likely to rate the parties as "not too influential" or
"not influential at all" in well-educated cities, again with a
reversal when we move past a median of 11 years of schooling.
When we look at manager and nonpartisan mayor-council

[26] These data are from the *Municipal Year Book*. Chicago: International
City Manager's Association (Annual), for the cities in the fluoridation study.

TABLE 5.

Community Educational Level and Political Structure

| | Educational Level | | | | |
|---|---|---|---|---|---|
| Political Structure | 8 years or less | 9 years | 10 years | 11 years | 12 years or more |
| Percent of cities with city manager government* | 30 | 43 | 46 | 59 | 55 |
| (N) | (229) | (259) | (259) | (166) | (174) |
| Percent of cities using commission governments* | 20 | 14 | 14 | 13 | 12 |
| (N) | (229) | (259) | (259) | (166) | (174) |
| Percent of mayor-council cities with non-partisan elections* | 41 | 44 | 25 | 49 | 36 |
| (N) | (113) | (120) | (110) | (58) | (50) |
| Percent of cities holding a referendum in past 12 years* | 44 | 49 | 47 | 54 | 54 |
| (N) | (129) | (136) | (159) | (104) | (112) |
| Of cities holding referenda, percent who held 6 or more in 12 years* | 37 | 33 | 47 | 55 | 57 |
| (N) | (53) | (64) | (74) | (58) | (62) |
| Percent of partisan mayor-council cities with "weak" parties | 14 | 32 | 58 | 67 | 50 |
| (N) | (22) | (22) | (31) | (9) | (8) |
| Percent of manager and non-partisan mayor-council cities with "weak" parties | 53 | 44 | 67 | 67 | 60 |
| (N) | (36) | (43) | (60) | (48) | (60) |
| Percent of cities with uncontested mayoralty elections* | 19 | 16 | 13 | 16 | 29 |
| (N) | (72) | (71) | (76) | (45) | (49) |
| Percent of cities with 3 or more candidates in last mayoralty election* | 12 | 15 | 27 | 29 | 19 |
| (N) | (72) | (71) | (76) | (45) | (49) |

* Data standardized by region.

cities as a second test, we see exactly the same pattern. In the next two rows we see that, as education increases, the number of uncontested mayoralty elections declines, again with a reversal at the end, and the number of elections with three or more candidates for mayor increases, again reversing at the end. Thus we have at least four bits of evidence that cities with moderately high levels of education are the ones with the weakest and most open and fluid political structures. Why? We think it is another corollary of the general theory.

We noted at the beginning of the paper that the well-educated population should show more attention to issues, less party loyalty, more support for reform and for direct democracy. So far, so good. But why should very high-status cities have strong parties, uncontested elections, and the absence of third party candidates? Looking again at our earlier discussion of the effect of very high levels of education and citizen participation, we see that several of the points made there would lead us to predict a greater structuring of politics in these cities. Political parties can be stronger because they have greater volunteer resources, because the leadership is better known, and because the leadership has a denser network of organizational affiliations to work through. There is also less danger of the party producing the sort of completely unacceptable candidate whose presence weakens party loyalty. And opposition may be suppressed because an organizational monolith has captured the available contributors and volunteer workers, or has permitted the incumbent to build a strong following. One case comes immediately to mind: the ward surrounding the University of Chicago was the only one of fifty in Chicago where the incumbent alderman was unopposed in 1967—despite the considerable heterogeneity of the area, which includes low-income Negroes and wealthy whites as well as University faculty and students. The incumbent alderman, whose base has been the local precinct organization affiliated with Americans for Democratic Action, was formally endorsed by both the Republican and Democratic parties, despite the fact that the incumbent is highly controversial, and is the white alderman of a ward which has a very large Negro population. In this case it seems reasonable that the willingness of the middle-class residents to participate at a very high level in amateur politics—and their loyalty to the independent party—has resulted in the growth of the functional equivalent of a political machine, has made it possible for the incumbent to be very well known in his ward, and has created a political climate which in another time or place might be called oppressively conformist.

## Negro Registration in Southern Counties

The next case is possibly the most difficult one to argue. One assumes that the governments of Southern counties are strongly opposed to the registration of Negroes. But if this is so, one must inquire why there are Negroes registered in the South at all? If some counties have been quite successful in disenfranchising the Negro despite the federal government, why have others not been as fortunate? When we consider the problem, it becomes clear that there are reasons why a local government might not resist a Negro registration drive: it may need Democratic votes; it may need to gain the support of Negro elites; it may believe the Negro vote to be deliverable in local elections; it may find resistance simply more trouble than it is worth. Whatever the case in any particular county, it does seem clear that if a prospective Negro registrant were given his choice of submitting his application to the local registrar of voters, or to a referendum vote by his already enfranchised fellow citizens, he would surely choose to take his chances with the former. If, then, the citizens are more strongly opposed than the government to Negro registration, we predict, consistently with the other material presented, that the higher the educational level of the whites in the county, the more reluctant the government will be to permit Negro registration. This curious generalization is precisely the finding of Matthews and Prothro. We cannot improve very much on their explanation of the finding: "The higher the average education of the whites in a county, the more actively and effectively they seem to enforce the traditional mores of the region against Negro participation in elections. An increase in average schooling for whites in the South seems to give them more of the skills they need to effectively express their antiNegro sentiment."[27] They go on to note that white citizens' councils are more common in counties with higher levels of education, as an example of this. We have reexamined their data, and have standardized them to remove the interstate variation in Negro registration rates; this does not affect the pattern. (See Table 6.) Note that one-half of the cases fall in the lowest-education group, which has the highest registration rate; above this point the curve is flat at the lower level. The data presented by Matthews and Prothro show that the counties with highest education have a slightly higher registration rate, but this finding disappears when state differences are removed by standardization.

TABLE 6.

Educational Attainment of White Population and Political Characteristics of Southern Counties*

| Political Characteristics | Median Years of Schooling of Whites | | | | |
| | 8 years or less | 9 years | 10 years | 11 years | 12 years or more |
|---|---|---|---|---|---|
| Percent of Negroes registered to vote | 34 | 27 | 28 | 28 | 28 |
| Percent of counties with segregationist organization | 15 | 27 | 30 | 34 | 38 |
| Percent of counties with racial violence reported | 6 | 8 | 18 | 23 | 40 |
| Mean percent of votes for Strom Thurmond for President, 1948 | 23 | 27 | 28 | 29 | 23 |
| (N) | (520) | (275) | (123) | (57) | (23) |

* Data standardized by region.

[27] Donald R. Matthews and James W. Prothro. *Negroes and the New Southern Politics.* N. Y.: Harcourt, Brace and World, 1966. P. 128.

Matthews and Prothro noted that segregationist organizations are more common in high-status counties; even when the data are standardized, this effect remains quite pronounced. This is as predicted by our argument, of course. More surprising, however, is the fact that incidents of racial violence are reported much more frequently from highly educated cities. The sources for these data are the *New York Times,* the *Southern Educational Reporting Service,* and the Southern Regional Council. It is possible that there is considerable over-reporting of incidents in high-status communities, but the relationship is so strong that we have included it despite our qualms about journalistic sources. Again we argue that high levels of literacy, willingness to participate in community affairs, and organizational skill make it easier to mobilize the human resources necessary to throw rocks at school children, or burn a cross. At a minimum, a sufficiently dense network of association to permit like-minded persons to organize informally for social support would seem to be a necessity.

In the last row of this table we see another curvilinear relationship, although not a very strong one: the lowest and highest educated counties gave the fewest votes to Strom Thurmond's States' Rights candidacy. Our argument is simply that in these counties social control mechanisms to maintain loyalty to the national parties were most successful. It is in the moderately well-educated counties that the candidate who best represented the values of the citizenry was most successful.

## Two Alternative Explanations

These data seem to lend little support to the most obvious alternative explanation—that the differences in the behavior of communities of differing status levels lie in the differences in the values of the residents, with the governments of middle-class cities doing "middle-class" things, while working-class cities produce working-class government outcomes. In the

case of fluoridation, Negro voter registration, school desegregation, and probably urban renewal and bonds for municipal improvements, the correlation at the community level
is the opposite of that at the individual level. The data strongly suggest that the community is a good deal more than the
sum of its parts.

What about the reversal which sometimes occurs at the
high end of the educational scale? It could be argued that, in
the case of fluoridation, for example, the greater support for
fluoridation among especially well-educated persons is sufficient to overcome the debilitating effects of high levels of
citizen participation. But in the case of party structure, we
see no way in which the reversal at the high end of the scale
could be attributed to the values of well-educated people;
certainly, we see no reason why well-educated people should
disapprove of three-way mayoralty races, or approve of uncontested elections and strong political parties.

A more difficult objection to deal with is the point that
the cities at both extremes are more homogeneous, and ac-
cordingly similar to each other and different from cities in
the middle. The argument might go as follows: heterogeneity
causes dissension and conflict, and conflict tends to make it
difficult for the government to act. The hypothesis seems
quite reasonable on its face—although no more so than the
one we have advanced—but there are two problems. First,
how do we explain the ability of city governments to act
contrary to the wishes of a homogeneous public, for example,
in registering voters in the poorest counties of the South?
Second, we could determine at which median educational
level the population is most heterogeneous in education only
if we assume that education is a metric scale measuring social
status—that the difference between five and six years of schooling is as important as the difference between 12 and 13 years.
Without this assumption, there is no obvious argument which
would establish that cities with a median educational level

of eight years are in fact more homogeneous in social status than a city with a median of 11 years.

The one important exception to our argument is Minar's[28] findings, and our own, regarding conflict over schools. Recall that we found that well-educated communities are more likely to approve school bonds. David Minar studied a group of Chicago suburbs, and found not only more favorable votes on school bond and tax referenda, but less competition in school board elections in the higher status suburbs. No doubt there are issues which are exceptions to our hypothesis, although we are disappointed that school board selection should be one of them. However, Minar's data are limited to a group of suburban school systems near Chicago: it may be that many of them are in the upper end of the ecucational distribution where the "reversal" might be in effect. At this time, we can only report that there is at least one apparent exception to our hypothesis.

## Conclusions

If examples of the ecological fallacy (the inability to generalize from group data to individuals) are difficult to find, examples of what we might call the contextual fallacy (the inability to predict group action from the characteristics of individuals) are apparently common.

We have examined eight different community issues and found twenty-two cases which support our hypothesis that a city with a well-educated population is partly immobilized by high levels of citizen participation which prevent the government from exercising the authority to make decisions. In addition, we have found in ten of these cases a reversal at the high end of the educational distribution, where, we argue, the educational level is high enough to permit a decision-

[28] David W. Minar. The Community Basis of Conflict in School System Politics. *American Sociological Review*. 31, December 1966, pp. 822-834.

making process in which citizens play structured, consistent and predictable roles.

No doubt there are certain issues in which the effect is different from the one shown here. We do not make any prediction, for example, about noncontroversial decisions, and some educational decisions may not follow the pattern of the issues presented here.

It should be observed that this paper only seems to give support to the idea that citizen participation is "bad." Granted the "intelligentsia" would conclude, on many of the issues described here, that citizen participation has had unfortunate results—damaging children's teeth and preventing racial equality, for example. But there are no doubt other issues in which widespread citizen participation leads to "good" results. The only value-oriented conclusion one can legitimately draw from these data is a mere tautology: If public officials are going to do the right thing, the people should leave them alone while they do it.

# How Much Neighborhood Control?*

Editor's note: *The following dialogue followed statements before the Subcommittee on Urban Affairs by Frederick Gutheim, consultant on urban affairs, Washington, D. C.; James Heilbrun, professor of economics, Columbia University; and Milton Kotler, resident fellow, Institute for Policy Studies, Washington, D. C. Senator William Proxmire, member of the subcommittee, presided at the session.*

Senator PROXMIRE. What you are saying is that you would like to give the residents of the poor community the authority to determine their own ordinances and to some extent their own laws, and in doing so wouldn't you then be making even smaller communities, within a community which so many people say is too fragmented now?

You would seem to be in direct conflict with Mr. Heilbrun, and Mr. Gutheim, and others, who have said what we need is a broader metropolitan government rather than one that is fragmented into smaller units.

Mr. KOTLER. I am in some agreement with Mr. Gutheim.

Mr. GUTHEIM. We need both, really.

Mr. KOTLER. I am giving the locality more weight. The reason for having face-to-face units of authority is not mere sociological nicety. It is what man's political nature requires.

* From Hearings before the Subcommittee on Urban Affairs of the Joint Economic Committee, Congree of the United States. 90th Congress, 1st Session—Sept. 27, 28, and Oct. 2, 3, and 4, 1967.

Further, there is great power today in locality. It must be legitimated by local authority.

Of course, this may frighten business and capital. Imagine, that they could be restricted by the local authority of a poor neighborhood! At some point, however, the neighborhoods of poverty require new forms of economic organization to fit their social conditions. I am sure we could live with a mixed economy.

Senator PROXMIRE. Are you talking about political or economic organization, or both?

Mr. KOTLER. There are many new possibilities, I suppose. I don't know what these new economic forms are, but local people would invent them if they had authority. They may be neighborhood corporation businesses, owned and operated by the neighborhood authority, either publicly or privately chartered.

I am not certain what kind of local economy will emerge. But, I am sure people with authority will invent new economic forms, that would be different from our familiar pattern of local business.

Senator PROXMIRE. Would that aggravate the kind of situation that has been described by Mr. Heilbrun, when he pointed out the central city is losing the people with better incomes who are moving away from the central city and attracting the people with lower incomes?

One of the reasons for this is because they don't have the opportunity to have a countywide, or metropolitanwide taxing unit.

Now, if you are going to fragment it even more narrowly and provide that the inner core of the central city is going to have its own community, its own antiusury laws, its own taxing power and so forth, aren't you going to make it that much worse?

Who is going to stay in there along with the poor?

Mr. KOTLER. I am not, by any means, advocating neighborhood separation. I do recognize the need for a larger city tax base and metropolitan organization for certain things. I merely emphasize the political importance of the neighborhood as a local unit of self-governing authority. This is quite in accord with the absorption of the suburbs into a metropolitan authority. There is agreement there, but let us give some recognition and attention to the political issue about which people are today warring; namely, local control.

And by the way, I would like some liberty, too. I live in Washington and have no political liberty, only a so-called mayor.

Senator PROXMIRE. It is not liberty. You don't have authority. You don't have any way of translating your desires and your needs into effective political action in Washington because we don't have an elected government.

Mr. KOTLER. I have never made a binding public decision in my life, except to say that once every four years I get into a booth to pull a lever. That is not public decision. That is not legal authority. That is a private and rather absurd act, which I do not expect to perform again. [Laughter.]

When Jefferson spoke of the word republic, he realized that you cannot have representation without democracy; namely, without local assembly that has authority over something, be it the trees on the public streets.

Senator PROXMIRE: I think all of us would agree with the sentiment of what you are saying, but it is a matter of defining the kind of areas where this is possible, and where it would be acceptable, perhaps, to the Congress and to the city government and to the State, and fighting for as much as you can get, by giving the people who live in these communities as much authority and dignity as you can give them, and at the same time providing the overall authority necessary to achieve the kind of thing Mr. Heilbrun is talking about.

Mr. KOTLER. Let's take the Model Cities Act.

It contains a very regressive feature. Unlike earlier Federal housing programs under which the Secretary of HUD could give grants to local nonprofit organizations—if they got the mayor's approval, the Model Cities Act contains no authority for this local funding relationship. The Secretary can only give money to the city public agency.

Now, that is a regressive feature. We are precisely moving our legislation away from doing the politically necessary thing. I think it would be very good to amend that act to permit the Secretary to fund neighborhood corporations as structures of citizen involvement in the model cities program.

Of course, there is a neighborhood corporation bill which is before your committee, Senator. Senator Ribicoff's bill S. 1433, would amend the Model Cities Act to provide for this decentralization of authority.

But currently we are moving to more and more centralization. As a result, you get Detroit—beautifully coordinated cities without any contact between the people and government. It is an error to think of coordination as the problem of fitting agencies together in a neat pattern. The coordination is between the people and government. This can only be done by the delegation of authority to neighborhood locality.

Senator PROXMIRE. You are an expert in this area of riots. Do you feel that this enigma that puzzles so many people, of a Detroit, which has done so much, and has seemed to have a very progressive nongovernmental organization, inasmuch as the UAW is the dominant union, and it is the union that has done more for civil rights, than any other union in the history of our country—at least in a big way.

Detroit had so many things going for it, and yet they had the riot.

Is this because these programs moved ahead in a way that left the people in the poor areas feeling that they had nothing to see about it, no control over it, no influence, didn't count?

Mr. KOTLER. There are two basic questions that our nation has to struggle with. First, is our economic organization able to get the 30 million poor into the flow of money, which has been holding this country together? Second, is money enough or do people need liberty?

Our inadequate antipoverty money does not get down to the people. I am familiar enough with poverty programs to conclude that their latent function of advancing new careers for the professional class prevails over their manifest aim to bring the poor into the economy. The reason for this is that structurally there is no room in the economy for them. Even if there were, I am not sure they wouldn't riot, too.

We have a 19th century notion which plagued every developed country: Can you possibly hold together a nation by economic organization? This is the dubious assumption of capitalism and communism. They merely differ on their strategies of economic control. The assumption is the same. If we can get everyone into a job, we do not need political liberty to bind a nation. We can merely control people by the manipulation of wages.

This worked for a while. As local government, the foundation of liberty, was being destroyed by our State governments. Well, now, we have a problem. For 30 million people there is no room in the economic system. As a matter of fact, there is no room for a lot of whites. Capital is becoming autonomous. Its technology is destroying the labor value of man and consequently more people are thrown out of the wage system.

What then, is to socially control them?

Today, we are trying desperately to squeeze them back into the economy, through manpower training programs. Frankly, this is nice, but certainly no political solution, let alone economically feasible. Although you can get one guy into a job, the political problem is, What are the rest doing? Waiting? Unless you get whole classes at a time into jobs, you face the fact of their political formation.

So, we have a problem now. The whole notion of controlling a nation by wages is being challenged by the dialectics of capital, which is displacing human labor value. We may have to turn to an older notion of binding a State in peace; namely, the proper distribution and arrangement of authority, or binding a State by political constitution rather than economic organization. We must give existing social powers the authority to make laws which they require for survival and advancement, and harmonize this arrangement in government, thereby harmonizing the society.

We must have local government because today urban locality is a major formation of social power. Witness the riots. We must give to those communities, which have no adequate economy, some kind of legal authority to build a viable economy. I am not an economist, but a political scientist. The beauty of legal authority, properly arranged, is that it publicly establishes man's creative and constructive solutions to survival and prosperity. That is the importance of political liberty and its local foundation.

Senator PROXMIRE. Mr. Heilbrun?

Mr. HEILBRUN. Mr. Kotler has stuck his neck out, which I think helps to further the dialogue here, and he raises questions which we can all discuss.

I avoided that by not endorsing any specific proposals.

Senator PROXMIRE. You said we need a redistribution of income in which the poor can share, in a sense, and yet you can't get it now, and you endorse shifting a greater level of financial responsibility to counties, States, and so forth.

Mr. HEILBRUN. Right. But I would like to come back to the issues which Mr. Kotler raises, because they are very fascinating ones.

In a sense I agree with him, but in another sense I do not, which, I think, is the same feeling that the chairman has. You can't be against participatory democracy. It is like being against motherhood, and I think anyone who lives in a large city—and I live in New York—is very much aware of the terrible problem of lack of communication between the central administration of the city and the people in the neighborhood. It is a very serious problem.

In New York we have a monolithic educational system which employs something like 55,000 teachers, and it is all run from one central office somewhere, where they have I don't know how many thousand central bureaucrats operating the system, and the neighborhoods, until very recently, had nothing whatever to say about how this thing worked.

I think we are all properly distressed by this overcentralization and this lack of communication or, more properly, of participation, at the neighborhood level.

The question that comes to my mind is, What kind of activities can—both usefully and feasibly—be decentralized? And, I have to admit that my initial reaction to most proposals of decentralization is that they would involve maintaining the central administration as it now is and creating another layer of bureaucracy underneath somewhere, which really wouldn't lead to the result that you want.

Nevertheless, I think Mr. Kotler is right, that we have to find some way of decentralizing some functions of government to the neighborhood level, but I question whether it can be anything as sweeping as he seems to suggest, because the ghetto areas are truly impoverished, and if you threw them on their own resources, they would have nothing.

They don't stand to gain by autonomy. They may stand to gain by having their local authorities subsidized from the outside, but that raises all kinds of other political questions.

Mr. KOTLER. Everyone else is subsidized. We are not talking about their own resources and their local secession from the city or nation. They don't want that either.

Mr. HEILBRUN. But then he raised the question on what conditions and terms they could get money from the higher levels of government. I don't think it is possible in a practical sense to conceive of neighborhoods going on in one direction in social policy, while the State of New York or the State of

Illinois is heading in another, because the State simply won't subsidize these efforts that seem to contradict the direction in which social policy has been determined by the majority, and you have to remember that the ghettos are a very, very small minority in the State or National Population.

They are only large in the central city, and even in the central city they are far from a majority in most cases. There may be some exceptions to that.

So, I think that we have to find those functions that can be centralized, and try to work experimentally toward decentralizing them.

Maybe education is one such function, but even there you have problems, because if you have neighborhood self-determination in the educational system, you invite segregation.

Public policy favoring segregation may involve moving students around from school district to school district.

But with neighborhood autonomy, you cannot have that.

There are a lot of conflicting end values here, and it is difficult to decide what is the best set of policies.

There are some functions of government which you certainly cannot decentralize. For example, smog control is something that has to be done not just on a city basis, but on a regional basis.

Garbage collection is another example. There is no reason why a neighborhood should want to control that, because the scale of operation that is necessary for an efficient system simply precludes any local autonomy, so it seems to me the practical way to go at this is to find those functions that can be handled on the local level and try to work toward that, but not to raise the hope of creating truly autonomous neighborhood governments, because I think that that is retrogressive in the larger sense.

I think you mentioned somewhere in your paper, Mr. Kotler, that you recognize the fact that society is increasingly organized on a horizontal scale that is nationwide.

For example, as an economist, I am in touch with economists in all parts of the country. I probably am in closer touch with the economists, let us say, in California, than I am with the physicists in my own university, whom I hardly ever see or speak to.

The same thing goes on throughout society. There are these horizontal layers of communication, which have been made possible by modern communication and transportation and the whole of society is organized on that scale.

This is not a new theory; it has been put forth by sociologists, like Scott Greer.

The locality for most people has less and less real meaning—

Senator PROXMIRE. What are the groups and the people within the ghetto communities who can identify with the people outside of it?

Mr. HEILBRUN. That is the problem that Mr. Kotler recognizes, you see.

Senator PROXMIRE. Maybe there are some social workers that do so. Perhaps you have some people who organize just on the basis of fighting for civil liberties and civil rights, as we have in the city of Milwaukee right now.

Mr. HEILBRUN. Mr. Kotler recognizes that the poor in the ghettos are not part of this national system of intercommunication. They are isolated, they are powerless, and they are not receiving the sense of participation or belonging which even the middle-class citizen in this country now has, and the question is, what can you do about it?

Well, he is proposing to give them a sense of political participation, but—

Mr. KOTLER. Also power. You know, there is nothing like 15,000 city votes held together by neighborhood self-governing authority to get some resources from the city, the State, and the Federal Government.

Senator PROXMIRE. May I interrupt you, or did you want to make another point?

Mr. HEILBRUN. I think the alternative attack, and I think the attack which most people would endorse as being, you know, just the ordinary way that we hope to go about these things in this country, is to incorporate the poor eventually into the national system by, as Mr. Kotler says, taking them one by one and training them for jobs which will not disappear by the day after tomorrow.

Now, that is an extremely difficult task, and I recognize, I think, as well as anybody, that it is necessary to organize the energy of the people in the ghetto to help themselves. It can't be done from the outside. They have to take action on their own to find their way into this system, with whatever help they can be given, and so I do not want to come down too heavily against what Mr. Kotler is saying, because I recognize that his proposal is really part of the same philosophy that endorses stimulation for self-help and self-determination, but I do question whether it can be done on as grand a scale as he seems to be suggesting, which is really to make a political revolution that runs counter to the whole sociological tendency, not just of the last few years, but of the last 400 years, or more.

Senator PROXMIRE. I know Mr. Kotler is anxious to get in, but I want to get Mr. Gutheim into it, and I would like, if possible, for you to come in on this angle:

You say the problem is not simply one of very poor people living in ghettos—that is part of it, and a very important part, and a dramatic part, but it is not the only important part.

There are many other people living in the metropolitan areas whose problems are increasing and perhaps it is going to get worse as time goes on, and as I recall your paper, you emphasized a kind of mindless lack of planning and direction and understanding which we have in our cities, just a tendency to grow like Topsy and grow very badly for that reason.

That is one of the points you make that I think is most helpful, and I wonder if there is anything the Federal Government can do by way of encouraging the development of planning and initiative.

You say that few, if any, of the cities have a great university, which by itself can provide a great deal of the assistance in defining goals, and providing understanding and perhaps organizing those who want to work to develop the city. As you put it:

Few metropolitan regions, for example, contain a great university that has accepted any significant measure of commitment to the solution of its urban problems.

What can we do to encourage this? And I would like to have the other gentlemen comment on this.

Mr. GUTHEIM. Perhaps I could give a little foreground to this.

Senator PROXMIRE. I just happened to settle on that, because that seems to me the immediate thing we could do in some of our cities. There may be other things we can do.

Mr. GUTHEIM. I am very glad you recalled that sentence, Senator, because I do think this is a problem of ideas and one that can be illuminated not only by research and by the accumulation of data, but by some fairly sustained thinking about it, and this is what I would think a university might be expected to undertake.

It is certainly something that cities are not undertaking now, and I think I spoke somewhere about the shortcomings of urban bureaucracies in terms of being able to deal with the kinds of questions that we are considering here.

I would like to provide a little foreground for this question by saying that in the last paragraph of my paper in the compendium, I tried to recognize that we needed the means to deal with the large metropolitan areawide systems, such as transportation, that are not only impossible to deal with in bits and pieces of the metropolitan mosaic, but which are also fundamental to overcoming many of the problems of the neighborhood, of the problems of isolation, for example, the separation of people living in city ghettos from the growing number of jobs that are found out on the periphery. You have to have something that deals in a more unified and effective way with the problem of the metropolis as a whole.

But you also have to have what we have been talking about here, the smaller grassroots democratic unit in which there may not be much power, but there certainly can be political recognition, and political influence, and in which there can be a response to these kinds of questions.

I am not so sure that they are all that economic, in terms of jobs, although I believe that is still the most fundamental thing. There is the poverty of affluence, of course, and there are many people that are not happy about the kind of life they have to live in city ghettos, who are not necessarily poor, who are not particularly unemployed.

It is the relationship between these two things that fascinates me. When I think of the problems that you referred to, of smog and garbage collection and so forth, while they are metropolitan problems, they fall unequally on various parts of the metropolitan area.

If there were a neighborhood government in Anacostia, the Kenilworth dump would have been closed down much earlier. In Watts, for example, the isolation of the city because of the deficient public transportation—

Senator PROXMIRE. Let me interrupt at this point and say that I think this is one of the reasons that it is important for a particular city to have a university, or an intellectual group, or planners who can zero in on that city's problem.

If we try to do it in Washington, we can miss the mark badly. We can't set the priorities for all the cities at once and do it wisely here.

If, on the other hand, we can provide some kind of stimulation, incentive, and support for a group that can do it in each city, it seems to me it might be a very wise investment for them to define goals and priorities for that particular city and area.

As you say, in Watts, for example, isolation and lack of

transportation is very vital. Perhaps this is of less importance in New York.

Mr. GUTHEIM. Or Detroit, the home of the automobile. I think if I had a few thousand dollars to experiment with, it might be useful to spend it in conducting a constitutional convention in one of the neighborhoods Mr. Kotler is concerned with.

Something like that, I think, would tend to put more pieces of this problem together than we see now in the single shot, "Give transportation to Watts," for example, or recognize some kind of voice for a neighborhood that simply allows it to blow off steam and express itself.

Senator PROXMIRE. If you are going to try to cope with the kinds of problems Mr. Kotler is suggesting, it seems to me you have to have some people who can plan, think, look ahead, examine, get into the area and ask the right questions, and then have the prestige to work with the city, the county, the State, to persuade them to go ahead with this kind of thing and grant this kind of opportunity for the people living in the area.

Mr. GUTHEIM. The people we are talking about are on one side of the street, and the brains are on the other.

Mr. KOTLER. I object to that statement. The brains are where?

Mr. GUTHEIM. On the university side.

Mr. KOTLER. That is why we have riots and rebellions? On what basis do you feel the brains are in the university? Biologically, there are brains all over the place. It is a highly prejudicial statement. I am shocked.

Mr. GUTHEIM. I said "brains," not "intelligence." Let's say that the people living in ghettos have found no way to express themselves effectively in terms of ideas, facts—

Mr. KOTLER. Excuse me. I don't wish to be ill-mannered, but how do you imagine that poor people without jobs have been able to survive unless they had brains?

The fact that they have expressed no neighborhood public

policy, though I think they have, may have something to do with the fact that there is no public authority in the neighborhood.

Senator PROXMIRE. Would you disagree, Mr. Kotler, with a notion that a great deal of the training and disciplines that have been achieved at the university can be useful and helpful?

I am not talking about—and I am sure Mr. Gutheim isn't either—certainly any moral superiority.

Mr. GUTHEIM. Biological superiority.

Senator PROXMIRE. But that there are people with techniques which can be helpful to the poor community in developing its own degree of self-government and developing its own opportunity to express its will.

Mr. KOTLER. Provided the university people work under contract from the neighborhood authority. They must be legally responsible to the community, if they are ever to be professionally responsible. Isn't that why people want to hire their own doctors and lawyers?

The communities want the professional help. They know they need skills. They want to hire technical ability. Or will we give that authority to the professionals, the so-called brains, to go in and experiment with communities to their own delight? Gentlemen, that cannot be done anymore without further warfare. I don't know what black community you can get into on that privileged basis.

Senator PROXMIRE. Well, unless we do something like this you are not suggesting anything that has very much chance of making progress. Unless you begin to get the skills in here somehow, and unless you provide a framework—

Mr. KOTLER. The minute you give authority, and I mean some kind of authority to govern something, to a neighborhood, and resources, the first thing that neighborhood assembly will do is invite and hire professionals to come in and tell them how to do things. They will listen, and weigh that advice.

That is the first thing that will happen.

Mr. GUTHEIM. Has this been done somewhere?

Mr. KOTLER. Well, you know, there are a lot of neighborhood corporations going on now and all have professionals in staff positions. I helped start the East Columbus Community Organization (ECCO) Corp. a few years ago. They have professionals on their staff, hired by the people. Since then we find, on the basis of partial returns of a survey, neighborhood corporations in some 30 cities with varying degrees of delegated authority over public programs.

This is a good development. It has a natural process of Federal programs accommodating to the political realities of local power. Congress can do more to affirm this process by passing legislation to help form more neighborhood corporations as well as amend existing community development legislation to fund neighborhood corporations as well as public agencies.

We are seeking an urban federalism.

Senator PROXMIRE. That is fine. I don't see any objection to that, but I do think there is great validity to the point made by Mr. Gutheim that it would be good to develop great universities, or have great universities—after all, every State has universities which have a great deal of competence—and to get them involved with the plan and a program for the entire metropolitan community, including the ghetto areas.

Mr. KOTLER. Let's take an old-fashioned case. Isn't the healing and curing power of a doctor stronger if a patient has the right to hire him? Isn't it stronger that way than when a doctor is a stranger and commands him to be cured?

All we want to know is this: On what basis does expertise relate to the community? I say if it relates to them through contract, under the authority of the community, it can do so much more. It is welcome. It is invited. Its power of expert purpose is so much greater.

Senator PROXMIRE. I do not see any necessary conflict here. You have to have both.

Mr. KOTLER. Let's face the fact. Much money in the poverty program is given out in contracts to universities in technical assistance.

Senator PROXMIRE. But, one difficulty here, Mr. Kotler, is that you are looking at this almost entirely from the standpoint of ghetto poverty. This is important, and all of us, in our hearts, feel it is the problem we would like to solve quickly, because the injustice is so clear, and it is on our consciences, but it is not the only problem, and the great university cannot only work in this area, but in other areas.

I don't want to put too much emphasis on this university concept. There are brains in our corporations and businesses that can be organized in this kind of area, too. It has got to be done through the city government, or the Governor's office—heaven knows.

What I am trying to say is that somehow we have to bring this technological competence, and by that I am talking, not just about engineering, but I am talking about in the area of training, education, and all kinds of areas, bring that to bear with the greatest possible force in the whole community.

In the ghetto you do have an understandable problem of human respect and dignity and intelligence. These people want to have a great deal to say about it, and they should have, but at the same time, it would seem to me you are obscuring the total problem if you focus totally on the notion that first you have to ask these people what they want, let them work on their own constitutional convention, and then call on expertise which is somehow going to be available.

Don't you have to have a total program that looks at the total program of the metropolitan area? Won't you solve your poverty problem best if you do it that way?

Mr. KOTLER. It is fine to have an overall view. All I am saying is that we must start these neighborhood authorities, too. We must give them some public authority. And that cannot wait for a total picture of what we should transfer and what we shouldn't.

As for pollution, remember nuisance law. There was an old-fashioned law to handle smog through nuisance law. But that was killed a while back. Localities can no longer restrict property from destroying their natural environment. Most national problems are in fact local—and only national by definition. Air pollution is something that shoots up from a chimney and falls down in the neighborhood. These national problems have local existence.

It is amazing how people have common sense in handling these problems. In ECCO, one of the first self-determined programs was a veterinary program. That seemed foolish. But, why did they want it? The reason was that there were lots of rats, and lots of dogs and cats to get the rats. They got rabies and you cannot afford shots for $10. So, you give shots to all the animals, and you have a public health program to prevent rats and rabies.

So, there is a community intelligence that knows how, practically, to meet certain problems. It can be informed and perfected by expert advice, you know, under contract.

Mr. GUTHEIM. You are really talking about what problems, what powers, what funds and resources might appropriately be given to these neighborhood organizations, and I think those questions are important to decide.

I think they are important to be clearer about than we are probably going to be this morning.

We have probably had enough experience now in these neighborhood corporations to begin to add it up and to analyze it and to make some contribution toward reviewing it and clarifying it. In the end, we are going to have to answer these questions within the framework of what metropolitan areas as a whole are going to need, because you require both a new conception of the powers to handle the large metropolitan systems aspects of the problem, and other powers to give voice, expression, and authority to smaller parts of the whole area.

I think that this is pretty close to being the heart of the problem that we're discussing this morning, and I would be very much interested in —

Senator PROXMIRE. Would you just repeat that, please? The heart of the problem is what, again?

Mr. GUTHEIM. To define the powers and the correct area for the neighborhood unit—for example, the authority which should be given to such a unit of government. It is certainly more than an election district, it is more than a ward, it is more than a concern only with the local environment. The traffic going through a neighborhood, for example, which is destroying its social and physical environment, doesn't originate there, and is not destined there, but it may be one of the most destructive things from the standpoint of hazards in the street, traffic, even the sense of isolation that you have in watching these big pieces of tin go by that don't belong to you.

So we must not look at the problems of the neighborhood as limited to the neighborhood.

They are part of something else. It is not just a question of giving people a possibility of a greater voice in their own lives and their destinies, but also a stronger voice in the decisions of the larger human community to which they belong.

Senator PROXMIRE. Why don't you have the same kind of problems in the suburbs? If they have it in the central city, why doesn't this problem develop in the suburbs?

Mr. GUTHEIM. You do have it, but one of the great attractions of the suburb to the people is the extent that they find a political unit which is reasonable in scale, and in which they can participate, play some kind of part.

They don't just go, as Mr. Kotler says, into a ballot box once every four years, but they are involved in community organization.

Senator PROXMIRE. A lot of them are not, of course. They leave their problems behind in the central city. They come into the city and work and go to live in the suburbs;

but they go back to their home, modest or substantial, and they live a residential life. And a residential life that, because they have the income, can be pleasant and doesn't have the terrible problems that the people who don't have much income and have to live in the central city have.

Is there something beyond this? After all, Mr. Kotler has raised a very clear point that has been in the minds of all of us. These people do feel dispossessed. They feel as if they do not belong. Many people in the suburbs don't do much either in terms of taking part.

The town meeting—that is something that, in New England and some other cities, people take part in.

I have found it is hard to get people to come to any meeting, whether you have a Governor there, a Senator, or mayor. People don't turn out anymore.

What is it peculiar about the poor neighborhood in the central city that gives people this terrible feeling of frustration, persuades them to riot, and persuades them to indulge in the violence which probably hurts them more than anybody else—anyway, it does do injury to them—whereas there is no disposition in the suburbs, though there is in smaller cities, as you brought out in your paper, Mr. Kotler.

But there doesn't seem to be much in the suburbs.

Mr. KOTLER. I think you raised the essential question. In the suburbs, money is a sufficient basis of power and they have a good degree of territorial control.

Senator PROXMIRE. Let me interrupt to say that it is not as if we have had a period of riots throughout our history. We didn't have complete tranquility, certainly, in our central cities, but until the last couple of years we didn't have anything like what we have had recently.

Why has this all of a sudden developed in such an acute and tragic way?

Mr. KOTLER. In the poor community, the only principle of power people have, because they don't have jobs, is their common strength territorially organized. The common action of all those people in the neighborhood is a political force, of some exchange value.

Senator PROXMIRE. What has happened lately that has made them feel this way? Why have we gotten riots in 1966 and 1967, whereas we didn't have them in the fifties and the forties?

More people were poorer. There were more people suffering from malnutrition.

Mr. KOTLER. Probably because the poor feel stronger today.

Mr. HEILBRUN. It is the revolution of rising expectations.

Mr. KOTLER. Those things are expressions of strength, too.

I don't know why the rebellions are going on now, and not 10 years ago. Violence is a very unpredictable affair, but the point is the value of "community" is so much greater in the poor neighborhoods today where there is no wealth as a lever of power. That is why the collectivity is so much more important in the poor neighborhood, and that is why they want territorial, or community control. It is the principle of their collective power.

This is a political fact. I am not proposing neighborhood government as a conscience statement. Compassion must not lead public policy.

This is a political problem. So, we must meet it with practical wisdom, prudence, not conscience. The problem is this: If people are organizing for local control and have local power, what do you do? You either crush them, or you give them the authority. I am saying politically, Congress, the constituted authority, must do the latter as the only way to peacefully catch up with political fact.

If people in the poor neighborhood need their local liberty to build a local prosperity and justice, if they need and want local control, Congress should give them some appropriate authority, if for no other reason than to lead the people. If you don't give authority you cannot lead, and the nation is split.

Political problems are never solved. They are only dissolved. The transfer of some legal authority to localities can dissolve the present fury and rebellion. With lawmaking authority the local community will build programs that will improve local life.

This neighborhood authority should be democratically constituted with assembly and council, so that each resident will have decision. That means liberty and citizenship. That is the sweet road to domestic peace.

In the meantime, efforts will be made toward metropolitan units based on neighborhood authority.